Doc Halligan's
What Every Pet
Owner Should
Know

Doc Halligan's

What Every Pet Owner Should Know

Prescriptions for
Happy, Healthy
Cats and
Dogs

Dr. Karen
Halligan

Illustrations by Liz Wells

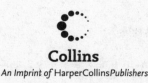

Collins
An Imprint of HarperCollinsPublishers

HarperCollins books may be purchased for educational, business, or sales promotional use. For information please write: Special Markets Department, HarperCollins Publishers, 10 East 53rd Street, New York, NY 10022.

A hardcover edition of this book was published in 2007.

FIRST COLLINS PAPERBACK EDITION PUBLISHED 2008.

Designed by William Ruoto

Library of Congress Cataloging-in-Publication Data

Halligan, Karen
    Doc Halligan's What every pet owner should know : prescriptions for happy, healthy cats and dogs / Karen Halligan. -- 1st ed/
    p. cm.
ISBN: 978-0-06-089859-5
    1. Cats. 2. Dogs. I. Title. II. Title: What every pet owner should know. III. Title: Prescriptions for happy, healthy cats and dogs.
SF442.H33 2007
636.8–dc22   2007060869

ISBN: 978-0-06-089859-5
ISBN: 978-0-06-089860-1 (pbk.)

08 09 10 11 12 WBC/RRD 10 9 8 7 6 5 4 3 2 1

JUN
2008

This book is dedicated to the cats and dogs that lost their lives in Hurricane Katrina, and to my beloved dog, Duke, whose unconditional love changed my life forever.

Contents

Introduction

One of the greatest loves you can experience is the unconditional love of a pet. Through my work of treating illnesses, injuries, and providing preventative medical care to pets, I give back some of the unconditional love I've received from animals in my life. I'm privileged to have a career that gives me the opportunity to share my knowledge of pets—learned in vet school and from years of practice—with their owners, thereby helping cats and dogs live long, happy, and healthy lives.

Animals have always been a part of my life. I grew up surrounded by loving dogs and cats, and learned to love animals through my experiences as well as by reading about them in books such as James Herriot's novels. Early on, I realized I wanted to devote my life to caring for animals. I followed my dream and graduated from veterinary school at University of California, Davis in 1989.

My desire to care for animals became more focused after I first started practicing. When I went to social gatherings, people would hover around me asking basic veterinary health questions and requesting information about their beloved pets. My neighbors would bring animals to my house, plying me with questions.

However, my desire to educate people about pet care crystallized as I worked at shot clinics on the weekends to supplement my income and to pay back my student loans. I was shocked at the condition of most of the pets I administered vaccines to—dogs barely able to walk because their nails were so long; cats and dogs with severe halitosis and thick green tartar covering their teeth; arthritic pets; unspayed females whose uteruses were just waiting to become infected; unneutered dogs who would one day run after a female in heat and get struck by a car. At these shot clinics I barely had time to vaccinate all of the animals that people brought in, let alone try to educate the owners about how to take better care of their pets. I was astonished as I discovered the majority of people lacked basic knowledge about pet health care, and from that day forward, my goal was to help change that. I decided that I would educate, to the best of my ability, all the clients I saw in private practice—at the very least.

Every pet owner must also plan for disasters. The importance of disaster preparedness for animals became painfully clear in the fall of 2005 when Hurricane Katrina brought her wrath to the Gulf Coast, followed by the destruction of Hurricane Rita. Thousands of animals lost their lives and thousands of owners were torn from their pets, never to be reunited. In the weeks and months of confusion surrounding these tragic events, thousands of pets were shipped all over the United States to various shelters for safekeeping. I was on the ground in Baton Rouge, Louisiana, dealing firsthand with these abandoned animals. Unfortunately for pet owners who failed to have an identification collar or microchip on their pet—sadly, this was the majority of animals I tended to—the odds of being reunited with their pets were slim. Your pet is an important family member and must be included in your disaster plan.

Another issue close to my heart is the frustration I feel about the millions of animals that are destroyed in our country every year due to irresponsible pet ownership. As a shelter vet, this fuels my desire to educate pet owners and hopefully put an end to the euthanasia of unwanted pets. We, as a nation that loves animals, must stop the irresponsible breeding of dogs and cats in the United States. My job as a vet entails euthanizing suffering animals, but having to kill them due to the lack of available loving homes is wrong. In the twenty-first century, we should be able to come up with a solution to stop the barbaric act of killing millions of healthy puppies, kittens, cats, and dogs in the shelters. I hope this book leads to a solution by raising awareness at the very least. I know we have a long way to go, but the well-known quote by Lao Tzu, "A journey of one thousand miles begins with a single step." is appropriate here. Each of us can make a difference by educating one person, saving one dog or cat.

My sincerest desire is that this book will become a resource that you refer to as your pet moves through its life stages: a guidebook to return to as questions come up so that you can enhance your pet's life to the fullest. If this book saves even one animal's life by encouraging people to adopt from a shelter instead of buying from a pet store—or helps owners recognize symptoms of illness early on, or makes them careful not to let their pet get poisoned by rat bait, or convinces them to neuter their cat or dog—then I have accomplished what I intended to do.

Chapter 1

Your New Four-Legged Friend

"Until one has loved an animal, part of one's soul remains unawakened."

—Anatole France, novelist, satirist, playwright, and poet

Loving a dog or cat is truly one of life's most rewarding experiences. Animals can melt our hearts. I've seen clients who consider themselves "dog people" have a kitten show up on their doorstep and change them forever by breaking down old walls and awakening the spirit, which led to a deep, meaningful, loving relationship with the kitten. I've seen families torn apart by death be reunited by the love of a puppy. In New Orleans I witnessed amazing heroic acts from people who were touched by the pain and suffering of animals and wanted to help.

Animals can bring out the very best in us if we let them. They have this ability because they love us unconditionally. They freely offer their love with no expectations.

Think First, Act Second

Okay, so you're sold on getting a pet. You really want to have a long, happy, meaningful life and have decided that owning a dog or cat would be just the right thing.

However, there are many factors to consider first. You may have owned a cat or dog in the past, but that doesn't mean your lifestyle suits having one now. You must take into consideration the huge daily responsibility it is to own a cat or dog. Don't buy a pet as a status symbol or because a cute puppy or kitten tugged at your heartstrings. Don't run out and buy a pet during the holidays or as a gift for someone who is ill prepared to own one.

If you do decide to get a pet, just make sure you've thoroughly assessed your lifestyle, living situation, and financial resources. Don't be hasty. This should be a carefully thought-out decision in which you've contemplated the enormous task it will be to have a living, breathing creature join your family. You will be responsible for your pet's every need.

Ten questions to ask yourself

1. What do you hope to gain from your relationship with this pet?
2. Do you have the financial resources to take on a new family member?
3. Will this new pet fit into your current family, four-legged members included?
4. Are you prepared emotionally if your pet has a medical problem?
5. Do you have the time commitment necessary to care for this pet?
6. Does your current living situation allow for a new pet?
7. Does your work or travel schedule interfere with owning a pet?
8. Has the whole family been involved in the decision to get a new pet?

9. Are you willing to give up some freedom to own and care for a new pet?
10. Are you physically able to handle this new pet?

Pets should be selected with the entire family in mind, including everyone's needs, concerns, expectations, fears, and medical issues, such as allergies. Will the family thrive from taking on and caring for a new pet, or will this caretaking become a burden after the initial excitement wears off? Keep in mind that children may not always fulfill the promises they make about caring for a new pet. Will a relationship with this pet enhance or detract from any human relationships that you may have, such as a spouse, children, or close friends, or even your job?

Kitten, Puppy, Cat, or Dog?

Without a doubt, owning a puppy or kitten requires much more work during the first year than adopting a mature dog or cat, but there are pros and cons of both. Raising a kitten or puppy takes a certain amount of commitment on your part to ensure you end up with a well-behaved pet that fits into the family. It's similar to raising a child, only at an accelerated pace. A kitten or puppy will age fifteen human years in one year and go through all the stages that a child would experience into their teens. It can be challenging, entertaining, daunting, and amazing all at the same time. The trouble that puppies and kittens can get into can rival that of a two-year-old child.

The key is to put in the effort initially so you don't wind up with an untrained, highly destructive, or obnoxious cat or dog. A pet's first year of life is crucial to developing a highly positive social bond with you.

If you don't have the time, energy, or patience to put into raising a kitten or puppy, then it's probably best to adopt an adult dog or cat.

Generally speaking, adult pets require far less work initially; however, if they have behavioral problems, you'll need to address those immediately so you can enjoy cohabiting with your pet.

It will invariably take some work to have your adult cat or dog adjust to your household. As in any new relationship, you must first get to know each other. By putting a good six months of effort into establishing ground with your new pet, you'll have a highly social, well-trained animal that fits properly into your home.

Cat Versus Dog

Naturally, there are certain differences in owning a cat versus a dog.

Advantages of owning a cat include:

- Easier to potty-train than dogs
- Can stay longer at home alone
- Fairly quiet
- Relatively small
- Don't need to be walked
- Fairly nonaggressive
- Typically less costly
- Require less exercise
- Need less socialization
- Need less training

Benefits of owning a dog include:

- Excellent companions
- Unwavering love and loyalty
- Provide sense of safety and protection

- Many different breeds to choose from
- Come in all sizes and shapes
- Some make great traveling companions

Choosing the Right Pet

It's critical that you research the particular breeds of dogs or cats before you actually go out and buy one. Different breeds have different characteristics and temperaments as well as maintenance requirements you must consider before choosing a particular breed. For example, Persian and Abyssinian cats are considered to be very affectionate; Siamese cats like to meow a lot. Long hair versus short hair is another consideration. Certain breeds of dogs, such as Maltese, poodle, and Lhasa apso, require grooming every six weeks.

Just because you buy a purebred doesn't mean you have a 100 percent guarantee of health and temperament. If you choose to buy a purebred, just make sure it comes from a reputable breeder and not from an ad in the newspaper or a pet store.

Even if you decide to choose a mixed breed from a shelter, it's a good idea to recognize the breeds that influence the pet you may choose and its breed characteristics. The American Kennel Club website is a good place to get information on more than 150 different breeds of dogs. Another great way to learn about different breeds is to ask pet owners with particular breeds about the temperaments and pros and cons of the breeds. Be prepared to get an earful.

Whether you choose a purebred or a mixed breed, just be careful to resist the urge to take the first cute dog or cat that looks at you longingly. Try to make the decision by being objective and selecting a pet that fits your budget, living conditions, and lifestyle. When you see a dog or cat that interests you, take the time to interact with it and see how its realities match yours. How did it interact, play with, and respond to you and/or the whole family? I remember adopting a dog out to a family with a child in a wheelchair. It was amazing how different dogs reacted when they encountered the wheelchair, and to finally see the dog that fit perfectly into that family.

Don't choose a dog or cat purely on the basis of physical appearance. Temperament and behavioral characteristics are far more critical in determining the suitability of a dog or cat for a given family and household.

First Impressions

Puppy/Kitten-Proofing

Before bringing your new kitten, puppy, cat, or dog into your home, you need to kitten/puppy-proof your house, garage, basement, and yard, as well as have the necessary supplies ready to make your pet feel comfortable. Puppies and kittens are little bundles of furry curiosity that can get them into a lot of trouble, but pet-proofing is necessary for adult cats and dogs as well.

Just like a child uses its hands and fingers to explore, a cat's or dog's natural instinct is to use its mouth and teeth to investigate all new things—which are plentiful in a new home. At around four months of age, the baby teeth begin to fall out, allowing the adult teeth to push through the gums. (See Chapter 5 on dental care.) This teething process can cause sore gums, leading puppies and kittens to chew more. Puppies especially will be tempted to bite and chew on almost anything they can get their mouth on, and they can swallow new objects. Since this is a natural behavior, you should provide pets with toys of their own to chew on and play with.

Keep in mind the lower vantage point that puppies and kittens have. They'll be attracted to things you won't see when standing, so you need to get down on all fours and see their environment through their eyes. This way, you'll see things at your pet's level and not overlook anything. Don't worry—you don't have to bark or meow! See Chapter 8 on avoiding the emergency room blues.

Common Dangers

Everyday dangers to puppies and kittens include plants, household garbage, food, cleaning substances, swallowable objects (this includes anything small enough for them to get a hold of), electrical cords and wires, curtain and drapery cords, plastic bags, shoes and clothing, children's toys and items, medicine, open fires, open doors, balconies and raised decks, pools and ponds, unsupervised small children, and other pets. Keep toilet lids, dresser drawers, trunks, and closets closed. Be careful when closing your refrigerator, oven, washer, or clothes dryer to make sure your kitten or puppy is not inside. Keep sewing supplies out of reach and never leave a hot stove unattended. Block off stairs and ledges with a baby gate. Keep poison and all medication in a locked cabinet or room that your pet can't access. Examine your house and furniture carefully for small holes, gaps, and spots where a small animal could squeeze into and get stuck. Watch out for heavy objects placed on unstable bases, such as an iron on an ironing board. See Chapter 8 on avoiding the emergency room blues.

Once you have puppy/kitten-proofed your home, keep in mind that the key to ensuring your pet's safety is to keep a watchful eye on it and know its whereabouts at **all** times. Just like you wouldn't let a toddler run around the house unsupervised, so it should be with your puppy or kitten. Make sure you have a small, safe room or crate in which to confine your pet when you're not able to directly supervise it.

Supplies

The basic supplies include an appropriate bed and bedding, a sturdy cat or dog carrier or crate, food and water bowls, brushes and combs, appropriate collar, harness, and leash, identification tag, litter pan and scooper, and several scratching posts for kittens or cats.

The First Day

The first few days a puppy or kitten is in its new home are exciting and demanding at the same time. Both the animal and your family are adjusting to new situations, so patience is a must. New puppies and kittens are vulnerable and impressionable, so routine and security will help them gain self-confidence. The whole family must agree on responsibilities, routines, and rules to be followed. For instance, if everyone agrees that the puppy will sleep in its new crate, then don't change your mind just because one family member wants the puppy to sleep in his bed.

Yes, you now have this incredible ball of fur with attitude, needs, and wants, and you're completely responsible for it. The first few weeks of a kitten's or puppy's time in its new home is so important in terms of socializing and bonding with humans and should be treated as a critical period in your relationship. This is the time for cuddling, holding, playing gently, and talking to your new kitten or puppy. I've always spent a lot of time talking to my pets. I also like to sing to them (but only to them, because they don't mind if I sing off-key!), which most pets really enjoy. Subsequently, all my pets have developed strong bonds with me. Properly handled, your kitten or puppy will associate their friendly, happy times with you and become a friend for life. You will be molding your pet's personality while strengthening your own commitment to cherish it for life. It's a symbiotic relationship.

It's important to make your puppy or kitten as sleepy as possible before it goes to bed, especially during the first few nights in its new home. Puppies will howl or cry when they're separated from whatever they're most attached to, and initially this will be the mother and/or littermates. After you bring your new puppy home, this attachment quickly transfers to its new family.

Confining your puppy at night is important. You want to withhold water for at least a couple of hours before bedtime, and make sure to take your puppy outside before bedtime. For a bed, you can use a box or crate with a blanket or carpet in it. If your puppy is exhausted because it has had a busy day, it should settle down, relax, and go to sleep. If your puppy starts to howl or cry initially, don't respond; if you do, it will learn that making noise will succeed in getting attention, thus prolonging the time it takes for the puppy to get used to being alone and sleeping at night. If your puppy awakens during the middle of the night, it may need to be taken outside in the beginning at least once to relieve itself.

It's important to remember that a kitten's needs are different from those of a puppy or an adult cat or dog. It's best to initially limit the area in which you first place your kitten. Confine it to a safe room with its bed, food, water, litter box, toys, and a scratching post. Cats naturally investigate their surroundings, so starting them out in a controlled area will eliminate unmanageable situations. After confining the kitten to a room for a couple of days, you should slowly allow access to the rest of the house.

Cats are nocturnal animals and like to play and prowl at night. To prevent your kitten from disturbing your sleep, be sure to play with it early in the evening to use up some of its high energy, have toys available, and never encourage or play with your kitten at night, especially if it wakes you up in the middle of the night. Confining your kitten initially will also allow any resident cats to become familiar with the kitten's odor and sounds, and keeping it separated from any other cats in the household will decrease the chances of spreading disease.

Ideally, your new kitten or puppy should be examined by a vet before you bring it home, but if this is not feasible, have your pet examined as soon as possible prior to introducing it to any other animals.

The First Six Months

The first six months of your pet's life are the most formative period, both physically and psychologically. In addition to being critical in shaping the relationship between the animal and the family, this is also the time when your pet is most susceptible to disease. Kittens and puppies are more vulnerable to various illnesses because their immune systems aren't fully developed yet.

Vet Exam

The vet should see your kitten, puppy, cat, or dog as soon as possible—ideally within twenty-four hours. With kittens and puppies, there will need to be more than one visit in the first six months. Puppies and kittens need to get started on vaccinations to protect them from deadly diseases. Some viruses travel through the air or may be brought into the house on people's clothing or shoes—or may even live in the environment.

Your veterinarian's advice is key to teaching you all about pet care and ensuring that your pet has a long, happy, healthy life. The vet will record your pet's weight, take its temperature, listen to the heart, look in the eyes, open the mouth, check the teeth and bite, look in the ears, check the skin, look at the belly button for umbilical hernias, watch it walk to check for limb problems, and run a fecal test and blood test to rule out parasites and other potential problems. All kittens should be tested for feline leukemia and feline immunodeficiency virus. These are common viruses in the environment that can be fatal, so it's good to know ahead of time if your kitten has them. This test is called the FeLV/FIV combo test and is done while you wait.

Seeing a veterinarian early is vital to the health and well-being of your pet. There are numerous potential health problems that your vet can treat effectively if caught early when animals are young. Ask your vet about any breed-specific illness you may not know about.

Deworming

Most kittens and puppies become infected with worms either before they're born or later through their mother's milk, so it's important to have their stool checked by your vet. Some veterinarians just routinely deworm kittens and puppies, as it's very common for them to have parasites. A microscopic exam of the stool sample, called a fecal, will help determine if your pet has worms and what type it has. The fecal will also rule out other common parasites that can occur in puppies and kittens, such as coccidia and giardia. Your veterinarian will prescribe the proper deworming medication, which is usually repeated. Avoid buying over-the-counter dewormers unless directed by your vet. See Chapter 12 on seasonal disturbances.

Vaccinations

I can't overestimate the importance of vaccines. Too many kittens and puppies succumb to infectious diseases that are entirely preventable by routine vaccinations.

A vaccine stimulates the immune system to produce antibodies, which are protein molecules that neutralize disease. Your puppy or kitten receives antibodies from its mother's milk. After weaning, however, it needs to receive a series of vaccines in order to develop proper immunity on its own. Puppies and kittens are vaccinated more than once because the antibodies they receive from their mothers at birth and in their milk, which wane over time, interfere with the puppy's or kitten's ability to produce its own antibody response to a vaccine. The time at which these maternal antibodies lose their effectiveness is different for each puppy or kitten, so it's important to start the vaccination series at seven to eight weeks of age. Kittens and puppies then receive a series of vaccines three to four weeks apart until they are sixteen weeks old. After that, boosters are needed yearly for some vaccines and every two to three years for others.

Typical vaccine schedule for puppies and kittens

AGE	PUPPY	KITTEN
8 weeks	parvo, distemper, parainfluenza	panleukopenia, feline rhinotracheitis, chlamydia, calici
12 weeks	parvo, distemper, parainfluenza, infectious hepatitis, bordetella	panleukopenia, feline rhinotracheitis, chlamydia, calici, feline leukemia
16 weeks	parvo, distemper, parainfluenza, infectious hepatitis, bordetella, rabies	panleukopenia, feline rhinotracheitis, chlamydia, calici, feline leukemia, rabies

Spaying and Neutering

Spaying or neutering at an early age prevents unwanted pregnancies and protects your pet against tumors of the reproductive organs. Early neutering in males also improves behavior by reducing roaming, urine marking, and aggression between male animals. Neutered pets live longer than non-neutered pets, have no risk of testicular cancer or torsion, and have a greatly reduced risk of prostate disease. Female dogs that are altered before they have their first heat cycle, which is usually at seven months, have at least a ninety percent decrease in developing breast cancer later in life. Spayed females have no risk of ovarian or uterine cancer or life-threatening uterine infections, and heat cycles and unpleasant behaviors are eliminated.

You can have your puppy or kitten spayed or neutered as early as eight weeks of age. It's recommended that the procedure be performed before your pet is six months old. See Chapter 4 on spaying and neutering.

Flea Control and Heartworm Preventative

Flea and tick control is relatively easy nowadays because of the high-quality products available through your vet, and can be started as early as six weeks of age.

Heartworm disease is caused by a worm that lives in the heart, major arteries, and lungs, where it interferes with the functions of these organs and causes serious disease and/or death. Heartworms are most commonly found in dogs and cats, although they can infect ferrets, sea lions, bears, foxes, wolves, coyotes, and even humans. They can only be transmitted from one animal to another by mosquitoes. Unfortunately, even strictly indoor cats can be infected because mosquitoes can come inside and bite the cat. The good news is that this deadly disease is 100 percent preventable. Heartworm is easy to control by simply giving your pet a monthly tablet, which you can start as early as eight weeks of age. See Chapter 12 on seasonal disturbances.

Puppy Potty-Training

It's important to remember that the biggest influence on how quickly your puppy becomes potty-trained is how much time and effort you put into it. Halfhearted efforts or intermittent training on your part can cause your puppy to eliminate in the house for months and seriously delay the process. Patience, confinement, and a regular schedule are the keys to successful potty-training. The more input your puppy receives, the faster it will be potty-trained.

Dogs, because they are born in a nest, have an instinctive desire to move away from the nest to relieve themselves. They will do so without being taught, as soon as they are capable. The key with potty-training is to teach the puppy that your house is the nest and that it should relieve itself outside of the nest. It's also important to recognize the physical limitations of puppies that are being potty-trained. Young puppies may need to eliminate every two to four hours during daylight hours when they are most active, but be able to hold it much longer at night. A simple rule of thumb to estimate how long a puppy can hold its urine is its number of months in age plus one. For example, a two-month-old puppy can typically hold its urine for about three hours. There is considerable individual variation on this, so you may need to get up in the middle of the night to take the puppy out to avoid accidents. You'll quickly learn your puppy's physical limitations and try not to exceed them.

Initially take the puppy outside to the same spot in your yard where you want it to eliminate at the following times:

- First thing in the morning
- Shortly after each meal
- At least once an hour
- After playing or exercising
- Immediately upon waking at any hour
- After any type of stimulation
- Last thing at night

It's important that you stay outside with your puppy. Be patient and wait. As soon as they begin to potty, choose a positive phrase and then praise them enthusiastically. If you've taken your puppy outside and nothing happens after a few minutes, take it inside and try again later. If you notice your puppy sniffing the floor or circling, interrupt it immediately and take it outside. Try not to carry it outside or it won't get in the habit of walking outside to eliminate. If you're unsuccessful, you must take your puppy to the vet to rule out any health problem that could be causing a failure in potty-training, such as a bladder infection or parasites.

Crate Training for Dogs

Crate training is one of the best ways to potty-train a puppy. Crates can also be used to prevent puppies and dogs from having the opportunity to be destructive or get into trouble when not supervised. Puppies shouldn't be confined continuously in a crate except at night. The crate should be big enough for the puppy to lie fully stretched out on its side, tall enough for the puppy to stand, and wide enough for the puppy to easily turn around. However, the crate shouldn't be so big that the puppy can become active. For large breeds of dogs, it may be necessary to purchase more than one crate as they grow, or at least block off a part of a large crate at first with cardboard.

One of the benefits of confinement is that it discourages activity, which can trigger elimination. When active movement is allowed, the puppy must be taken to the chosen site for elimination regularly. For very young dogs, it's desirable to take them to the elimination site once during the middle of the night until they can make it through an entire night.

Start by having the crate accessible and leaving the door open. Place pieces of food inside and your puppy will quickly become very comfortable going into the crate. Crates are very natural for dogs because they fit into their den concept, and most dogs that have their own crates consider them a place of security, much like having their own bedroom.

Litter Box Training

Cats have a natural proclivity for using a litter box. Most were trained by their mother as kittens to use a litter box, and the ones that weren't catch on quickly. Kittens begin using the litter box by their third week of life. They will follow their mother to the litter box and begin to imitate her bathroom etiquette.

The first step in successful house-training is to make sure you have the right equipment. Try to find out what litter material was used by the mother and buy that if possible. There are lots of choices regarding litter. If you're unsure, start with unscented litter because some kittens dislike the scented kind. If you already have cats at home, provide an additional box for each new cat. The litter box should be made of a washable material such as plastic, and the side must be low enough for a kitten to enter but high enough to contain the litter. Some litter boxes come with hoods that help control the odor as well as keep the litter in the box. The box should be placed in a relatively quiet area of the house with minimal traffic. Be sure the box is easily accessible and not too difficult for your kitten to find. When your kitten stops playing and begins sniffing around, gently carry it to the litter box. Simply place your kitten in the litter first thing in the morning, after meals, after periods of energetic play, after long naps, and last thing at night.

This basic training is usually adequate. Most adult cats only need to learn where the new litter box is located. Again, I recommend one litter pan per cat. Confining your cat to a small room initially is the best way to foster good litter box habits. Remember to provide a quiet, secluded spot for your cat's litter box. Do not let your kitten or cat roam freely in the house until you're certain your pet is using its litter pan regularly.

Make sure the litter box contains enough litter for digging and burying—about two to three inches is sufficient. Also, most kittens will automatically use kitty litter in preference to other surfaces, except for the soil of a potted plant. Be sure to keep plants out of the kitten's reach or cover the soil with pinecones or decorative rock. Once you've found a litter that your new kitten likes, avoid making sudden changes.

Keep in mind that the number one reason a cat stops using its litter box is because the box is dirty. If your cat continues to make mistakes, the behavior can actually become a habit, so don't wait on litter box issues.

* * *

To keep your cat happy with its litter box and avoid mishaps:

- Clean the box daily.
- Keep fresh litter in the box at all times.
- Wash out the litter pan weekly.
- Never frighten your kitten near the box.
- Try to prevent anything unpleasant from happening near its box.

If accidents occur, be sure that your kitten is checked for any underlying medical problem that may exist.

Socialization

Puppies and kittens go through a pattern of growth from infancy to maturity. Kittens especially have high energy and intense curiosity, so there's never a dull moment with them. Spending time with your puppy or kitten will help develop a strong foundation for a long, loving relationship. One of the most critical periods of development is called the socialization period, which occurs from three to twelve weeks of age in puppies, and two to twelve weeks of age in kittens. During this time your puppy or kitten is very impressionable with regard to social influences.

Try some events that are pleasant and nonthreatening. Invite friends over to meet your new puppy or kitten, including men, women, children, and seniors. If your pet has good experiences, it's likely to accept people throughout its life. Expose your puppy to as many types of social events as possible, and with kittens, acclimate them to other cats and friendly dogs as well. With puppies, try to avoid dog parks, beaches, and other areas where there are a lot of dogs, as puppies that are fewer than four months of age are highly susceptible to disease.

Stimulating play is vital during this time. Stalking and pouncing are important behaviors that are necessary for proper muscular development. If you give your puppy or kitten a sufficient outlet for these activities using toys, your pet will be less destructive and less likely to use family members or furniture for these activities. The best toys are lightweight and movable. Avoid any toy that is small enough to be swallowed. All kittens and cats must have scratching posts available to deter them from using your furniture.

Felines and Furniture

Cats are unique in that their nails are sharper and more curved than any other mammal. They are also carnivores, so in the wild this would help them grip their prey. Now that they are domesticated, sometimes that prey becomes your furniture. Cats scratch for a variety of reasons. This includes marking their territory (both visually and with scent glands in their pads), stretching, and sharpening their nails. But not to worry—with patience and training cats can coexist very nicely with a $2,000 couch. Here's how:

- Kittens tend to use their nails more than adult cats, so start working with your kittens as soon as possible.
- Try different scratching posts to see which surfaces your cat likes.
- Make sure the post has a wide base and is stable enough for the cat to stand up and pull down on the post.
- Spray the post with catnip if your cats like this smell.
- Attach dangling toys around the post to entice your cats.
- Play with your cats around the post.
- Praise your cat or give a food reward after it uses the post.
- Put scratching posts in locations where your cats like to scratch. Many cats like to scratch when they first wake up, so if they sleep with you, put a post by your bed.
- Train your cat to stay away from your furniture by putting aluminum foil, bubble wrap, or double-sided tape on the furniture where they scratch.

- Spray your furniture with lemon cleaner. Cats usually dislike the smell of citrus.
- Use loud noises or a squirt bottle with water to discourage your cat from scratching the furniture. Repetition is important.
- Trim your cat's nails on a regular basis. Your vet can show you how.
- Try Soft Paws. These are plastic coverings for your cat's nails that you can buy from your vet. Soft Paws are vinyl nail caps that are glued to your cat's claws, which effectively cover their nails so no damage occurs when your cat scratches. They need to be changed every four to six weeks.

Most cats can be trained to use a post, so don't give up! Remember, cats have a natural instinct to scratch. This is a very normal behavior. With a little bit of guidance you can teach your cat to scratch its post instead of your furniture.

Nail Trims

Start trimming your pet's nails early on. This will establish a very important routine that must be maintained for life, much like your own need for nail trimming. Puppies and kittens have very sharp nails, so ask your vet to trim them at your first visit. Then, if you feel comfortable, have the vet teach you how to perform nail trims. If not, you must decide where and how you will have this done on a regular basis. See Chapter 3 on prevention.

Puppy Principles/Kitty Kindergarten

Both puppies and kittens need socialization as well as training to help them fit nicely into your family and society. Unfortunately, a recent study showed that fewer than one out of five dog owners have taken their dog to obedience training. This is akin to only one out of five parents sending their child to school. Imagine that!

The goal of early puppy training is to give your pet the best possible start in life. Learning takes place rapidly during the first six months of a puppy's life, so anything a puppy experiences at that time will make a greater impression than it ever will again. Therefore, you should capitalize on this critical time and set the patterns for a well-behaved dog. By seven weeks, a puppy's brain has developed sufficiently to allow it to process everything it needs to learn.

Puppy class will show your puppy that learning is fun and will establish a very special bond between you and your pet. Positive training techniques will teach your puppy manners and prevent it from displaying unwanted behaviors. Puppies should enjoy the learning process and become confident and curious about life. Most puppies are eager to learn, and when they really begin to mature at around six to twelve months of age, they are in the middle of the most independent, challenging phase of their life. Beginning early gives you a jump start in shaping good behavior. But don't expect to graduate from puppy-training class with a fully trained dog. You'll be laying the foundation for a lifetime of training and, as your puppy grows and matures, it will be able to tackle more complicated tasks. To help establish a trusting relationship with your puppy, you should reward behaviors that you like, prevent annoying behaviors from happening, and teach it that acquiescing to your requests is the smartest way to go.

Just like with puppies, training kittens is important so your kitten grows up to be a happy, well-balanced cat. In fact, there are even "kitten kindy" classes where owners take their kittens and learn about normal feline behaviors and needs, how to prevent problems, how to play with a kitten correctly, as well as teach kittens to come, sit, and even do tricks such as a high five. Owners are taught never to use their hands to play with a kitten and to stop playing if it gets too intense or rough. Studies have shown that kittens that attended such classes formed stronger bonds with their owners and had fewer behavioral problems.

Indoor versus Outdoor Cats

Outdoor cats have significantly shorter life spans than indoor cats. The life expectancy of an outdoor cat is only three to four years, compared to fourteen to sixteen for an indoor cat. Outdoor cats have a fifty percent chance of being killed by a car. Cats are incapable of understanding the danger of cars and will cross roads assuming they can outrun any vehicle. Outdoor cats are also prone to be injured in fights with other cats and dogs, eat poison, drink antifreeze, get exposed to extreme weather, receive abuse from angry neighbors, become lost, or get fleas, parasites, or infections passed on by other cats.

I always recommend that cats be kept indoors. It's okay to let them into an enclosed area in your backyard as long as they're being supervised. You can even train a cat to walk on a harness and leash. With the proper stimulation, indoor life provides all of the pleasures of outdoor life without all of the dangers. Besides, cats spend up to sixteen hours a day sleeping! Unlike dogs, cats do not have to run around to explore their environment; instead, they take in their surroundings visually. They use their sensitive hearing to detect subtle changes. Cats also spend a considerable amount of time grooming, stretching, sunbathing, and moving from one lounging place to another. These simple acts are integral to a cat's life. Nice window ledges, cat trees, and safe cat toys all add to an enriched environment and a safe haven for your indoor cat.

Proper Identification

Proper identification can be a matter of life and death. All pets should wear a collar and name tag at all times. Make sure the collar is not too loose or too tight, and remember to adjust or change the collar as your pet grows. Small breeds of dogs that are predisposed to tracheal problems do better with a harness rather than a collar and breakaway collars are safest for cats.

Another very important form of identification is microchipping, in which a tiny device is implanted beneath the skin. The chip has a number that can be read by a special scanner, and that number is registered in a national database with your name, address, and telephone number. If your pet gets lost and is turned over to a shelter or vet clinic, a scanner can be used to find out your information. As long as the information is current, you'll be contacted and reunited with your pet. See Chapter 9 on outfitting your pet.

Feeding for Life Stages

Always feed your puppy, kitten, cat, or dog for its life stage and breed. Kittens and puppies develop at an amazing rate and therefore need a lot of calories, fat, protein, and vitamins to grow properly. After weaning, they require about twice the nutritional energy of an adult dog or cat. Because of these needs, you should feed your pet a high-quality puppy or kitten food. You don't want to feed an adult diet or a maintenance diet because these don't have enough fat or protein for a growing pet. Once your pet is spayed or neutered, its caloric requirement will drop about ten percent initially and will continue to gradually decrease until it becomes an adult at around one year of age.

Tips for feeding:
- Feed only food that states it's for puppies or kittens.
- Wet food is okay as long as it's for puppies or kittens.
- Do not feed table scraps, tuna, or milk.
- When changing the diet, always mix the old and new food together for a couple of days so your puppy or kitten won't get diarrhea or stomach upset.

The time at which you will switch your pet to an adult or a maintenance diet varies depending on when your pet is spayed or neutered, the breed of your pet, and its lifestyle and activity level.

Six Months to One Year

Puppies and kittens have a lot of growing to do in their first twelve months. Not only will they grow up physically, but their personalities will also develop. You can help your pet fulfill its potential as a loving companion by setting up the perfect environment. As it grows you can teach it the necessary skills for safe interactions with humans. Give your pet a variety of experiences that allow it to build self-confidence. For example, you can help your pet develop a positive self-image by enrolling it in puppy- or kitten-training classes. Take your pet for car rides and introduce it to safe feline- and canine-friendly dogs to foster a solid social foundation. Make sure your kitten or puppy develops confidence in people by having it play with children, adults, and seniors, both men and women. This teaches your pet that strangers are friendly and come in many different shapes and sizes. After about six months, a kitten's enthusiasm for play generally declines, but you should continue to have two fifteen-minute regular play sessions a day.

Dental Care

Veterinarians now realize the importance of taking care of an animal's teeth. Tartar and plaque not only lead to gingivitis and tooth loss, but the bacteria present can cause damage to such organs as the kidneys, liver, and heart, shortening your pet's life significantly. Brushing your pet's teeth just three times a week will prevent serious health problems and extend your pet's life. If you start getting your pets used to brushing while they're young, they may even learn to look forward to their poultry-flavored toothpaste and brushing. See Chapter 5 on dental disasters.

Grooming

Kittens, cats, puppies, and dogs should be brushed frequently to minimize shedding and promote healthy skin. A poorly groomed cat or dog is at risk for external parasites, tangles, mats, and skin problems. Although cats clean themselves thoroughly, brushing the coat will reduce shedding on furniture and increase the health of the coat. Brushing will also decrease the amount of hair ingested by the cat, which will help reduce hairballs. Long-haired cats need to be brushed daily while short-haired cats can be brushed once or twice a week.

Developing a Routine

Cats and dogs thrive on routine, so this is your chance to get your pets accustomed to receiving a weekly once-over. By handling your pet early on, it will get used to and even enjoy being touched and having its mouth, ears, and eyes examined. This will make trips to the vet much less stressful and you'll discover abnormalities early on, which can even save your pet's life. See Chapter 3 on prevention.

Environment Enrichment

Domesticated dogs and cats need to feel stimulated to have a quality life and prevent boredom. If left alone, their natural instincts to hunt, explore, play, or socialize are rarely engaged. Instead, most dogs and cats spend their days eating, sleeping, pacing, or getting into trouble. These "latchkey" pets often obsess about food, which is sometimes their only form of stimulus. More than forty percent of cats and dogs are overweight. See Chapter 6 on obesity.

For dogs, try to socialize them often to stimulate their instinctive need to interact. This includes frequent walks, hikes, or romps at the dog park or the beach. You can take an agility course or a fly-ball class with your dog. You can place pieces of kibble in specially designed rubber balls, which will keep your dog busy for hours. Leaving a radio or television set on can be a real comfort to dogs and cats. You can also buy pet videos showing life-size images of animals cavorting around.

For cats, invest in a kitty condo. Cats love to climb and jump, and cat trees provide the perfect platform for their natural athletic as well as acrobatic abilities. Cat trees come in all sizes and shapes with sisal rope and studded platforms for perching, climbing, and scratching. Cat toys are available for all kinds of activities, such as batting, stalking, pouncing, and interactive play. Some toys have catnip in them, which can really add to your cat's enjoyment. There are kitty-teaser toys that simulate the natural prey drive, feather toys, windup toys, and laser pointers that offer cats a chance to chase. The list is endless. Just invest in a few, find out what your cat likes, and play with your cat for at least two fifteen-minute sessions a day. You can provide visual stimulation by putting a bird feeder outside a window with a cat ledge for satisfactory viewing. Of course, the best way to prevent boredom is to interact with your cat and spend time playing, grooming, petting, and just plain old loving it!

Latchkey Dog

This term is used to describe a dog that's left alone in the house all day while its owner is at work. Latchkey dogs often become bored, lonely, and unhappy. These feelings can lead them to cause mischief and destruction. This can be especially problematic for some dogs, especially those with separation anxiety. These dogs will chew carpet and furniture, soil floors, eat trash, scratch doors, and bark.

It's important that dogs—especially puppies—have an outlet for natural behaviors; they need to run, jump, play, and explore. Failure to provide enough activities leads to behavioral problems.

What do you do with your dog while you're away at work all day? A good solution is to hire a professional dog walker who makes sure your unsupervised pet gets plenty of exercise and attention. Latchkey service is perfect for pet owners who work long hours (or get stuck in long meetings) and don't want to leave their dogs unattended for extended periods of time without adequate potty and exercise breaks. The service provides a welcome relief for the pet and peace of mind for the owner, knowing the dog is receiving personal care during the day. The dog walker can simply take the dog outside to potty and get some fresh air, or for a walk to stretch its legs or to a dog park to run around. Exercise is crucial for all dogs, whether small or large, purebred or mixed breed. It keeps dogs healthy, but it also helps them relax.

Dog walkers should have insurance and a contract that specifies the exact services that will be provided. Set up a consultation and meet with the walker before you hire him or her, and make sure the person has a rapport with your pet.

Behavioral Problems

The purpose of training is to formalize the learning process so the family and pet will get along and build a bond that lasts a lifetime. You need to teach appropriate behaviors and discourage those that are inappropriate so your pet truly becomes a family member—one that you are proud of because it is obedient, faithful, well-mannered, playful, a joy to live with, and something to brag about.

In the first year of life, kittens and puppies will pick up most, if not all, of its habits, both good and bad. This is the best time to nip future behavioral problems in the bud. What might be cute behavior for a tiny kitten or puppy is not so cute for a ten-pound cat or sixty-pound dog. Laying the groundwork for expected behavior when your pet is young and impressionable is far better than attempting to break the habits of an older animal.

If your puppy or kitten develops behavioral problems that you can't resolve, it's best to enlist a trainer or specialist to help correct them. Ask your veterinarian for a recommendation or talk to other pet owners to get a referral.

Obedience Training

Dog obedience training is crucial to raising a well-behaved companion and can stop some behavioral problems. It should be a mutually pleasurable experience for the dog and the whole family. The quality time and individual attention you spend while training your dog will foster mutual love and respect. You'll learn how to have fun with your dog while establishing control. No dog is too old to learn. You'll teach your dog how to respond to your commands, like "come," "sit," "down," "stay," and "heel." You should be able to walk your dog down the street without it dragging you, or vice versa.

Happy Dogs Are Tired Dogs

There are also a number of fun dog sports for your pet to try, such as agility, fly ball, and obedience trials. Agility is a physical sport in which you guide the dog through an obstacle course. The dog has to navigate through tunnels, jumps, and suspended tires. It also has to climb a six-foot-tall A-frame, as well as weave in and out of a series of ten to twelve poles. There are different levels of difficulty from beginning to advanced.

Fly ball is a sport where dog teams compete against one another in relay races to obtain fly-ball titles and win tournaments. Each team consists of four dogs. Every dog on a team must jump over four hurdles and hit a box that will eject a tennis ball. The dog must bring the ball back over the hurdles. Once that dog is back, then the next dog goes until every dog on the team has completed the course. Each team is racing not only against the clock, but one another. Dogs win titles based on the speed of their team.

Obedience trials test the dog's ability to willingly perform obedience commands. There are three levels of competition: Novice, Open, and Utility. In Novice, the dog must heel on and off leash, stand still for an exam by a judge, come when called, and perform a sit-and-down stay for a few minutes with the handler in sight. In Open, the dog must heel off leash, drop on recall, retrieve a dumbbell on the flat as well as over a high jump, jump over a broad jump, and perform a sit-and-down stay for a few minutes with the handler out of the room. The Utility exercises are the most complex. Almost all commands are by hand signal and all are off leash. This level includes scent discrimination, directional retrieving, and directional jumping. Once a dog completes all three levels, it can continue competition for points toward its Obedience Trial Championship.

These are just a few of the dog sports available out there. Remember, a tired dog is a happy dog, both physically and emotionally, and you *can* teach an old dog new tricks.

Recognizing Illness

The following are all signs of illness. If your pet shows any of these signs, a trip to the vet is necessary.

- Abnormal discharge from the nose, eyes, or other body openings
- Abnormal behavior, sudden aggression, or lethargy
- Abnormal lumps, limping, or difficulty getting up or lying down
- Sneezing and/or coughing
- High temperature
- Vomiting, diarrhea, or constipation
- Straining to urinate or defecate
- Blood in the urine or stool

- Loss of appetite, marked weight loss or gain, or excessive water consumption
- Difficult, abnormal, or uncontrolled waste eliminations
- Excessive head shaking, scratching, or licking or biting any part of the body
- Dandruff, loss of hair, open sores, or a ragged or dull coat
- Foul breath or difficulty chewing or opening and closing the mouth
- Convulsions, muscle spasms, or paralysis

The End of the Day

Having a dog or cat can dramatically improve the quality of your life and, as studies have shown, even extend your longevity. Giving and receiving love is an essential component to a great life. With love, patience, and a little effort, your cat or dog will become an amazing companion.

Owning a cat or dog is a lot like having a child—it will enrich your life, but it's a big commitment that requires time, emotion, and finances. Just be sure you have thought through the decision extensively, done your research, and asked the right questions. Then pick a dog or cat that suits your lifestyle, budget, and living conditions. Choosing the right pet will lead to a win-win situation with an abundance of fun-filled days for you and your four-legged furry friend.

Chapter 2

Make No Bones About It: Your Pet Is What It Eats

During sixteen colorful years of veterinary practice, I got into the habit of asking pet owners whose animals outlived their average life expectancy how they fed and cared for their pets. These amazing long-lived cats and dogs included Mrs. Wiley's sixteen-year-old lovable white German shepherd Penny, who exceeded the average life span of twelve years, and Mr. Bates's cantankerous twenty-year-old chocolate poodle, Taffy, who lived beyond the average fifteen-year life span. There was also Danner, a stoic twelve-year-old harlequin Great Dane whose normal life span would be seven years, and Sammy, Tiffany, and Peanut—all twenty-three-year-old persnickety domestic shorthair cats whose average life span should have been fourteen years. And these are just a few examples.

I queried these lucky pet owners partly out of curiosity, but partly because I had a vested interest: I wanted my chocolate Lab, Duke (I often felt like I gave birth to that dog), to live as long as possible.

While their answers varied, including yoga, an overabundance of walks, acupuncture, herbs, meditation, and unlimited hugs and kisses, there was a common denominator: They didn't give table scraps or people food.

They all fed their beloved cats and dogs pet food.

What a novel idea!

Some gave dry food only, some canned only, and some a mixture of both. As much as we want to spoil our pets with tidbits of our tasty food, the lesson learned from this is: We are actually causing them more harm than good when we do. Of course, genetics play a part, but you can extend your pet's natural life expectancy by being careful about what you feed it.

Cuisine Control

More than sixty percent of all vet bills and vet visits for vomiting and/or diarrhea are due to illnesses resulting from something a pet ate! Every year hundreds of well-meaning pet owners spend thousands of dollars in unnecessary vet bills because of what they gave their precious cat or dog to eat. This ranges from bones to burgers, pizza, avocados, and chocolate. You name it, and someone has given it to their pet—usually with disastrous results.

Just because your pet likes eating something doesn't mean it's good for them, and in some cases it can be harmful. Did you know that tuna fish can cause serious heart disease in cats? (I never understood why cats—which don't enjoy swimming or even like water, for that matter—love tuna so much.)

Feeding pets is similar to feeding children. You can't let your pet dictate the menu. Cats and dogs don't know what's good for them and they'll eat just about anything you give them or that they can get access to. Fast food tastes great, but you know how horrible it is for you—imagine how horrible it is for your pet. So an easy rule of thumb is: If it isn't particularly healthy for you, it's most likely harmful for your pet.

Pets Will Eat Anything

If your pet consumes something it shouldn't, you could be making matters even worse without realizing it. For example, one of my clients, Mr. Cotter, called me one evening to say that his Lab, Bubba, had gotten into some rich food and now had the "squirts," as he called it. I prescribed a few days of a bland diet for Bubba—a 50/50 mixture of cottage cheese and white rice—to help bind him up. If there was no improvement, I explained, Mr. Cotter should bring Bubba in to see me.

A couple of days later, I received another call from Mr. Cotter. He was annoyed that the stools had not improved but were, in fact, worse. Upon questioning him, I came to learn that he was giving the right mixture, but not cooking the rice! From then on, I've always prescribed *cooked* white rice and cottage cheese.

Pica

Our pets will eat many bizarre things. In fact, there is a condition in dogs and cats (and children) called pica, in which they ingest inappropriate nonnutritive objects. This can include fabric, sticks, stones, dirt, mulch, jewelry, plastic toys, eyeglasses, and hats. I personally have removed stones, scissors, shoulder pads, dinosaur-print panties, diamonds, and a Mickey Mouse hat from pets with this condition.

While it's normal for puppies and kittens to orally explore their environment, it's abnormal for them to actually consume foreign, inappropriate objects. Pica can occur in young or adult animals and can cause serious medical complications such as severe oral burns from chewing on electrical cords (not to mention electrocution), poisoning from ingesting noxious substances, and even perforated or obstructed stomachs and intestines, which requires emergency abdominal surgery to repair tissue and remove the offending foreign object. Sometimes an underlying disease will cause this behavior, but most of the time the cause of pica is unknown. Recent theories suggest it is a form of obsessive-compulsive disorder or that it may be caused by boredom. In any case, if you suspect your pet has pica, it's best to consult with your veterinarian immediately.

Coprophagy is a specific form of pica where pets eat stool—either their own or that of another animal. This behavior, while not necessarily dangerous to the animal, is unacceptable and can lead to parasites and other intestinal upsets. Coprophagy is common in dogs but rare in cats. Again, the exact cause of this condition is not known, although some experts feel it is seen more often in dogs that tend to be highly food-motivated, or that it might be carried over from normal parental behavior of ingesting the waste of young offspring, or that it's a natural evolutionary behavior used by wild dogs to sustain themselves during times when food was unavailable. Dogs may also eat bowel movements from cats living in their household or from farm animals.

Coprophagia may be a behavioral problem or secondary to a medical illness such as hormone/endocrine imbalances, malabsorption disorders, parasites, diabetes, and/or disorders of the thyroid gland. Once your veterinarian has ruled out a medical cause of coprophagy, there are some steps you can take to curb this nasty behavior.

The most effective way is to eliminate access to the offending feces itself. This can be done by immediately picking up after your pet. Another suggestion is to keep your pet on a leash anytime it goes outside.

Behavior modification can also be an effective tool. At the time of defecation, distract your pet with a food reward so it will become conditioned to expect food at defecation instead of looking for feces to eat.

Alternatively, you can treat your pet's food with a commercial meat tenderizer, MSG, or a product called For-Bid to make feces taste unpleasant. You can also sprinkle cayenne pepper or a commercial product such as Bitter Apple spray directly on the stool to create a taste aversion. However, for this method to be effective, every stool your pet has access to must be treated in order for your pet to learn that eating stool results in unpleasant consequences.

Twenty Things You Should *Never* Feed Your Pet

The following list contains twenty foods that are commonly given to pets—usually with devastating results.

1. Bones

Bones are very dangerous for animals. Every year thousands of animals end up in the emergency room from eating bones, usually given by their owners as a treat. The fact is that dogs are omnivores, not carnivores. Most dogs and cats can't tolerate bones, since they can splinter or lodge in the intestinal tract with disastrous results, usually requiring surgery.

Bones can also get stuck in your pet's mouth or throat, which is just as dangerous. Bones of all kinds are bad; this includes pork, chicken, and beef. So the next time you feel the urge to give

Cats LOVE needles and thread, string of any sort, rubber bands—all kinds of fun stuff. Unfortunately, they will not only play with these things, but also eat them! Keep these items and others that your cat may seem attracted to in a safe place.

your dog a bone, just make sure it's a Milk-Bone™ or a Nylabone™. Your pet will love you for it.

2. Chocolate

A potentially lethal dose of chocolate for a sixteen-pound animal is only two ounces of baking chocolate or sixteen ounces of milk chocolate. Chocolate contains theobromine, which causes increased heart rate, central nervous system stimulation, and constriction of arteries in pets. Clinical symptoms range from vomiting, diarrhea, restlessness, and excitability to cardiac failure, seizures, and death. A serious reaction can occur as quickly as four to six hours after ingestion.

3. Alcohol

It doesn't take much alcohol to intoxicate a pet. Animals will stagger and bump into things, hurting themselves; alcohol also causes them to urinate uncontrollably. In high doses, it will suppress the central nervous, respiratory, and cardiac systems, and can even lead to death. It's best to just give your pet water.

4. Milk and Cheese

Many pets are lactose-intolerant and get diarrhea when drinking milk. Pets lack the enzyme that's required to break down milk sugar, and will experience vomiting, diarrhea, or other gastrointestinal symptoms. Even though your pets like milk and were nursed on their mother's milk, don't give it to them. Cheese, even in small amounts, is too high in fat and can lead to a life-threatening pancreatitis (inflammation of the pancreas).

5. Ham and Other Fatty or Salty Meats

Like cheese, ham and other fatty meats are high in fat, which can lead to pancreatitis, a potentially fatal condition. In addition, these foods can be very salty and can cause serious stomach upset if eaten by your cat or dog. Furthermore, large breeds of dogs that eat salty food may drink too much water and develop a potentially fatal condition called bloat. The stomach fills up with gas and within several hours may twist on itself, causing the animal to die. So avoid giving ham and rich, salty meats to your pets.

6. Onions and Garlic

Onions and garlic contain toxic ingredients that can damage pets' red blood cells and cause fatal consequences. Pets may develop vomiting and diarrhea, which may progress to anemia, weakness, and labored breathing. Onions, either raw or cooked, are more dangerous; a cat or dog can be seriously harmed by only a small amount. Garlic is less toxic, as pets need to ingest large amounts to cause illness.

7. Caffeine

Refrain from giving your pets coffee, as caffeine is unsafe for them. It contains methylated xanthine that, like chocolate, stimulates the central nervous and cardiac systems and, within several hours, causes vomiting, restlessness, heart palpitations, and even death. So make sure your pets stay away from that early morning brew.

8. Avocados

First, avocados are high in fat and can cause your pet stomach upset, vomiting, and even pancreatitis. Second, the pit, besides being toxic, can get lodged in your pet's intestinal tract, leading to a severe blockage that may require surgery. Symptoms of toxicity include difficulty in breathing, abdominal enlargement, and abnormal fluid accumulation in the chest and abdomen.

9. Tuna Fish

A cat's heart muscle requires an amino acid called taurine to maintain normal strength and function. Canned tuna fish doesn't have this amino acid, and cats that eat too much tuna will develop heart problems. If you want to give your cats the taste of tuna that they love, just make sure it's tuna fish for cats, which has taurine added.

10. Raisins and Grapes

A recent study found that raisins and grapes can cause gastrointestinal problems like vomiting and diarrhea, and can lead to life-threatening kidney failure. Symptoms start about twenty-four hours after ingestion. Small dogs can also choke on grapes.

11. Macadamia Nuts

These tasty nuts contain an unknown toxin that can seriously affect a pet's digestive tract, nervous system, and skeletal muscles. Clinical signs include vomiting weakness, depression, diarrhea, panting, difficulty walking, and muscle tremors. Dogs have become violently ill from ingesting as few as six macadamia nuts.

12. Tobacco

Tobacco contains nicotine, which rapidly affects the digestive and nervous systems of pets. This may lead to salivation, vomiting, diarrhea, hyperactivity, shallow breathing, rapid heartbeat, collapse, coma, and even death.

13. Liver

Eating large amounts of liver can cause vitamin A toxicity, which severely affects muscles and bones. Hypervitaminosis A causes severe changes, including constipation, deformed bones, weight loss, anorexia, and neck, joint, or spine stiffness due to excessive bone growth on the elbows and spine.

14. Fat

A pet's consumption of fat trimmings can cause pancreatitis, which leads to vomiting and diarrhea. Pets with pancreatitis are usually lethargic with severe stomach pain, and often become dehydrated. If left untreated, the condition can be fatal.

15. Potato Peels and Green-Looking Potatoes

Potato peels contain oxalates, which adversely affect pets' digestive, nervous, and urinary tract systems. Symptoms include lethargy, depression, vomiting, diarrhea, and seizures.

16. Yeast Dough

If ingested, yeast dough will expand in a pet's stomach or intestines and produce large amounts of gas in the digestive system, causing severe pain and even rupture of the stomach or intestines. Second, as the dough ferments, it produces alcohol, which can be toxic as well. Symptoms include vomiting, abdominal discomfort, lethargy, and depression.

17. Moldy, Spoiled Food

Dogs and cats can get food poisoning just like humans, and can actually die from eating moldy or spoiled food that may contain multiple toxins, causing vomiting, diarrhea, tremors, shaking, and seizures. Garbage gut is definitely dangerous, so don't feed anything you wouldn't eat to your pets.

IMPORTANT NOTE

If you think your pet has ingested any of the above food items, call your veterinarian immediately.

18. Rhubarb and Tomato Leaves or Stems

These plants contain oxalates, which adversely affect the digestive, nervous, and urinary tract systems. Pets will experience vomiting, diarrhea, labored breathing, abdominal cramps, weakness, convulsions, muscle twitching, and seizures from ingesting these.

19. Mushrooms

Mushroom toxicity can be fatal if certain species of mushrooms are ingested. These can contain toxins that may affect multiple systems in your pet's body, leading to shock and eventually death. Clinical signs include abdominal pain, seizures, hallucinations, depression, vomiting, and diarrhea.

20. Plums, Peaches, Pears, Apricot Pits, and Apple Cores

The pits and cores of these delicious fruits contain cyanogenic glycosides, which can result in cyanide poisoning when eaten by pets. Signs of toxicity include salivation, apprehension, dilated pupils, difficulty breathing, dizziness, collapse, coma, seizures, hyperventilation, and shock.

Times Are Changing

Dogs and cats have diverse nutritional needs, and how and what we feed our pets have evolved dramatically over the past thirty years. It used to be thought that dogs needed lots of meat or other protein in their diet to survive. As a consequence, dogs were

fed high-protein diets that resulted in poor coats, malnutrition, metabolic imbalance, hair loss, and weakness. We now know that dogs are really omnivores, which means they need meat as well as nonmeat foods to survive.

Cats, on the other hand, are true carnivores. They have the highest requirement for protein of all domesticated species. Because of this greater knowledge, we have made huge advances in understanding pets' nutritional needs and, because of these great advances, pet food manufacturers now make some excellent high-quality, formulated diets. However, there are huge differences between the different brands and varieties of generic, popular, and premium foods. Generally speaking, though, you do get what you pay for.

Feeding for Life Stages

Cats and dogs come in all shapes, sizes, colors, and ages. Most pet foods are made for three specific life stages, and this is exactly how you should feed your pet. Dogs and cats in different life stages require very different amounts of nutrients and calories.

The first stage is pediatric. Puppies and kittens under one year of age (for most breeds) should eat puppy or kitten food. At this life stage their bodies are constantly growing, so they need more protein, fat, vitamins, minerals, and calories than adults or seniors. It's very important that during this life stage they receive the correct balance of vitamin D, calcium, phosphorus, and high-quality protein needed for normal growth. If this doesn't happen, serious problems such as vitamin deficiencies, bone deformities, and malnutrition may occur, which can permanently scar them.

The next life stage is the adult or maintenance stage. This occurs when a dog or cat reaches full maturity, usually around one year of age. The object at this time in their development is to maintain a healthy body condition while supplying needed nutrients and energy. The activity level of an adult cat or dog will vary dramatically from one animal to another, so the amount they eat will vary, but they should all be eating an adult or maintenance diet until they reach the next life stage.

The senior or geriatric stage in dogs begins at five to seven years of age, depending on the breed. In cats, this occurs between the ages of seven and ten. Older dogs and cats are more susceptible to developing certain medical conditions such as diabetes, cancer, obesity, high blood pressure, constipation, arthritis, kidney disease, and heart disease. Senior diets that contain less protein, sodium, phosphorus, and fat are designed to help decrease the workload on the kidney, heart, and pancreas. Some senior diets have added fiber to help with constipation, and glucosamine to help improve joint function. Senior pets, just like elderly people, have a slower metabolism and can quickly gain weight, which leads to a higher likelihood of developing such conditions as arthritis and heart disease. In general, seniors need fewer calories to maintain their weight. It's best to avoid excesses.

Kibble versus Canned

There are currently three types of food to choose from. Canned food (sixty-eight to eighty percent water) is available in moist form and in individual portions. Semimoist food (twenty-three to forty percent water) is available in individual portions or in bulk. Dry food (six to ten percent water) is available as kibble, meal, or expanded particles. The type of food you should feed your individual dog or cat depends on its age, its predisposition to dental disease, and its lifestyle. In general, I recommend feeding dry food, but you should also ask your veterinarian for his or her opinion. Although the three food types are quite different in form, the biggest difference is in the water content.

Canned food is approximately seventy-five percent water, which is an essential nutrient, but the downside is that your pet has to eat more canned food to fulfill its nutrient requirements. Wet food has a low caloric density and higher packaging cost, so it's more expensive per calorie to feed. Depending on your pet, it can also lead to tartar buildup. Wet food is also the most palatable. Just open a can of wet dog or cat food and you'll see!

Semimoist food, like canned food, tastes good, but it's not as messy and doesn't spoil as quickly. You don't need to refrigerate it after opening, and it usually comes in single-serving sizes. The drawbacks are that it's usually high in sugar and preservatives, and can contribute to dental disease in some animals.

Dry food has the lowest water content and is the most popular because of its convenience and its crunchy texture, which can help reduce the amount of dental disease in some pets. It usually has preservatives added to reduce spoiling, so it lasts the longest, and has a high caloric density, which means it's the most economical to feed.

How Often to Feed

Of course, there's the issue of how often to feed your pet. I'm a big proponent of controlled feeding. My cats, Kinky and Nathan, each get two small scoops for breakfast and two small scoops for dinner. In place of extra food, I give them lots of love, playtime, and petting. This keeps them from being finicky and also lets me know exactly how much they're eating.

Obesity is now a problem in more than one third of all household pets. An easy way to avoid this growing epidemic is to use controlled feeding. If you see your pet's waistline vanishing, you can immediately cut down on its food intake. If your pet is too thin, you can add more food to its diet.

I believe in twice-a-day feedings for several reasons. First, twice-daily feedings are better for digestion than one large meal. Too-infrequent feeding leads to slow metabolism and even vomiting of bile from an empty stomach. Second, I think pets enjoy eating twice a day versus only once. They see us eating at least three meals, and by feeding them twice a day you'll resist the urge to feed them from the table, and your pet will be happier and healthier, and will live longer.

How Much to Feed

The feeding directions on the pet food have been specifically developed for that particular food. These are guidelines to help you choose what amount to give your cat or dog. You need to know how much your pet weighs to follow the instructions on the label, and I recommend starting at the lower amount given for the range of food to be fed. You want your pet to have an ideal body condition. This occurs when an animal looks well-proportioned with an observable waist behind the ribcage, and ribs that can be felt but not seen. There should be a small amount of fat covering your pet's ribs. If you're unsure about your pet's weight, ask your veterinarian. When I tell clients that their pets are overweight, they usually look at me in disbelief. See Chapter 6 on the battle of the bulge for more information.

Homemade Diets

Just like humans, cats and dogs have complex nutritional requirements to stay healthy. Although the concept of cooking for your pet may be enticing, at this time I don't recommend homemade diets unless instructed by your veterinarian. There are numerous problems with cooking for your pets. First, formulating your own cat or dog food is a difficult task. It's time-consuming and much more expensive to try and produce quality foods that provide better nutrition than you'd get from a premium brand of cat or dog food. Second, the nutrients in the formulation may not be the right quantities or proportions that your pet needs. Incorrect preparation and cooking may also deplete certain nutrients and result in a deficient diet. Third, homemade diets haven't been tested to document performance in cats and dogs over long periods of time. With so many excellent commercial brands available, I don't see any benefit to homemade diets right now. With that said, though, in ten to twenty years I wouldn't be surprised to find readily available homemade cooking packets for your cats and dogs in your grocery aisle!

How to Read Labels

Learning to read labels will teach you a great deal about the food you're feeding your cat or dog. You can also call the phone number on the bag or can, or go to the website for information. This way the company can offer explanations of what's listed on the label. It's important to know that one company's product may be very different from another's. Pet food labels are strictly regulated by AAFCO (Association of American Feed Control Officials), the federal government, the Food and Drug Administration, and the Department of Agriculture, and must follow strict guidelines like human food labels. If the pet food follows the guidelines set forth by AAFCO, the label will include a statement that says the food provides complete and balanced nutrition for that life stage, and it will also list whether the food is intended as a treat or a supplement.

Higher-quality diets with excellent protein sources cost more, but cheap ingredients are less efficiently digested. Your pets have to eat more of them to meet their nutritional needs, if that is even possible.

This translates into higher costs and, you guessed it, more poop to scoop.

Things You Want on the Label

1. Look for a pet food that conforms to minimal AAFCO standards.

2. Choose a pet food that has a highly digestible source of protein. Meat-based diets such as chicken, turkey, beef, or fish are much better because the protein is of a higher quality and is easier to digest. Look closely because many foods are vegetable-based, like soybean, corn, or rice, all of which contain incomplete proteins.

3. The first two or three ingredients on the label should be some type of animal protein such as chicken, beef, fish, lamb, or turkey. They should not be animal by-products (the leftover part of the meat), grains, or vegetables.

4. The pet food can or bag should have an expiration date. Don't feed foods past their expiration date.

5. There should be a phone number and/or website so you can contact the company and ask questions.

6. Look for natural preservatives like vitamin C or E.

Things to Avoid

1. Generic-label or store-label brands. Feeding cheap food to your pet is the equivalent of people eating fast food. It's cheap and it tastes good, but it's not good for them. It's much better to eat a well-balanced meal with high-quality ingredients like lean meats, vegetables, and fruits.

2. Purchasing food past its expiration date.

3. Food that has preservatives that are controversial. These include BHT, ethoxyquine, BHA, and propylene glycol.

4. Unidentified meat, bone meal, or meat by-products listed on the label.

5. Vegetables or grains listed as the first several ingredients.
6. Cheap or low-quality foods with fancy labels.

Dealing with Treats

A treat should be just that: something special that's given on occasion. Treats aren't necessary for most cats or dogs, and can even be harmful in certain instances. Most dog and cat treats are not complete foods and are extremely high in fat and sugar with very little nutritional value. Try to choose treats that have protein and/or carbohydrates as the first few ingredients. Too many treats can lead to imbalances in the diet and even malnutrition. Dogs and cats filling up on too many treats are like kids eating too much candy—it's unhealthy. Try to stick with treats that match your pet's lifestyle and life stage.

Another potential problem from too many treats is weight gain. A small dog or cat fed two to three treats a day may become overweight in less than a year, unless the intake of regular food is decreased to compensate for the added calories. When using treats as a reward during training, just break off a small piece instead of giving the whole thing. Using treats only as a training tool or to enhance your close bond is great—but if you give them all the time, they won't be special! Just be sure to keep them to less than ten percent of your pet's daily food intake.

Will a Pill a Day Keep the Vet Away?

To supplement or not to supplement—that is the question. Vitamins have been around for more than twenty years, and in the spirit of treating pets as part of the family, it seems like any vitamin or supplement you can buy for yourself is also available for your cat or dog. But how safe are vitamins and supplements, and are they really necessary?

There's a large amount of anecdotal evidence, some of which dates back to ancient times, supporting the benefits of nutritional supplements. However, there's a lack of scientific studies to validate these anecdotal claims. Furthermore, just because supplements work for people doesn't necessarily mean they will promote health and well-being in pets.

Yes, vitamins can play a key role in keeping pets healthy—ensuring proper nutrition and rehabilitating an injured or sick animal. However, veterinary nutritionists agree that if your pet is eating a well-balanced, nutritionally complete dog or cat food, there's no reason to add a vitamin or mineral supplement.

There are times, however, throughout an animal's life when it may need a higher than normal amount of nutrients, including:

- Being under stress from illness or injury
- Recovering from surgery
- Having a poor appetite
- Experiencing bone and joint problems
- If the pet is an active and working dog
- When on a restricted diet
- When taking certain medications
- When it's very young or very old
- When pregnant or nursing

Always check with your vet before adding vitamins to a pet's diet on your own, because doing so can actually be harmful to the pet's health. While it's tempting to believe that a pill a day will keep the vet away, arming yourself with knowledge will help you make the right decision with regard to adding vitamins or supplements to your pet's diet.

The bottom line is that each pet and situation is different and must be treated on an individual basis. The following is a summary of tips to help you make the right decisions about giving supplements to your pet:

- Talk with your veterinarian before adding *anything* to your pet's diet. Your vet can guide you and give you an objective opinion on the effectiveness, safety, and toxicity potential of the supplements.
- Read labels and avoid products that make outrageous claims. Chances are, if it sounds too good to be true, it probably is. Beware of product labels that make wild claims to cure disease.
- Always give recommended doses.
- Don't forget to tell your vet about *any* supplement you're adding to your pet's diet, especially if your pet is being treated for a medical condition.
- Always choose a reputable company, check out the manufacturer's reputation, and look for quality ingredients.
- Call the manufacturer and ask questions.
- Avoid high levels of supplementation of any single nutrient unless specifically prescribed by your vet.
- Be suspicious of terms like "natural," "holistic," "wholesome," and "organic."
- Be wary of pet foods that are okay for all stages of life.
- Be sure to check with your vet about discontinuing all natural remedies two weeks prior to surgery.
- Cats tend to be much more sensitive than dogs and should *never* be given supplements without the advice of a vet.

Animals with Special Needs

There are many cats and dogs that have illnesses or conditions that require prescription diets. Some of these diseases are feline lower urinary tract disease (FLUTD), kidney disease, heart disease, food allergies, inflammatory bowel disease, and obesity. Veterinarians routinely use prescription diets for these specific health conditions. Sometimes I will put animals that are at risk for developing a particular disease on a diet to prevent this problem.

Male cats with FLUTD are at risk of making crystals in their urine, which can lead to urethral obstruction and death. Both my cats eat urinary tract formulas as a preventative to this disease; I simply don't want to risk the odds of them developing it. These are diets with reduced minerals such as ash and magnesium that contribute to the formation of crystals. They also promote a urine pH level that further inhibits FLUTD. When in doubt, ask your vet if a prescription diet is right for your pet.

Food for Thought

Feeding your pets should be enjoyable and easy. Again, I want to stress the importance of properly feeding your cat or dog. Their health and longevity depend on it! Deficiencies and excesses of the six basic nutrients in your pet's diet can cause irreversible damage, scarring your pet for life. So read labels, use controlled feeding, discuss your choices with your vet, and, most important, find a brand in your pet's life stage that it loves. Instead of varying your cat or dog's food, try changing the toys they play with and giving lots of love and attention. Don't forget fresh water at all times. My cats run to their bowl every morning and every night to eat the same kibble I've been feeding them for six years, and they've had no health problems. Stick with one brand and avoid table foods, and you'll not only save money on your vet bills, but your pet will live a longer, healthier life as well!

Chapter 3

Prevention Pays, Neglect Costs

I'll bet if I said I knew how you could increase your pet's life span by about twenty percent, you'd say, "Great, doc—tell me what to do!" Well, it's called *prevention*—which simply means defending against disease by taking care of your dog or cat the way you take care of yourself. Prevention is one of the reasons many dogs are living into their late teens and cats are living into their early twenties. Another reason for this increased longevity is improved technology and medicine. Kidney transplants, MRIs, prosthetics, hip replacements, dialysis, root canals, pacemakers, chemotherapy, and even brain surgery are all real options now for cats and dogs. In fact, almost any procedure that can be performed on people can now be performed on pets. The key is that veterinarians need to make an early diagnosis—before it's too late and the disease process is so far along that treatment is ineffective.

The trouble is, the initial changes in your dog or cat that indicate illnesses are often very subtle and can easily be missed. It's deadly to show signs of illness or disease in the wild; therefore, animals often instinctually hide their symptoms, which can make minor changes more difficult to detect.

Many common diseases in pets are preventable and inexpensive to treat if identified early. Therefore, as a pet parent you play an integral role in prevention and early detection. You must take your cat or dog's health into your own hands by:

1. Quickly recognizing signs and symptoms of disease.
2. Taking your pet to the veterinarian at least once a year for a physical exam and, if needed, teeth cleaning.
3. Complying with the veterinarian's medical directives for course of treatment and follow-up care.

Common Sense and Vigilance

Animals meow, bark, hiss, and howl, but since they can't talk, they can't tell you when they don't feel well. Be vigilant. You must become aware of your pet's normal routines and habits. This is an easy yet indispensable way of picking up on early warning signs, such as changes in your pet's diet, behavior, activity level, and regular routine. These changes communicate volumes about your pet's well-being.

Also, by learning to do a weekly "once-over" physical exam on your pet at home, you can catch health problems early, which is an essential component in keeping your pet healthy and your vet bills low. Another big benefit of home exams is that your pet will get used to being handled and examined. This decreases your pet's anxiety when receiving yearly physical exams at the hospital. Of course, they will probably always dislike the rectal thermometer, but it's a lot easier and faster to make an accurate diagnosis on pets that willingly allow the vet to examine them.

The Weekly Once-Over

When performing your weekly at-home exam, you want to take a systematic approach and do it the same way every time so you don't miss anything. Be sure to sneak in lots of hugs and kisses so your pet learns to enjoy it; you might even find a special petting spot during the once-over. I discovered that Kinky loves to be scratched under her chin and Nathan adores body rubbing.

Face

It's been said that the eyes are the windows to the soul. This is true for animals as well—you can tell a lot about their health by looking at their eyes. You're probably already looking into your pet's eyes lovingly, but you also want to look for signs of illness or injury. Dogs and cats get many of the same diseases that we do, including cataracts, glaucoma, conjunctivitis, and dry eye, but if caught in the early stages, many of these conditions can be prevented from progressing and your pet's eyesight could even be saved. Cats and dogs can even develop tumors in the eyes, so look closely with a good light. Both pupils should be the same size and the eyes should be clear, bright, and shiny, not cloudy.

The whites of the eyes, or sclera, should be white, not red. Dogs and cats have what's called a "third eyelid," which helps protect the eye as well as lubricate it by producing tears. The third eyelid should not be showing. When a cat or dog is sick or in pain, you will suddenly see this white-colored membrane covering the lower part of the eye. You should not see redness, discharge, or squinting, as these can all be signs of infection, foreign objects in the eye, or pain.

Check to see if there is an increase or a decrease in tear production by noticing how moist your pet's eyes look and how often they tear up. Certain breeds of dogs such as the cocker spaniel, shih tzu, Lhasa apso, Pekingese, miniature schnauzer, and bulldog are predisposed to developing a very common condition known as dry eye, where tear production is greatly reduced, leading to red, itchy, and painful eyes.

The eyes should not appear sunken or excessively protruding, and your pet should not be rubbing or pawing at its eyes. If your cat or dog has a small amount of normal discharge in the corner of its eyes, go ahead and gently wipe this out with a soft tissue. You can also use eye wash solution, a saline solution available over the counter at drug or pet stores, to remove this.

Lips

Some dogs that have lip folds, such as spaniels, are especially prone to inflammation and skin infections on their lips. Lip tumors can develop on both dogs and cats. Check your pet's lips to make sure there are no crusts and there is no scaling, and that the skin isn't dry and cracked like your lips when they are dry. Be sure to look for redness and hair loss around the mouth as well.

Nose

It's a common fallacy that a warm nose means a dog or cat has a fever. Humidity, body temperature, and flow of tears through the ducts into the nose all help determine whether your pet's nose is dry, moist, warm, or cold. There are no sweat glands in the nose and the moisture is caused by the mucus lining. During sleep and in certain climates, a dog or cat's nose may become warm and dry, but this doesn't mean it has a fever. However, the nose should be smooth and without any scaling or roughness. Sneezing or nasal discharge can be signs of an upper respiratory infection, quite common in cats. Also look for color changes on your pet's nose. There should be no loss of pigmentation on a dark nose. White noses can get sunburn and even skin cancer. See Chapter 12 on seasonal disturbances for directions on applying sunscreen.

Ears

Since cats and dogs have much longer ear canals than people do, infections usually start way down at the eardrum and work their way upward, so by the time you actually see debris, the infection has most likely been there a while. Dogs and cats are susceptible to ear infections because of their long, L-shaped canals; some dogs have wax-trapping hair lining the canals as well. And dogs that have moisture-sealing earflaps provide the perfect swamplike environment for bugs to thrive.

Look at your pet's ears. They should have very little odor or discharge, but a small amount of wax is normal. If you see debris, redness, hair loss, or crusting, or your pet seems to be in pain when its ears are touched, it could be a sign of an ear infection. Look for abnormalities on the outside of the ears, a happy home for some parasites. Hair loss, crusting, and redness can indicate mites, allergies, or infection. Ears should be flat, not swollen. Flies will sometimes bite at the tips of dogs' ears, so carefully check along the edges. Cats and dogs will paw at their ears or shake their heads when their ears are bothering them. Also, if your pet is prone to ear infections, learn how to properly flush out the ear canals. Have your vet show you how to do this. I've also given some tips below.

How often to clean depends on the pet and how many predisposing factors it has. I usually recommend ear cleaning at least every two weeks for dogs, and only if instructed by your vet for cats. Regular ear cleaning can drastically reduce the number of infections your pet develops.

How to clean the ears:

Use an ear-cleaning solution made for dogs and cats. Squirt the solution into the ear, filling the *entire* canal, and gently massage the ear base for sixty seconds. The solution should hit the eardrum and flow back out of the ear if you have completely filled the canal. Wiping or cleaning only the upper portion of the canal does nothing for the lower portion, which is where infections usually begin. Let your pet shake its head, and then use a cotton ball to wipe out any debris. Repeat the whole process until cotton balls come out clean.

Things to avoid when cleaning:

- Never use Q-tip-type swabs, since they can easily break off and get lodged in your pet's ear canal.
- Never clean ears with peroxide, soap, water, or oil, as these can irritate the skin lining the canal or set up the perfect environment for an infection.

The bottom line is to learn what your pet's ears normally look like so you'll spot a problem early—before a severe infection or illness sets in.

Mouth

Notice if your pet has any trouble opening and closing its mouth. Look for any drooling or difficulty chewing and swallowing. Hopefully you're brushing your pet's teeth daily or at least three times a week. Refer to Chapter 5 on dental disasters for instructions. Check your dog or cat's mouth for tumors, swelling, bleeding gums, tartar, and foreign objects like string (cats) and sticks (dogs). Look at the teeth. Are they white, brown, or green? There should be no broken teeth and **no odor**.

Look at the color of the gums. They should be nice and pink, not white or red. You can check your pet's circulation by using your thumb and briefly applying pressure to the gums and releasing. The area that you pressed should turn white and then rapidly return to the normal pink color. This is called the capillary refill time. For dogs and cats, one to two seconds is considered normal. If the refill time is less than one second or more than three seconds, it could indicate a serious circulation problem and necessitates an immediate trip to the vet.

Before moving to the skin, feel under your pet's throat. Dogs and cats have lymph nodes in their bodies, just like humans do. Feeling for lumps, like the doctor does to you, can help detect enlarged lymph nodes, which can be the first sign of cancer or infection in dogs and cats. Dogs that get lymphoma, a common type of cancer, will have enlarged lymph nodes that are easily felt. Other lymph nodes that are readily detectable when enlarged are located at the shoulder, under the forearm, and on the backs of the rear legs.

Excessive panting or coughing is abnormal, and your pet should not cough when you touch its throat. This can be a sign of a sensitive trachea or a common upper respiratory disease in dogs known as kennel cough. The trachea, or windpipe, is a long, hollow tube that connects the nose, mouth, and throat to the lungs. The normal trachea is tubular and it maintains its shape because of a series of circular rings made of cartilage. Certain breeds of dogs have weak cartilage, which leads to a flattening of the cartilage rings. Tracheal collapse is a common disease of toy breeds of dogs including chihuahuas, Lhasa apsos, Pomeranians, poodles, shih tzus, and Yorkshire terriers.

Skin and Coat

The skin is the largest organ of the body and is also the first line of defense against disease. Look closely at your pet's skin by parting the hair in several spots or blowing gently. It should be clean and dry. Look and feel for areas of swelling, heat, scrapes, pain, hair loss, crusting, or redness. Some pets have pigmentation or freckles on their skin, which is considered normal. Now run your hands all over your pet's body, including all four legs, and lift up the tail. You'd be amazed at how many animals develop tumors or infections on the underside of the tail. And don't forget to look at the tummy. (You never know—this could be a favorite spot for petting!) Check for lumps, bumps, and growths of any sort. Look closely under the fur because small bumps can be hard to see. The most common sites for tumors to grow are on the skin, mouth, mammary glands, and lymph nodes. Check under the coat for flakes, ticks, fleas, and flea dirt—small flecks of black debris that look like black pepper. This is actually flea poop, and if you get it wet, it will turn red—pretty disgusting! See Chapter 12 on seasonal disturbances for more information on fleas.

Your cat or dog's coat should be sleek and glossy, not dull, dry, or greasy. Run your fingers through your pet's hair. There should be no buildup or odor on your hands. Also check between the toes and look at the pads. Dogs and cats can get burrs, gum, and other foreign objects lodged there. During the summer months, dogs can easily burn their pads. See Chapter 12 on seasonal disturbances for more information.

Proper hydration is very important. A good check to see if your pet is drinking enough water and is adequately hydrated is to gently pull up on the skin over your pet's shoulder blades, then release the skin. If your pet is hydrated, the skin will snap back quickly into position. If your dog or cat is dehydrated, it will take much longer for the skin to release; sometimes, it will even stay tented up. This can be a serious problem and requires a phone call or a trip to your vet right away.

Anal Glands

The anal glands are two dime-sized sacs located on either side of the rectum, at the four o'clock and eight o'clock positions, and are found in a variety of animals. Their biological function is to impart a distinct odor to the stool that is unique to pets, and consequently they serve very little purpose in domesticated dogs and cats. This odor is very foul and pungent. The secretion from the glands is normally expressed when a pet has a bowel movement or is frightened, due to tightening of the rectal muscles. However, if the stools are too soft or too hard, or the substance in the gland is too thick, the glands will not get expressed and can get very full or become abscessed and impacted, causing pain and discomfort. A small percentage of dogs and cats genetically produce anal gland secretions that are too thick to pass through the small ducts that extend from the sacs to the anus.

When the glands become full or impacted, pets may scoot on the ground, lick their anal area, or exhibit strange behavior such as tail chasing, reluctance to allow you to touch their tail or rear end, reluctance to lift the tail, or circling; sometimes cats will groom themselves excessively beneath the tail. At this point the glands need to be manually emptied, usually by your veterinarian, although many groomers are adept at expressing the anal glands. If the glands are infected, antibiotics may be necessary.

Toenails

Keep those toenails short. Dogs and cats with overgrown nails are like women in stiletto heels. Walking is very difficult, and lameness, bone, or joint problems can occur as a result. Also, the nails can grow so long that they curl under the foot, embedding into the pads or skin, which is extremely painful for your pet. Nail trims need to be done regularly, depending on how active your pet is and how fast its nails grow. You should have your cat's or dog's nails trimmed on a regular basis, either at a vet hospital or at a groomer's. If you want to attempt it yourself, have a professional teach you how. Cats and dogs can get quite ornery if it isn't done properly, and accidentally cutting the nail too short will result in lots of pain and bleeding. It's best to start trimming your pet's nails early on, as a puppy or kitten, to get them used to this routine grooming procedure.

Weight

Last but not least, check for weight gain or loss. This can be crucial in determining early signs of disease or illness. I recommend weighing your pet weekly. Using your home scale, just weigh yourself holding your pet and then subtract your weight that day. Even just a few extra pounds can be significant in animals, leading to arthritis, heart disease, diabetes, and breathing difficulties. Chances are if you can pinch an inch, your pet is overweight and should see the vet to get started on a weight-loss program. See Chapter 6 on the battle of the bulge for more details. Some long-haired cats and dogs can appear healthy, when in reality they have lost weight, but because of their luxuriant coat, the loss may not be readily apparent. Catching weight loss or gain in the early stages is far better than waiting until it has progressed to something more serious that's much harder to treat.

Again, be aware of what's normal for your pet, so when changes occur, you can address them immediately by calling or visiting the vet to get the problem checked out and treated before it becomes severe.

The Brush-Off

Regular brushing is good for your pets, both mentally and physically. The earlier in life you start brushing, the better. Get your pet used to having its paws looked at, too, and to being handled in general. If your pet is an adult, you'll have to start out slower and spend more time initially getting them used to this. Brushing helps reduce shedding and improves the quality of the coat, which is a magnet for all kinds of things including gum, burrs, paint, fleas, and ticks.

Brushing your cat or dog is important for a number of reasons:

- It makes your pet feel good.
- It prevents hair from snarling into painful mats.
- It helps prevent hairballs in cats.
- It removes dead hair and stimulates new hair growth.
- It invigorates the skin and coat, keeping your pet healthy and its coat shiny.

Ten Most Common Ailments

A large percentage of ailments that afflict cats and dogs can be prevented with proper diet, care, and exercise. Here's a list of the ten most common medical conditions reported in dogs and cats, and the ways you can help prevent them.

1. Dental disease: daily tooth brushing and annual dental exams by your vet.
2. Ear infections: regular ear cleaning.
3. Bladder infections: feeding a proper diet and ensuring adequate water intake.
4. Stomach upset: feeding a proper diet and not giving table scraps.
5. Skin irritation: providing adequate flea/tick control, brushing, and feeding a proper diet.
6. Kidney disease: feeding a proper diet and ensuring adequate water intake.
7. Arthritis: exercising (slows onset by preventing weight gain).
8. Upper respiratory disease: proper vaccinations (prevents some infections).

9. Diabetes: keeping your pet lean with a proper diet and exercise.

10. Intestinal disease: feeding a proper diet and not giving table scraps.

Creatures of Habit

Cats and dogs are creatures of habit. They like eating from the same bowl, sleeping on the same pillow, and staring out the same window day in and day out. One clue that your pet might not be feeling well is any sudden change in its normal pattern of behavior. It's important for you to observe your dog or cat's normal routine and make a mental note or jot it down. I recommend a journal to keep a record of your pet's health. It can prove invaluable in early diagnosis of disease.

Sometimes changes can be very obvious, and other times, quite subtle. A dog that usually loves its walk but is now suddenly lying in the back room where it never goes is obviously not feeling well, yet another sick dog might be going on those walks but just lagging behind or drooping its head or tail a bit. These are warning signs that something isn't right. Cats, with strong evolutionary habits to mask indications of illness, might just not want to be petted when they feel sick, or might start vocalizing more.

Be a Pet Detective

Train yourself to observe your cat or dog like they observe you. Believe me, they know all of your patterns, habits, and rituals. Use all of your senses: sight, sound, smell, and touch (okay, no taste involved here). Watch the way your pet moves,

breathes, and pants or meows. Use your nose to detect any unusual odors. Any changes in your pet's daily habits might be a clue that a health problem is present. Cats and dogs can be quite stoic about pain, and may not show you they're hurting until the problem is so advanced that they can no longer hide their discomfort. Dogs are sometimes just so overjoyed to play that they will often ignore pain.

Behavior changes that signal something is wrong include:

- Hiding
- Irritability
- Increased sleeping time
- Decreased interest in playing
- Aloofness
- Apprehension
- Tiring easily
- Not wanting to be petted
- Hyperactivity
- Decreased alertness
- Clinging more than usual
- Reduced interest in you
- Vocalizing

As a veterinarian, I rely heavily on owners' observations to help me detect problems and steer me in the right direction to a proper diagnosis. Remember, we can't ask our patients questions. (Well, we can ask all we want, but we'll be waiting a long time for the answers.) You and your pet share a life together, whereas I only get to see your pet maybe once a year for an examination. If you bring your cat or dog in once a year and I spend fifteen to thirty minutes for each exam, and your pet lives to be twelve years old, that's only a total of three to six hours spent with your pet in its lifetime. Not much time for me to adequately get to know your pet!

Your observations are extremely important, as you will be

answering questions on your pet's behalf as well as providing information that will assist the vet in keeping your pet healthy. So your weekly once-overs, keen observations, and written records are invaluable.

Yearly Physical Exam

One of the most critical actions is taking your pet to the vet at least once a year for a complete physical and dental exam. Of course, it's important to visit the vet when your dog or cat is ill, but many pet owners don't recognize the value of taking their pets to the doctor even when they aren't sick. Remember that animals are programmed to conceal illness in the wild—where it's about survival of the fittest and the weakest animals are preyed upon first—so cats and dogs don't always show you when they're not feeling well. In addition, unfortunately, life spans of dogs and cats are much shorter than ours, and many diseases in the early stages are not readily apparent, such as abnormalities of the heart, kidney disease, thyroid problems, and even cancer.

Never underestimate the importance of your cat or dog's yearly exam. Your veterinarian is doctor, dentist, and surgeon all rolled into one. If you take your pet in once a year for a checkup, it's the equivalent of you seeing your own doctor and dentist once every five to seven years, because animals age approximately five to seven years for each year of human life. And the longer a problem persists, the more difficult it is to treat. Waiting until your pet is showing obvious clinical signs means waiting until some internal damage has begun.

Important reasons for regular checkups include:
- Early disease detection. The goal is to prevent disease, or at least detect it early.
- Vaccinations to prevent common life-threatening diseases such as rabies, distemper, and parvo in dogs; rabies and feline leukemia in cats.

- Obesity/nutritional counseling. One out of every three pets is obese. It's the most common nutritional disease. Many owners think their pet's weight is normal when it really isn't. See Chapter 6 on the battle of the bulge.
- Discussion of behavioral problems.

Owner Compliance

Pet owner compliance is of paramount importance in treating illness and disease. This is where owners often make a big mistake: They either stop medicating their pets early because they think the problem has been resolved or are not administering the medicine properly in the first place.

Many owners stop giving medications early because outwardly their pet appears to have been cured. In reality, the ailment is under control, but not necessarily gone. Discontinuing antibiotics or any medicine early is never a good idea unless instructed by your vet. Especially with antibiotics, the most resistant bacteria are killed off last. If you stop the antibiotics too soon, before the infection has completely cleared up, the most resistant bacteria remain and will produce an infection that's more difficult to treat than if you had given all of the medication appropriately in the first place. To make matters worse, there's now a risk of antibiotic resistance, in which bacteria have mutated or changed so the antibiotic that previously killed them or slowed their growth doesn't affect them anymore. As more bacteria become resistant to various antibiotics, there are fewer medications that have an effect on them; thus, newer and stronger antibiotics will need to be used, if they exist. Inappropriate antibiotic usage includes not giving it at the right time, skipping dosages, not following instructions such as giving it with food, not giving it for the appropriate length prescribed, or giving it too often.

If your vet prescribes antibiotics for seven days, you must give the antibiotics for the full seven days. Do not stop on day three because you think the problem is over.

Some owners stop the medications because they're having trouble giving them to their cats and dogs. Administering pills or liquid to your pet can be frustrating for both parties. A recent market survey revealed that only ten percent of cat owners and thirty percent of dog owners succeed in medicating their pets correctly. Therefore, a lot of prescriptions sent home by veterinarians end up in the owner's cupboard rather than in the pet. Sometimes owners are embarrassed to admit failure. Don't be. Veterinarians and their staff understand how difficult it can be, both physically and emotionally, to give a cat or dog medicine. Because of this battle—where pets are hiding under the bed and owners are prying mouths open—drug manufacturers have gotten smarter and are now offering tablet and liquid medications in delectable flavors like chicken potpie, bacon, tuna, cheddar cheese, and even banana bread. You need to communicate with your vet if you're having trouble medicating your pet, because you must give all medicines as prescribed. Your pet's health depends on it!

Leftover prescriptions should be discarded unless otherwise instructed. Pet owners might think they'll save money by reusing the medication at a later date. But in fact, they're actually promoting chronic disease by not treating the problem completely in the first place, and besides, the leftover pills or liquids will expire. Trust me, when writing prescriptions, veterinarians only prescribe the amount of medication for the minimum amount of time it takes to treat the particular illness.

Follow-Up

The following is a common scenario. An owner brings a pet in because it has been shaking its head. I diagnose an ear infection and, after flushing the ear canals, I send home eardrops and oral antibiotics. I tell the owner to bring the dog in for a recheck in two weeks to make sure the infection has been completely resolved. The dog never comes in for the follow-up, and instead I see the pet three months later for another ear infection, which is more severe this time. The owner tells me they didn't come in for the recheck because it seemed like the infection had cleared up; the dog stopped shaking its head and appeared to be fine. The owner is now frustrated that the infection is back. Of course, the problem is that the infection had never gone away in the first place, and now it's more serious.

That one- to two-week recheck is essential to making sure the infection has been completely resolved. In order to determine this, the vet must use an otoscope, an instrument with a long plastic cone attached, to actually see the eardrum. Without the otoscope it's impossible to tell whether the infection has cleared up. So don't drop the ball. Keeping your follow-up appointments is vital.

Go to the Vet

The following are all signs of ill health and necessitate a trip to the vet:

- Any discharge from the eyes, nose, mouth, or other body opening
- Foul odor from the mouth, ears, or skin
- Fever of any kind
- Any sudden increase or decrease in water consumption or appetite
- Head shaking or pawing at eyes, face, or ears
- Excessive licking, scratching, or biting at the skin or any other body part
- Any lumps and bumps
- Any change in attitude or energy level
- Any change in potty habits or stools
- Sudden weight loss or gain
- Stiffness or difficulty rising
- Sleeping more or other behavior changes
- Open wounds, sores, loss of hair, and/or dull, dry, or greasy coat

Paw and Order

Get to know your pets. Be observant of their habits and routines on a daily basis and the way they look and smell. Understand them both emotionally and physically. The ultimate goal of preventative medicine is to discover diseases early and treat them before they become serious, causing irreparable damage. Performing your own physical exam on your pet once a week is so important in the early detection of illness.

Because pets age so much faster than humans, their life spans are short and their health can change a great deal over the course of even a few months, so always bring your pet in for its yearly exams and give all prescribed medications. Taking your pet to the vet sooner rather than later will not only save you time and money in the long run, but can also save your pet's life!

CAUTION

You *must* take your cat or dog to the vet whenever it gets into a fight with another animal. The skin is the first line of defense against disease, and if a puncture wound occurs, bacteria and viruses can enter the bloodstream, leading to disastrous and sometimes fatal consequences. I remember performing an autopsy on a client's pet that had died unexpectedly. The cause of death was an endocarditis, or infection of the heart valve. Unfortunately this pet had gotten into a fight with another dog and the owner declined antibiotics, recommended by the emergency vet, which proved to be a fatal mistake.

Chapter 4

Love Your Pet: Spay or Neuter Your Pet

Cats and dogs don't share our sexuality. They don't have sex for fun or romance, or because they're lonely, angry, or jealous. Animals don't fall in love. They're not motivated by sexual pleasure, but rather by instinct or a hormonal drive to breed. When their reproductive organs are removed, they don't miss their sexuality nor do they worry about the loss of their ovaries or testicles. They don't have a "sex drive"—they're simply responding to hormonal changes to ensure survival of their species. These hormonal changes can, in fact, cause great discomfort, torment, and even premature death.

Many pet owners project their own emotional or physical needs onto their animals (a phenomenon called anthropomorphism), when, in fact, there's absolutely no benefit from sexual activity for either male or female cats or dogs. Spaying (for the females) or neutering (for the males) effectively eliminates the development and progression of numerous objectionable and sometimes dangerous sexual behaviors.

Most people think veterinarians recommend spaying and neutering to help the overpopulation crisis. Tragically, about every four seconds an animal is killed by euthanasia because it has no home. While this is certainly a major reason to spay or neuter your pet, there are numerous health and behavioral benefits, too.

In fact, the single most important decision you can make for your cat or dog is to spay or neuter them.

Spaying or neutering your pet eliminates or reduces a wide variety of health problems that can be very difficult and expensive to treat, such as many types of cancer, tumors, and other serious health complications. Spayed and neutered animals no longer feel the need to roam seeking a mate, so they have less chance of being involved in fights or traumatic injuries. Also, infections, abscesses, such diseases as feline leukemia virus and feline AIDS (transmitted by fighting), and other contagious diseases are greatly reduced in altered cats, which helps avoid expensive vet bills while extending their life span.

After euthanasia, cancer is the number one killer of cats and dogs. Yet a onetime surgery can prevent most of these deaths. I can't tell you how many times devastated owners have said to me, "Nobody ever told me about the health risks of *not* spaying or neutering my pet."

It's not unnatural or unkind to spay or neuter your pet. Contrary to popular belief, spaying and neutering do not alter basic temperament, personality, or intelligence. In fact, many undesirable qualities that occur under hormonal influence actually resolve following surgery.

Pets that are spayed or neutered will not become less affectionate or playful, nor will they resent you. In fact, the opposite is likely to occur. Neutered cats and dogs are more responsive to their owners and spend less time marking their territory and more time at home where they belong. Neutered dogs, however, retain their natural instincts for guarding their family or home, and both neutered cats and dogs indulge in less intermale aggression.

Dogs that are spayed or neutered have much better concentration and can focus on the task at hand instead of constantly being distracted by hormonal stimuli. With a longer attention span, they perform better during training or fieldwork. Virtually all service dogs are spayed or neutered for this reason.

Spaying or neutering your cat or dog leads to better health, longer life, peace of mind, and foolproof birth control that lasts a lifetime. The average life span of an altered pet is forty percent longer than one that's not spayed or neutered, and the overall effects of spaying or neutering will positively influence your pet's behavior. This simple procedure will save you and your pet from unnecessary suffering and unexpected financial burdens. No need to hesitate, ponder, or ask a friend—just do it!

Spaying

Spaying (ovariohysterectomy is the technical term) is the complete surgical removal of the reproductive organs in a female. Both the uterus and ovaries are removed through an incision made in the abdomen. (Fallopian tubal ligation and hysterectomies, in which only the uterus is removed, are only performed on humans.)

In women, great efforts are made to maintain or restore hormone production in the body if the ovaries are removed, but the same is not true for dogs and cats. The sex hormones estrogen and progesterone, which are excreted from the ovaries, play a key role in reproduction; however, they also stimulate and control heat cycles and are responsible for many unwanted and life-threatening side effects. For every heat cycle a female pet endures, her odds of having medical problems later multiplies by ten. In addition, infections of the uterus called pyometra are very common and life-threatening in unspayed females, so the uterus is removed. An ovariohysterectomy ensures that the hormones that cause health and behavior-related problems are no longer produced, and at the same time many cancers and other medical conditions are reduced or eliminated. It prevents the animal from getting pregnant and also eliminates heat cycles.

This procedure can be safely performed on animals as young as eight weeks of age. Animals in heat and pregnant animals can also be spayed. Puppies can become pregnant as young as six months of age and kittens as young as four months.

Unspayed female dogs and cats are at risk for developing a number of medical problems such as:

- Ovarian cancer
- Uterine cancer
- Cervical cancer
- Breast cancer
- Mastitis
- Uterine infections
- Uterine torsion and uterine prolapse
- Vaginal hyperplasia and prolapse
- Cystic endometrial hyperplasia
- Chronic endometritis
- Cystic ovaries and hyperestrogenism
- False pregnancies
- Difficult pregnancies
- Transmissible venereal sarcoma
- Skin conditions

The most common and life-threatening health problems seen in unspayed female dogs and cats are breast cancer and uterine infections.

The Heat Is On

Sexually mature female dogs and cats will only accept a male and become pregnant during their heat cycle. The heat cycle is different in dogs than in cats.

Sexually mature female dogs have a heat cycle where they ovulate, are receptive to male dogs, and can get pregnant once or twice a year, every four to twelve months (the average is every seven months, but it's quite variable), starting as early as six months of age. Each heat cycle lasts for three weeks during which bleeding occurs for about ten days. Female dogs will drip blood on the floor, carpet, and furniture.

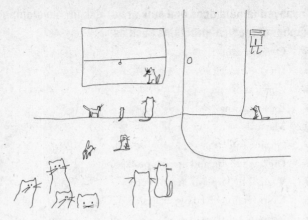

The more heat cycles an unspayed pet goes through, the more susceptible she is to serious disease.

The heat cycle for dogs is divided into three parts, each one lasting an average of one week.

- **Week 1 (proestrus):** The female vulva swells and secretes blood
  and pheromones that drive male dogs into a frenzy, and on a warm
  summer night will attract males from up to three miles away.
  Unaltered male dogs are adept at detecting this aroma. Females in
  heat will also spray to mark their territory, especially if there are
  other pets in the household. Vaginal bleeding can lead to stained
  carpets and furniture. Pets may break house-training. The female
  dog may act moody toward people (including her owners) during
  this stage as well as to other dogs, with mood swings ranging from
  affectionate to snappy. Some female dogs will even become
  aggressive and damage furniture or attack strangers. Dogs may
  refuse to eat as their bodies undergo hormonal changes.
  Sometimes, a female dog will tease the male, lifting her tail and
  allowing him to sniff, but will bite the male's head off if he tries to
  mount. Even if a male is successful at mounting a female during
  this time, she is unlikely to get pregnant.

- **Week 2 (estrus):** The vulva is still swollen, but the vaginal discharge will usually stop having visible blood in it. Here the female ovulates and will usually allow the male, any and all, to mount her. She will most likely then become pregnant. If more than one male mates her, she could have puppies from different fathers.

- **Week 3 (diestrus):** This is the last stage of the heat cycle. The female has already ovulated and is losing interest in sex even though males will still be determined to mate. She is unlikely to allow this to happen, but if it does, it's doubtful that she will get pregnant.

Unlike cat sex, which is "wham-bam-thank-you-ma'am," dog sex takes much longer as the dogs actually get locked in what is called a *tie*. The male dog has a bulbous gland at the base of the penis that swells, locking it into the female's vagina. The dogs usually move around and end up with rumps next to each other. This is the tie, and it lasts anywhere from three to twenty minutes. If you catch a pair of dogs in a tie, you can cause great injury to both the male and female genitals and possibly even get bitten if you try to pull them apart. Drenching them with cold water usually separates them, but it's probably too late to prevent an unwanted pregnancy.

Dogs and cats in heat are also at risk for accidents. Roaming is not only a problem with unaltered males, but females in heat will go to great lengths to escape from the house or yard to find a mate. Mating can even occur between fences. Dogs in heat have been known to run through glass doors, jump out of moving cars, and be hit by cars as they attempt to find a mate. Owners of female dogs and cats in heat have to deal with a sudden influx of male dogs and cats around the house and yard. These obnoxious visitors leave numerous droppings, spray plants and trees with urine to mark their territory, and engage in fights with other dogs and cats in pursuit of the female.

Sex and the Kitty

The feline reproductive cycle is unique as cats are capable of multiple pregnancies within a single reproductive season, making them one of the most prolific domesticated species. Female cats become sexually mature when they reach at least eighty percent of their adult weight and are unusual in that their heat cycles are influenced by seasonal changes in the amount of daylight. Thus, a female cat may have her first estrus anytime between four and twelve months of age. The onset of puberty varies depending on the breed, time of year, social environment, health, physical condition, and nutritional state.

Cats usually begin their heat cycles in January and continue every two to three weeks until September. This period, known as being in heat, generally lasts an average of three weeks. Starting around January, a female cat will keep coming back into heat every fourteen to twenty-one days until she becomes pregnant, is spayed, develops a serious illness, or the amount of daylight decreases, which is usually around October. Anoestrus, the no-heat period, lasts from October until the new season begins in January or February.

When a female cat goes into heat, she becomes very vocal, loudly calling for a male cat. She'll roll on the ground and constantly rub against furniture or your leg. She'll assume a breeding posture with her head and front legs near the ground and her rump held high. She'll become very affectionate and may start urinating frequently. I've had numerous clients at emergency hospitals with their cats in heat, fearing something was dreadfully wrong.

Female cats will be in heat and accept a male for three to sixteen days. They are induced ovulators, which means they ovulate when they have sex. In order for the heat cycle to stop, a female cat must have sex, at which time the chances are high that she will become pregnant because she will release her eggs at the time of mating. Female cats will actively search out males and attempt to escape from the house and yard. They will also spray urine when in heat. Once this behavior begins, it can be difficult to stop. Female cats can become pregnant again as soon as ten days after giving birth, while still nursing the first litter.

Save Money, Save Lives

Dogs and cats have their own sexually transmitted diseases, many fatal and some potentially contagious to humans. Spayed pets are rarely exposed to these diseases.

Spaying also eliminates the heat cycle and associated mood swings, undesirable behaviors, messy bleeding, and the attraction of all available males to your yard (even if the female is kept indoors). Unspayed females are more likely to display aggression related to sexual behavior than pets that are spayed.

There are numerous complications associated with pregnancy, having babies, and raising a litter, such as infections, emergencies, costly Cesarean section surgery (an emergency C-section can run well over $2,000), and seizures due to calcium deficiency. In fact, more than fifty percent of all canine breeding results in the death of the mother or one or more of the pups. The risk of pregnancy and rearing a litter is far greater than the risk of anesthesia and spaying.

To summarize, spaying your cat or dog will:

- Greatly increase her life span
- Decrease her chance of developing breast cancer to almost zero if you spay *before* her first heat cycle (usually at six to seven months of age)
- Eliminate the risk of dying of uterine or ovarian cancer
- Eliminate the chance she will develop a pyometra (uterine infection)

- Decrease your vet bills
- Increase your pet's quality of life
- Prevent mood swings and undesirable behavior caused by heat cycles, including pacing, crying, and trying to escape
- Curtail bleeding on carpets and furniture
- Help decrease pet overpopulation
- Make your pet more social
- Make your pet happier and give her a better overall temperament

Neutering

Although many men cringe at the mere mention of the word, neutering a male dog or cat is the number one thing you can do to increase his longevity. Dogs and cats that are neutered live an average of forty percent longer than dogs and cats that aren't neutered. Statistically, neutered dogs and cats are just plain healthier. Many of the conditions that develop in unaltered dogs and cats significantly shorten their life span.

But neutering can be a touchy subject for men, because to them, those organs are an important aspect of their own body, and they assume their male pets feel the same way they do. But cats and dogs are not people, and they don't have the same feelings about castration, raising a family, or falling in love. Unaltered dogs and cats are obsessed with the urge to mate because their raging hormones are compelling them to reproduce—not to have a family of their own, but to ensure survival of the species. Male dogs and cats don't miss their testicles, nor do they hold a grudge against their owners, as some people surmise. They aren't angry because you took away their ability to reproduce. Instead, these pets are happier because they no longer have to feel sexually frustrated or think about breeding or fighting other animals for their turf. They will focus more on you.

Some owners also fear that a male dog will be "less of a male," act more like a female, or not be as tough or intelligent if neutered. Thankfully for dogs, cats, and men, the reproductive organs do not control their intelligence level or their toughness, loyalty, or character!

Neutered male cats are less likely to spray, roam, and develop testicular cancer or urethral obstruction. They have fewer litter box issues. Neutering drastically reduces their chance of contracting deadly cat viruses that are usually acquired during cat fights. It also means you'll spend less money on vet bills from fight wounds.

Activity level, appetite, playfulness, and socialization with humans are not changed and your neutered male dog will guard, hunt, work, and retrieve like always. The behaviors that do change are unwanted and destructive ones that are influenced by male hormones, such as obsession with the great escape, battling over turf, urine-marking inside and outside the house, inappropriate mounting, and digging. Dogs that resist training also benefit from neutering because they are more likely to accept the owner's leadership. All guide dogs, assistance dogs, and many police dogs are neutered.

You should also neuter dogs with hereditary conditions such as hip dysplasia or other congenital problems to make sure that these undesirable traits and diseases are not passed on.

It really is kinder to neuter a male dog or cat for so many reasons. With their reproductive organs removed, the flow of testosterone is gone, and most male cats and dogs become less aggressive and more people-oriented, and have fewer medical problems.

Neuter for Health

More than eighty percent of all unaltered dogs develop prostate disease, and the evidence is quite conclusive that the best time to neuter your dog or cat is before sexual maturity or puberty. This is considered practicing preventative medicine, and it also keeps your pet from developing bad habits. If dogs or cats are neutered at an early age, they will not sense or respond to female pheromones, and will be less stressed and want to stay home where they are safe.

Neutering is a term used to describe the surgical removal of a male animal's reproductive organs, or testicles. A small incision is made either directly over the testicle in cats or just in front of the scrotum for dogs, which allows surgical ligation and removal of the testes. Vasectomies are not performed because the procedure doesn't reduce the testosterone level and its harmful effects, so the males would still have secondary sex characteristics that are undesirable, as well as frustration living at home with the strong hormonal urge to go out and reproduce. Secondary sex characteristics such as roaming, fighting, inappropriate urination, and humping are all decreased or eliminated by neutering.

Neutering greatly decreases or completely eliminates certain health problems such as:

- Testicular cancer
- Testicular torsion
- Rectal cancer
- Benign prostatic hyperplasia
- Prostatic abscess
- Prostatic cancer
- Epididymitis (infection of the epididymis)
- Perineal hernia (abdominal organs bulging out of rectum)
- Inguinal hernia with potential organ strangulation
- Perianal gland adenomas (benign tumors)

- Orchitis (infection of the testicles)
- Venereal tumors
- Acute or chronic prostatitis

Testosterone Trouble

The effects of testosterone cause many diseases and health problems. Neutering provides relief from such hormone-driven urges as:

- Aggression toward other animals and people
- Territorialism, which is the tendency to be overprotective about the home ground
- Roaming, which is the desire to escape and seek sexually active females in heat
- Dominance
- Marking territory with urine and or feces
- Unwanted sexual behavior such as mounting, sniffing, or arousal

Many intact male dogs, responding to the overwhelming hormonal urge to reproduce, feel aggravated and will act nervous or irritable, pick fights with other dogs, or even become lethargic and less responsive to their owner and may stop eating.

Before cats and dogs were domesticated, they needed high levels of testosterone to seek out females to breed with, forage for food, and fight other males. Now that we have domesticated them, they no longer need these high levels of testosterone circulating in their body that do them much more harm than good, making them frustrated, ornery, and essentially unhappy.

Roaming

Studies show that of all the positive behavioral changes that neutering ensures, roaming shows the biggest change, with a ninety percent reduction in neutered animals. Fertile cats and dogs are driven by their hormones to seek out receptive females, even if they are confined indoors. Pets have been known to jump through glass windows, break down doors, dig holes in yards, or jump fences to get to a female in heat. Females in heat release airborne chemical attractants called pheromones, which male cats and dogs can sense for miles, and it drives them wild. Along with this comes the potential for pets to get lost, get hit by a car, contract a deadly contagious disease, or become injured in a traumatic accident while looking for a female. Terrible bloody fights can occur when several males pursue a female in heat, even if she is confined indoors. The resulting vet bills can be staggering, let alone the damage to the poor animals.

About ninety percent of the millions of cats and eighty percent of the dogs that get hit and killed by vehicles are unaltered. Roaming cats and dogs get into trash containers, defecate in public areas or on private lawns, drink contaminated water, consume garbage, get lost or stolen, suffer severe injuries from fighting, ruin shrubbery, and create noise and other disturbances while posing a risk of injury and disease to

FACT

More than eighty percent of dogs hit by cars are unneutered males who are frustrated and sexually driven to find a female in heat.

themselves and to the community at large. Again, neutering reduces this behavior by ninety percent!

Aggression

Another big advantage of neutering is that dogs and cats will be less aggressive toward other pets as well as people. The degree to which neutering suppresses aggression varies from one animal to another and is dependent on the age at which it is done. Generally speaking, it has its greatest effect if done before one year of age, with aggression toward other males being reduced by sixty percent.

Unaltered males and females are much more likely to display aggression related to sexual behavior than are neutered animals. As males mature, they become increasingly protective of their territory, which includes urine-marking and aggression toward other animals, particularly males that enter this self-established territory. Fights often result in severe injury to one or both animals involved. Your home or yard may become a magnet for noisy, fighting, bothersome male dogs or cats trying to mate, and these territorial instincts will override any social behavior they may have learned. They will defend their turf, sometimes to the death.

The intensity of other types of aggression, such as dominance aggression, is also likely to be reduced. About twenty-five percent of dogs displaying dominance aggression show up to a ninety percent level of improvement after being neutered. Specific diagnosis of the type of aggression displayed by your pet, identification of the situations that trigger it, and retraining your pet to behave differently are still essential.

Neutered cats and dogs have fewer injuries and deaths related to roaming. Once altered, they no longer feel the chemical drive to reproduce, so they are content to relax, stay home, and enjoy being part of the family. Altered pets are less likely to cry, howl, nip, growl, hiss, mount furniture or people's legs, climb on visitors, or knock down small children. They are also better able to learn and become more obedient.

One of the biggest behavioral advantages of neutering for male cats is to prevent aggression between cats and therefore eliminate or greatly decrease the chance of life-threatening consequences of these battles, including viral diseases such as feline AIDS and feline leukemia, and complications from abscesses or infections from cat bites.

Big Bite

Every year millions of people, often children, are bitten by dogs—usually their own. About eighty-five percent of dog bites involve unaltered dogs (usually males), which are two to three times more likely to bite than their sterilized counterparts.

Urine Marking

Unaltered male cats are notorious for spraying a foul, potent, musky-smelling urine. This is a normal sexual behavior of unaltered male tomcats; they scent their territory to affirm their dominant status. These cats will indulge in territorial urine marking on every upright surface they can find. This obnoxious smell will permeate anything it is sprayed on. Many intact house-trained male dogs and cats will urine-mark inside and outside the house on walls, curtains, shoes, handbags, couches, bedspreads, carpets, furniture, doorsteps, windows, flowers, and shrubs—yours and the neighbors'. Unfortunately, stains and odors resulting from urine spraying can be difficult, if not impossible, to remove. Luckily, this behavior is decreased by at least fifty percent in neutered cats or dogs.

Mounting

Mounting or humping outside of actual breeding should not be confused with sex; it's about dominance. Seeking to fulfill their sexual drive and dominance, dogs that are not neutered will often hump anything or anyone that moves, including children. Some dogs will hump a toy or sofa cushion incessantly. Much of the humping you see in puppies is actually play for them, but dogs can get obsessed with this behavior and it can turn into a strong habit. Fortunately for dogs and cats, this undesirable behavior is decreased seventy percent with neutering. If a dog persists in humping another dog in a social situation and it is neutered, the best thing to do is to distract the dog that is doing the humping and channel his energy into another activity.

To summarize, you should neuter your pet because:

- Approximately eighty percent of all pets hit by cars are males that are not neutered.
- Neutered pets are more social with other pets and thus have less aggression, which in turn means less fighting.
- Neutered pets live longer because they have fewer health problems such as prostatitis, testicular or rectal cancer, and perineal hernias.
- Neutered pets have fewer veterinary bills.
- Your neutered dog won't be seeking romance with your company's legs anymore.
- Neutering eliminates sexual frustration, so your pet will be friendlier and more relaxed.
- Neutered cats and dogs are less likely to urine-mark their territory.
- Neutered dogs are better animals for protection and security because they're not worrying about roaming the streets to mate.

- Neutered pets have fewer behavioral problems like digging, fighting, and escaping.
- Neutered pets need fewer calories to sustain their body weight.
- Neutered pets will increase the importance of *you* in their lives.

Vagrancy

The community at large benefits enormously from having dogs and cats that are spayed and neutered. Homeless, intact cats and dogs are usually unvaccinated and can be a source of rabies and other serious diseases that can be a huge public health hazard. In addition, wandering stray animals can become a public nuisance, soiling parks and streets, ruining the landscape, frightening both children and adults, creating noise and other disturbances, causing automobile accidents, and sometimes even killing livestock or other pets.

Certain laws hold you, as the dog owner, responsible for any and all of your dog's actions. This includes such property damage as trashing the neighbor's garden and automobile accidents in which there was swerving to miss hitting a loose animal.

Early Spaying or Neutering

Pediatric spaying and neutering (sterilizing pets between eight and fourteen weeks of age) has been practiced in North America for more than thirty years to help control the pet overpopulation epidemic. Numerous studies have shown it to be safe and that younger puppies or kittens actually do better with the appropriate anesthesia as well as the surgical process. Those neutered at a very young age often have less bleeding and faster recoveries than those neutered when they are older. Early spaying or neutering does not affect the growth rate and there are no appreciable differences in skeletal, physical, or behavioral development between those animals spayed or neutered early versus those spayed at six months.

Following the recommendation of the American Veterinary Medical Association that all pets be sterilized before adoption, including puppies and kittens as young as eight weeks of age, most animal shelters require adopted cats and dogs to be spayed or neutered. However, according to the American Humane Association, only sixty percent of adopters comply, despite implementation of spay/neuter contracts, coupons, and other incentives.

Myths and Misconceptions

There are many mistaken beliefs regarding spaying and neutering, some of which were touched upon earlier in this chapter. Here are other common myths.

MYTH #1:   *Spaying/neutering will change my pet's personality.*

FACT: A dog's or cat's personality is formed more by genetics and environment than by its sex hormones, and the only changes you'll see will be positive ones. Pets become less aggressive, anxious, and distracted, thereby focusing their attention on their owners rather than on trying to find mates. They are less likely to wander, fight, howl, spray, and mount. They will be more loving, protective companions because they're not worrying about breeding, fighting, or escaping—so they are much happier.

MYTH #2:   *Neutered or spayed dogs are not good family guardians.*

FACT: Spaying or neutering does not affect a dog's natural instinct to protect its home and family or be a good watchdog. Most pets will be more reliable and responsible after neutering and are easier to train because of stabilized hormones. Training—not hormones—makes a dog a good guard dog. Neutered dogs are better at protection and security because if an intruder opens the door and there is a female in heat in the neighborhood, your dog will choose to mate rather than to protect your house.

MYTH #3:   *Spaying/neutering is too expensive.*

FACT: The cost of spaying or neutering your cat or dog depends on its sex, size, and age. The price varies from one vet to another, but there are numerous low-cost clinics and even some mobile spay-and-neuter facilities that perform the surgery for free. But whatever the actual price, spaying or neutering your pet is a onetime cost that's relatively small when you consider all of the benefits. It's really a bargain compared to the cost of huge veterinary bills from fights, unwanted pregnancies, or being hit by a car, not to mention all of the health benefits.

MYTH #4:   *Neutering/spaying is very painful and my pet might die during the surgery.*

FACT: Neutering and spaying are the most commonly performed surgeries in veterinary medicine, and with today's quality anesthesia and pain-management medication, these surgical procedures are considered safe. In fact, most dogs and cats return to normal within twenty-four to forty-eight hours after the surgery. Although there's always a risk during a surgical procedure, the risks associated with *not* spaying or neutering your pet are far greater.

MYTH #5:   *My pet is special and her personality is so good that I want her to have puppies.*

FACT: Just because your dog or cat is special doesn't mean that her offspring will be anything like her, as you have the father's genes to consider as well. An entire litter of puppies or kittens might receive all of the mother and father's worst characteristics. There are absolutely no guarantees that you will get what you want out of a litter.

MYTH #6:   *It's better to allow your female pet to have at least one litter before she is spayed.*

FACT: Medical evidence indicates the opposite is true. Your dog or cat will have much less chance of developing cancer of the reproductive organs and mammary tissue if you spay before her first heat cycle. Letting her have even one litter predisposes her to breast, uterine, and ovarian cancers.

MYTH #7:   *Preventing pets from having litters is unnatural.*

FACT: We have already interfered with nature by domesticating animals. Domesticated dogs and cats mate more often and have larger litters than their wild ancestors, but cannot survive well on their own. Because of this, we euthanize millions of cats and dogs every year.

MYTH #8:   *Siblings will not mate with each other or their parents.*

FACT: Dogs and cats will readily mate with their mother, father, sisters, brothers, aunts, or uncles.

Overpopulation

Every year hundreds of thousands of puppies, kittens, dogs, and cats are euthanized due to pet overpopulation because these pets have no home to go to. Statistics show that eight to twelve million cats and dogs enter animal shelters nationwide and approximately five to nine million are killed annually in the United States. Here is an example to illustrate the enormity of the problem: An unspayed female cat, her

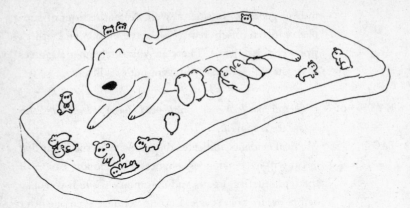

mate, and all of their offspring, can potentially produce 420,000 off-spring during a seven-year period, and one unspayed female dog and her offspring can reproduce 67,000 dogs!

Overpopulation and its many repercussions reach into our homes, neighborhoods, shelters, rescues, and local and national governments. Every person in this country is affected by animal overpopulation, even those who do not own pets. Local governments spend more than two billion in taxpayer dollars annually to care for lost, abandoned, and unwanted pets, and then to kill those that don't get adopted, which is approximately fifty-five percent of dogs and puppies and seventy-one percent of cats and kittens entering shelters. The average cost per stray animal to catch, feed, house, and ultimately destroy it is $100—and the money comes out of our pockets.

In addition to the financial impact, communities are affected by animal overpopulation in other ways: animals running loose and caus-ing traffic hazards, quarantines, bites, fighting, destruction of property, and loud yowling and barking.

Although the perceived high cost of spaying and neutering is of-ten thought to be the problem, the reality is that it's the lack of educa-tion regarding the tremendous benefits of spaying and neutering as well as ignorance about the huge volume of animals that are killed in our country every year. Every day, roughly 70,000 puppies and kittens are born in the United States, and only one out of five puppies and kittens stays in its original home for its entire life. The other four will be abandoned on the street or end up at a shelter. Every year millions of homeless animals live short, hard, hungry lives on the streets, only to die a miserable death from disease, injury, poisoning, exposure, starvation, or predation.

Euthanasia of healthy unwanted cats and dogs remains the leading cause of death in these species. As a pet owner, you can make a difference by spaying or neutering your pet and advising others to do the same so that we stop this barbaric act and change these tragic statistics. You can help all pets by reducing the number of dogs and cats condemned to live without homes and without love.

Neutering or spaying your pet is a small price to pay when you consider the overwhelming benefits: reduction or elimination of diseases, reduced aggression, decreased vet bills (and carpet- and furniture-cleaning bills), prevention of unwanted animals, and so much more. Fewer health and behavioral problems mean a longer and happier life for your pet. So be a responsible pet owner and make an appointment with your vet.

Chapter 5

Dental Disasters

Oral disease is the number one health problem diagnosed in dogs and cats. According to the American Veterinary Dental Society, more than eighty percent of dogs and seventy percent of cats have some form of gum disease before reaching age three.

If you haven't been taking care of your cat or dog's teeth on a regular basis and your pet is at least three years old, there is a good chance that some signs of dental disease are already present, including mouth odor, brown spots, and red, inflamed gums. Those teeth need cleaning immediately! Stop right now and check your pet's teeth. You'll probably be shocked by what you see. Something as simple as brushing your pet's teeth at least three times a week will not only save you hundreds of dollars on vet bills, but will extend your pet's life as well.

Oral hygiene is one of the most overlooked areas of medical care for cats and dogs. Proper dental care doesn't just make your pet's breath smell better; it's essential for long-term quality of life. Dental disease is a preventable problem. Most owners wait too long to get their dog or cat's teeth professionally cleaned, usually when their pet has bad breath. In fact, teeth cleaning should be viewed as a way to *prevent* disease and illness, not to treat it.

If your pet has excessive tartar buildup, gingivitis, or rotting teeth, chances are you have already waited too long. Good dental care in pets, just like in humans, revolves around controlling the bacteria under the gum line where it isn't readily apparent.

Gum disease follows the same path in pets as it does in people. It can be excruciating. Sadly, animals often mask their signs of pain. Your dog or cat can't report a toothache, but believe me, a large percentage of pets I see in the clinic have terrible teeth and really need a good dental cleaning along with tooth brushing on a regular basis. I have personally examined dogs and cats whose tartar buildup is so thick, it's literally the only thing holding the teeth in the sockets. When the tartar is finally removed, these teeth actually fall out. To make matters worse, years of chronic bacteria released into the bloodstream wreak havoc with internal organs such as the heart, liver, lungs, brain, and kidneys, eventually causing premature organ failure. An average-size dog that has its teeth brushed daily can live to be fifteen to seventeen years old; that same dog without any dental care will only live to be eleven to thirteen years old.

Dental disease is rampant among dogs and cats. Yet, with a little effort, you can keep your pet's teeth shiny and white for years to come.

Dental Disorders

The two main types of dental problems in puppies and kittens are traumatic damage to the baby teeth and
improper eruption of the adult teeth.
Baby teeth, unlike adult teeth, are
very thin and fragile. They are not
firmly anchored in place and can be
easily broken or pulled out of position. Puppies are very oral and often
explore the world with their mouths.

Avoid giving them hard objects to chew on or playing games such as tug-of-war. By pulling or chewing on hard objects, puppies can fracture or luxate (pull out of position) their baby canines or fang teeth. This, in turn, can damage the adult teeth that are lying under the gums, which can lead to delayed eruption, lack of eruption, or improper positioning of the adult teeth. Even adult teeth can be broken or damaged by hard objects like indestructible bones and rocks, so always be careful of what you allow your pet to chew on.

Abnormalities of bite, relatively rare in cats, are common in dogs. Any condition where the teeth are not positioned correctly is called a malocclusion. An undershot jaw, where the lower jaw protrudes beyond the upper jaw, is common in small dogs and in breeds such as shih tzus, Lhasa apsos, boxers, pugs, and bulldogs. An overshot jaw, where the upper jaw protrudes beyond the lower jaw, is called buckteeth. This is seen most often in collies, shelties, dachshunds, Russian wolfhounds, and dogs with elongated noses. Usually these malocclusions do not interfere with normal mouth functions.

On the other hand, what does interfere—and is common in puppies—is a baby tooth that doesn't fall out after the adult tooth has erupted. These teeth should be removed because they will cause displacement of the permanent teeth as well as excessive tartar buildup. Most puppies have these extra teeth (more than the normal forty-two teeth) removed when they are spayed or neutered.

Again, dogs and cats have teeth similar to ours, and the same conditions that lead to your tooth and gum problems also occur in your cat's or dog's mouth. But unlike us, dogs and cats do not have the option of replacing their teeth with dentures, so *we* must take care of their only adult set of teeth.

Pets suffer from dental tartar, tooth root abscesses, loose teeth, gingivitis, extra teeth, and tumors of the gums and teeth. Dogs and cats seldom develop cavities, but they often develop a far worse condition called periodontal disease: inflammation and destruction of the tissue that surrounds and supports the teeth. Periodontal disease is the cause of ninety-five percent of cases of bad breath—and can be life-threatening.

Good Pets, Bad Breath

Your pet should be able to get up close and personal with you without knocking you over with bad breath. Bad breath, or halitosis, is a sign of ill health. Shedding, drooling, and licking are normal, but halitosis is a symptom of disease.

Halitosis follows the same progression in animals as it does in people. Bacteria-laden plaque is attracted to the surface of the teeth within hours of teeth cleaning, and within days this plaque hardens to form tartar on the surface. This leads to gingivitis and eventually periodontal disease. As the bacteria destroy the bone, they produce hydrogen sulfide, a smelly gas that causes halitosis.

Bad breath in dogs and cats is most commonly a symptom of dental disorders like periodontal disease, gingivitis, plaque buildup, abscesses, sores, tumors, and ulcers of the mouth. But there are other diseases that can cause bad breath as well, including skin disease around the mouth, tumors or foreign objects in the mouth, and such metabolic diseases as diabetes, autoimmune disease, and kidney disease.

It's imperative to investigate the cause of your pet's halitosis rather than assuming it's natural for them to have bad breath. It is *not* natural. If your pet has halitosis, you need to take them in for a dental exam right away. If the cause is dental disease, once treated you can prevent the recurrence of bad breath in your pet with daily brushing and yearly professional dental cleaning.

The Root of the Problem

Dental problems begin when food particles, saliva, and bacteria form a filmy mixture on the teeth called plaque. Billions of bacteria living in the plaque begin to irritate and inflame the gums, causing gingivitis. If this plaque is not removed, it eventually hardens into brown-colored material known as *tartar*.

Just because your pet's teeth are white doesn't mean there aren't bacteria hiding under the gums just waiting to cause a problem. If you're not brushing your pet's teeth every day, chances are some bacteria are already present.

Early stages of gum disease should never be ignored because it is actually at this point that you can do the most good by preventing progression of the bacteria to other, more serious stages in which you can't reverse the disease process, such as infections on the heart valve, which will definitely shorten your cat's or dog's life span. Pets that have bacteria in their bloodstream will become internally ill and experience pain from the bacteria spreading to internal organs. These animals are in jeopardy of internal organ failure.

Good dental health will help your pet live a longer, happier life and save you lots of money in the long run.

Brushing Up on Dental Care

The goal is simple: Keep your pet's teeth clean. Brushing your pet's teeth is the easiest and most cost-effective way to prevent dental disease and the other health problems that come with it. Proper brushing will also save you money by decreasing the number of times your pet will need professional cleaning over its lifetime.

You want to start brushing as soon as the baby teeth erupt, usually at around three to four months of age, or as early as possible. The sooner you begin brushing, the more accepting your pet will be. Remember that most animals are not used to having someone's fingers in their mouth. But with a little patience, practice, and persistence, your pet may actually look forward to bonding with you through tooth brushing or, at the very least, accept it as the norm. Your cat or dog can't do it alone, so it's up to you to do it for them.

How to Brush Your Pet's Teeth

First and foremost, keep tooth-brushing sessions short and fun. Make your pet think of it like getting a treat. You need to make the process as pleasant as possible. Try not to restrain your pet too tightly. Brushing should be a bonding experience reinforced with praise and rewards. It should never be traumatic for you or your pet.

You will need a toothbrush and toothpaste made especially for pets. It's important never to use a toothbrush meant for people, not even a child's size, as the bristles are too hard. Cat and dog tooth-brushes are designed for pets and are extremely soft. There are several choices of styles, including a straight or angled toothbrush that's similar to the one you use; a finger brush that fits onto the end of your finger; and even an electric one with vibrating bristles. Each pet should have its own toothbrush to prevent the spread of germs and bacteria. (If any out-of-town guests are staying with you, don't forget to warn them that your pets have their own toothbrushes and toothpaste!)

Pet toothpaste comes in yummy flavors such as tuna, poultry, malt, and beef. Since cats and dogs don't spit out the toothpaste or rinse like we do, they need to use toothpaste that is made for pets. Look for brands that contain enzymes to help control plaque. Toothpaste made for people contains detergents that may cause stomach upset in pets when swallowed, and besides, all of the excess foaming may scare your pet—so stick to toothpaste that is made for dogs and cats.

Start by just handling your pet's mouth for several minutes a day to get your cat or dog used to its mouth being touched. If your pet seems reluctant, you can dip your finger in beef bouillon or tuna water to enhance the experience. Once your dog or cat is accustomed to having you play with its mouth, start rubbing the teeth with your fingers. Next, try rubbing the teeth and gums in a circular motion and start adding in the flavored toothpaste, which should taste good. You really only need to worry about the outsides of the top and bottom teeth, and you can keep the mouth closed by placing your hand around your pet's muzzle. Once this is working, you can try using the toothbrush. Lift the cheek on one side of the mouth and brush the outside surface of the teeth just as you would brush your own. The brush movement should be in a circular pattern with ten short motions that cover three to four teeth at a time. Placing your index finger directly behind the bristles will help stabilize the brush. Increase the number of teeth brushed each time until your pet accepts the routine willingly. Keep the sessions at fifteen to thirty seconds initially.

If your cat or dog is reluctant, don't try brushing all of the teeth right away. Just start with one or two teeth a day until your pet realizes that tooth brushing is okay, and then work your way up to eventually brushing all of the teeth. It should only take thirty seconds of brushing on each side of your pet's mouth. That's a small amount of time for such a huge investment in your pet's health and well-being—and is well worth the effort.

In time you will be surprised by how easy it is to add brushing to your pet's daily routine without interrupting your life. Find a convenient time when your pet is relaxed, such as after a walk, or after eating or napping. Try brushing while you watch TV together, or if your pet is most at ease while sitting on your lap, brush then.

You need to work up to brushing every day, or at least every other day; anything less than that is not helping your pet. The best time to brush is either in the morning or at the end of the day. Try getting into the habit of brushing your pet's teeth either before or after you brush your own.

Your pet still needs to have its teeth cleaned professionally, just like you do, but proper brushing will greatly reduce the number of times this has to be done. By brushing every day, your dog or cat will have sweeter breath and healthier teeth, and you will have lower vet bills.

Dental Disobedience

Sometimes, no matter how hard you try, your cat or dog will not allow its teeth to be brushed. But don't despair; even if you can't brush your pet's teeth, there are other ways to administer at-home dental care.

1. There are sprays and gels available that can be easily applied to the tooth and gum surfaces.

2. In lieu of a toothbrush and toothpaste, you can opt for dental pads or wipes that you wrap around your finger to brush the teeth with.

3. There are different chew toys and treats for your pet to gnaw on that simulate brushing. These include chew strips, rawhides, dental bones, and rubber chew toys. Some manufacturers add tartar-reducing enzymes to these products to help further prevent plaque buildup.

4. Diets are now available that can help reduce the formation of plaque deposits. These special foods have abrasive particles that will help mechanically remove plaque.

Professional Cleaning

People are supposed to get a dental exam every six months, floss daily, and brush after every meal. So if you think about oral hygiene and how nasty your pet's mouth will become after years without flossing and brushing, you'll realize how crucial it is to visit the vet at least once a year in addition to brushing. Proper dental care involves more than just scraping tartar off the teeth—which may make the teeth look better, but isn't addressing the culprit: bacteria under the gum line. Thorough dental care involves scaling, flushing, fluoride treatment, and polishing.

The only way the vet can properly clean your pet's teeth is when your cat or dog is completely anesthetized. Trying to perform these procedures on a pet that is awake is unrealistic, even with the best-behaved animal. The oral cavity must be examined extensively in order to assess all of the teeth, gums, and roots for signs of disease.

Many people balk at anesthesia due to the perceived risks, but in truth, the risks are negligible compared to those of letting your pet develop dental disease. Numerous precautions, including the use of safe short-acting anesthetics, a complete physical exam, knowledge of your pet's medical history, blood work, antibiotics, painkillers, and X-rays, make the dangers of anesthesia low in contrast to the risks of disease that can occur by not cleaning your pet's teeth. This is true even in the geriatric patient.

Even before (and certainly after) your pet has accumulated tartar, it's time to have the teeth professionally cleaned by your veterinarian. Virtually all equipment that dentists have for people, veterinarians now have for cats and dogs.

The vet's first step is to remove heavy tartar with special dental instruments like the ones your dentist uses. Next comes scaling the teeth rapidly with an ultrasonic scalar. This vibrating tool removes the tartar with minimal damage to the tooth enamel and cleans under the gum line without irritating the gums. The tip vibrates eighteen

SIGNS OF DISEASE

Symptoms of dental disease include bad breath, drooling, pawing at the mouth, listlessness, trouble swallowing, mouth sores, heavy plaque or tartar buildup, red and swollen or bleeding gums, movement of gums away from the base of the teeth, loose teeth, reluctance to chew hard food, abscesses, facial swelling, reluctance to eat or be patted on the head, and even a runny nose or sneezing.

Unfortunately, many pets do not show any symptoms of dental disease until the problem is severe with irreparable damage. Once a pet is actually showing signs of disease, it is not only causing discomfort or pain, but is affecting other body organs as well. Even when teeth appear healthy, bacteria may be building up in the spaces between the teeth and gums. Therefore, cats and dogs need regular dental exams by a veterinarian at least once a year.

thousand times per second, so it cleans the teeth much faster and more safely than doing it by hand. The teeth are then checked for fractures and other abnormalities, and the gums around the teeth are probed for pockets. If deep pockets are found, periodontal surgery may be recommended to heal the defect, eliminate infection, and restore the tissues around the teeth to good health. If necessary, severely damaged or loose teeth are extracted. Polishing comes next to smooth off the enamel surface in order to make it more difficult for bacteria to adhere. Finally, an application of fluoride is applied to prevent cavities. Once the bacteria get reestablished, the cycle of plaque leading to tartar and gingivitis starts all over again.

Routine preventative care is critical for proper dental hygiene. This protects your pet from painful dental problems and protects you from the expense of veterinary care needed to treat advanced periodontal disease.

Tooth Truths

When I began working as a veterinary technician more than twenty years ago, I never dreamed of encouraging pet owners to brush their cat's or dog's teeth. All of that has changed.

In 1987, the Academy of Veterinary Dentistry and the American Veterinary Dental College were formed in the United States. The American Veterinary Medical Association (AVMA) now recognizes veterinary dentistry as a specialty, and board-certified specialists are trained to perform procedures such as crowns, caps, implants, root canals, fillings, periodontal surgery, and even braces. Veterinary dentistry has truly evolved during the past two decades and vets now realize the tremendous importance of oral health. This, coupled with the "pets are people too" attitude, has created a new understanding and appreciation of cats' and dogs' pearly whites.

The bottom line is that pets are living longer because we see the value of taking care of their teeth. Don't sabotage your pet's life by realizing the importance of oral health when it's too late. Just imagine what your teeth would look and feel like if you didn't brush regularly! Your pet's oral hygiene needs shouldn't be any different than yours. Start brushing your cat's or dog's teeth today and schedule an annual dental exam to keep your pet's bark or meow healthy for many years to come.

Chapter 6

Battle of the Bulge

I t shouldn't be surprising that our pets have mirrored our own difficulties with weight control. One major difference, however, is that their diets are completely regulated by their owners (unless your pet has learned how to open the refrigerator and is sneaking late-night ham-and-cheese sandwiches).

Across the country, dogs and cats are battling the bulge, and their owners are mostly to blame. Many people who leave their pets home alone all day overcompensate for their guilt by sharing food or offering treats. How can a pet resist? No matter how many calories or how much kibble a cat or dog has already consumed in a given day, a pet will rarely meet a high-calorie snack it doesn't like. Overconsumption of calories leads to excess body fat, which is the most prevalent form of malnutrition in pets of Westernized societies. Ironically, pet obesity is happening because we love our pets so much—but we are inadvertently killing them with kindness.

As a pet owner, you hold the power of longevity in your hands. Studies have shown that lean pets live an extra fifteen percent longer and enjoy delayed signs of aging such as graying muzzles, impaired gaits, and reduced activity. You must use discipline and diet restriction to feed your pet so it will maintain its ideal body weight throughout its life—a task that is difficult for many pet owners who use food as a source of love.

By definition, obesity is the accumulation of an excessive quantity of fat. Since the late 1970s, the percentage of obese adults in the United

States has doubled (it has tripled among children), and obesity statistics for pets are mirroring this epidemic, with a rise in diabetes, heart attacks, and hypertension as well. More than forty percent of dogs and cats are overweight or obese. Carrying an excess of body fat is not just unhealthy—it's dangerous. It's a fact that the greater an animal's caloric intake over the course of its life, the shorter its life span will be.

Obesity is just as serious as cancer, but even more prevalent and life-threatening. It's the most common nutritional problem seen in veterinary hospitals today, yet is **completely preventable**. It's an avoidable condition that leads to avoidable diseases.

Tough Love

Pets gain weight for the same reason people do: too many calories and not enough exercise. Far too many of us are watching TV and surfing the Internet with our pets by our side. And our lack of willpower toward our own diet often extends to our pets, ruining their bodies and health. We give in to certain tasty, high-calorie foods, and we offer treats to our pets. Although an occasional treat is fine, oftentimes one treat turns into another and another . . . and before you know it, your pooch is pudgy. If given the chance, most pets will eat more than they need—just like people. Unfortunately, most owners are unsure of exactly how much food their pet should eat, and how much is actually being consumed.

Luckily for our pets, they can't serve themselves—unless you leave food out. This gives you a tremendous advantage in helping your cat or dog trim down. Now if only you can resist those big, soft, longing eyes! Surprisingly, most owners have *created* their pets' habit of begging by giving into them in the first place! If you give your cat or dog a treat every time it demands one, it reinforces this behavior. Cats often vocalize, roam restlessly, and act as if they need something. This is normal interactive behavior for a cat and has no relationship to hunger or food. When you reward this behavior with food, it tends to continue because you are, in fact, training the cat and reinforcing this particular behavior. Instead, you should try playing with your cat to distract it and help it burn calories.

Not all pets have eager appetites. Most obese pets have slow metabolisms due to inactivity and don't readily burn calories. Because of this overweight, cats and dogs don't require very much food to maintain their fat stores, and just a few extra calories make a huge difference over time. As little as one percent extra caloric intake can result in a twenty-five percent increase over ideal body weight by middle age (between five and ten years old for most cats and dogs). The owners who are successful with their pets' weight loss understand the importance of helping their cat or dog shed those extra pounds and thus have developed a "tough love" attitude where they learn to resist the temptation of loving their pets with food. What's good for you is good for your pets, and that means plenty of exercise and a suitable diet. If your pet is overweight or obese, a complete weight-reduction program is in order, including a proper feeding plan, an exercise plan, and a recheck or follow-up plan.

Prevention Is Key

It's much easier to prevent weight gain than it is to lose weight. Willpower is a big problem for most people, but thank goodness cats and dogs can't pick up the phone to call for pizza, use a can opener, or grab the car keys for a fast-food run!

Preventing obesity relies on a few sound principles that are well known to most dieters. It also entails feeding your pets well-balanced food for their life stage in proper amounts from the first day they enter your life. Like humans, cats and dogs may struggle to achieve that ideal physique, but with a little knowledge and discipline, your pet can be svelte all year long.

Recipes for success:

- Feed a balanced, nutritionally complete diet tailored to the life stage of your pet (see Chapter 2, Make No Bones About It).
- Begin by feeding the amount recommended by the manufacturer and tailor it to your pet's lifestyle.
- Always measure the amount of food you feed your pets. Use measuring cups for accuracy and never eyeball the amount of food you're giving.
- Once pets have been spayed or neutered, they have lower energy requirements and should have their food amount reduced accordingly.
- Never feed table scraps of any kind. They add calories and will unbalance your pet's diet.
- Give dog or cat treats sparingly and incorporate these extra calories into your pet's total daily allotment. Treats should account for less than ten percent of total calories.
- With multiple pets, it's best to supervise feeding times to ensure that each pet is getting the right amount of food.
- Don't allow pets into the room where you're preparing or eating food.
- Weigh your pet on a regular basis on the same scale.
- Make sure your dogs and cats get plenty of daily exercise.
- Feed your pets two or more smaller meals a day instead of one big meal.
- Make sure each pet has its own food bowl.
- Never leave food out in unlimited quantities.

Overfeeding puppies and kittens causes an increase in their number of fat cells and predisposes them to obesity as adults. Therefore, puppies and kittens that become obese during growth will often have a problem with obesity throughout life. After maturity, fat cells do not increase in number as readily, but instead increase in size. In addition, overfeeding puppies may accelerate the growth rate that in particular breeds may increase a predisposition to certain skeletal diseases, including hip dysplasia.

Live Fat, Die Young

Packing on additional weight places extra demands on virtually all the organs in the body, leading to disease and early death. Obesity should be viewed as a medical problem and, once diagnosed, treated immediately. As with other illnesses, the earlier you start treatment, the more favorable the outcome—and the lower your vet bills will be. Some of the serious consequences of obesity, similar to those in overweight humans, include heart disease; high blood pressure; diabetes; breathing difficulties; arthritis; exercise intolerance; pancreatitis; skin and hair coat problems; joint, bone, and ligament damage; decreased immune system; heat intolerance; increased surgical and anesthetic risk; digestive disorders; cancer; liver disease; and mental irritability.

Pinch an Inch

Your pet is overweight if it's ten to fifteen percent over its ideal weight, and obese if it's fifteen to twenty percent above ideal weight. How do you tell if your pet is over its ideal weight? There is so much individuality even among the varying breeds  that the best way to tell is to look at and feel your pet. Chances are if you can pinch an inch, your pet is overweight. If you're not sure, take your pet to the vet and ask for the doctor's opinion. Don't rely on "experts" at the dog park or family and friends reassuring you that your chubby domestic shorthair feline is okay.

Remember, when it comes to cats and dogs, a small amount of extra weight can be significant. For example, an eighteen-pound dog or cat that should normally weigh fifteen pounds is considered obese, even though it's only overweight by three extra pounds! Those three extra pounds to that eighteen-pound animal are the equivalent of forty extra pounds on an average female. An extra five pounds on a cat or dog that should weigh, say, seventeen pounds are the equivalent of fifty extra pounds on a 170-pound person.

You should be able to easily feel, but not see, your pet's backbone and ribs. Start by moving your fingers back and forth across your pet's sides or rib cage. If you can't feel the ribs, or more than a thin layer of fat is covering them, your pet is probably overweight. The fatter your dog or cat becomes, the thicker this layer of fat will be. Fat will also deposit in the "love handle" areas over the back, hips, base of tail, and abdomen. Actually *feeling* your cat or dog is important, because in animals with thick or long-haired coats, it can be difficult to tell if your pet is overweight just by looking.

Next, do a profile check. Your pet should have a "tuck" in its tummy, beginning just behind the last ribs and going up into the hind legs or thighs. In an obese pet, the stomach will hang down and there will be no tuck. Viewed from above, your pet should have an hourglass figure with a noticeable waist just before the hips at the end of the rib cage. Animals that are overweight do not have discernable waists and often have abdomens that protrude from their back and sides; they also have a distinct waddle as they walk.

Putting your cat or dog on a scale is certainly a good way to compare and contrast its weight as well as give you a starting point and a target goal. However, the problem with weighing your pet as the sole measure of determining if it's overweight is that there's so much variation among breeds, and with so many mixed breeds there are no accurate body weight charts. Also, since fat is lighter than muscle, if your pet has less muscle and more stored fat on its body, the resulting weight may seem normal, when in reality your pet is still visibly overweight. Conversely, a muscular, lean, well-toned dog or cat may actually weigh more than a chubby, less muscular dog or cat of the same size. Therefore, it's more accurate to look at your pet's appearance and to actually feel its body.

As a rule, the body weight of your cat or dog when it was young (between one and two years old) is considered to be its ideal weight. Look at pictures of your pet when it was younger. Do you see a noticeable difference?

Preparing for Success

Before embarking on any weight-loss program for your pet, you must take it in for a complete physical exam, blood test, and urinalysis to rule out any disease process that could be contributing to the excess weight and correct it *before* altering your pet's diet or routine. It's paramount to make sure your pet is healthy before making any significant changes to its diet and exercise regime.

Your veterinarian will help determine your pet's daily caloric requirements, select suitable food, and calculate the exact amount to feed so you'll know what, how often, and how much to feed. The vet should also help supervise the maintenance of your cat's or dog's weight condition coupled with an exercise plan and follow-ups.

It's vital that your veterinarian rule out conditions that can look like obesity, such as excessive fluid accumulation in the body, and confirm that your pet really is overweight or obese and not exhibiting symptoms of heart, kidney, or other metabolic diseases. Medical conditions that impact hormone balances in pets may contribute to the development of obesity. These consist of diabetes, and thyroid or pituitary gland dysfunction, including hypothyroidism and hyperadrenocorticism.

Brain disease and pancreatic tumors known as insulinomas can also influence metabolism and appetite. Certain medications that are frequently prescribed by veterinarians can also affect metabolism and appetite, including glucocorticoids like prednisone and dexamethasone, barbiturates such as phenobarbital, and benzodiazepines such as Valium. Also, spaying and neutering, which in and of itself does not make a pet fat, does decrease the amount of certain hormones present in the body, which can affect metabolism (see Chapter 4, Love Your Pet).

Genetics plays a role in metabolism as well, with certain breeds more predisposed to obesity. In cats, mixed breeds are more susceptible than purebreds, and dog breeds such as Labrador retrievers, cocker spaniels, Cavalier King Charles spaniels, Shetland sheepdogs, dachshunds, beagles, pugs, cairn terriers, basset hounds, and hound breeds in general are all more likely to suffer from obesity. Also, pets more than four years of age and pets belonging to obese owners are more prone to excess weight gain.

Work with your vet to develop a diet and exercise plan that's tailored to your individual pet's lifestyle, age, and medical history. A historical review of changes in your dog's or cat's body weight can be useful in establishing a pattern of weight gain and may help identify a particular event or change in environment that relates to the increase in body weight. Be sure to analyze your pet's eating and exercise habits. If your pet is eating too much and exercising too little, a change is in order. You should make a diet history of your pet that lists the types and amounts of food your cat or dog is receiving. Be sure to include all snacks, treats, biscuits, kibble, wet food, supplements, people food, and any other edible item that your pet is consuming.

Write down how much exercise your pet is actually getting. Sitting on the cat tree or walking to the food bowl does not constitute exercise. Swimming, running, walking, chasing toys, scratching a post, catching a ball, and running around the apartment all burn up calories and can be documented as exercise.

Bear in mind that it most likely took weeks, if not months, for your pet to gain weight and it may well take just as long for them to lose it. Dogs should only lose one percent to two percent of their initial weight per week, and cats should lose less than one percent per week. This equates to two to three pounds per month for the average dog, and half a pound per month for the average cat. For example, a ten-pound cat losing one to two ounces per week is healthy, and a 100-pound dog can safely lose about a pound per week. Shoot for a cat or dog reaching its ideal weight in six months to a year.

In particular, weight loss in cats must be gradual to avoid complications from hepatic lipidosis, or fatty liver syndrome (FLS), an accumulation of fat in the liver that may result in death if left untreated. FLS is particular to overweight felines and is one of the most common liver diseases diagnosed in cats (this condition is not recognized in overweight dogs). The typical scenario with FLS is that the overweight cat has gone through a period of anorexia or not eating. The chances of FLS occurring are greater if the cat is obese before the anorexia begins. Next, the excess fat stores are rapidly broken down to supply nutrients for the anorexic cat, with this fat being deposited very swiftly in the liver, failing to be adequately processed. The fat becomes stored in and around the liver cells, resulting in liver failure. The cat will often become icteric, or jaundiced, with the whites of their eyes, skin, and mouth turning yellow. This is a life-threatening illness that must be treated immediately or the cat will die. Treatment is aggressive with intravenous fluid therapy, nutritional support, and hospitalization until the cat's appetite returns and the liver starts functioning normally. Always take your cat to the vet if it fails to eat for at least two days.

Cutting Calories

There is no magic weight-loss pill for people or pets. Once a pet is obese, it will remain obese even if extra caloric intake stops, because fat stores take very little energy to maintain. In order for your cat or dog to

lose weight, **their caloric intake must be less than the calories expended through exercise and metabolism.** As I said, there's no magic involved—just discipline and common sense. Most pets are overweight because of too many calories and too little exercise, so physical activity and proper food choices are critical.

I strongly advise controlled feeding, regardless of whether your pet is obese. This method lets you control the amount of food your pet receives and allows for easy adjustments. Free-choice feeding has been an especially significant factor in feline obesity, because cats are hunters and aren't accustomed to eating whenever they want.

Dieting is an essential part of every weight-loss program. You have two choices when it comes to reducing your pet's caloric intake: You can decrease the total amount of the pet food your cat or dog is currently eating, or switch to a brand that's lower in calories. A twenty-five percent reduction in total food given can often work for a pet that is mildly overweight. For example, if you're currently feeding one cup per day, you would now feed only three-quarters of a cup (divided into two daily feedings) for your pet's allotted ration, and nothing else. Even one additional treat will slow down weight loss. I prefer to eliminate table scraps and treats altogether. Yes, eliminate! I've seen many cats and dogs lose weight simply because their owners stopped all treats and table scraps. The pets were happier, the owners were delighted, and I was thrilled when the scale showed suitable weight loss from this simple change in owner behavior.

Don't use food as a substitute for attention or a cure for guilt. Bond with pets during playtime and on walks instead of with treats. Think of treats as candy bars that are high in fat and calories. Instead, reward your pet with love and praise, or if you must give them something to eat, use a piece of food from their daily ration or a low-calorie treat. For cats, think in mouse-like portions.

With obese pets, which may need a more severe calorie restriction, simply decreasing the amount of regular food could restrict too much protein, vitamins, and minerals, and could actually cause nutritional imbalance. Therefore, a reducing diet is in order. Your cat or dog still needs a high-quality, meat-based diet that's high in protein but low in fat. Read labels and choose a low-fat food that's still animal protein-based (see Chapter 2, Make No Bones About It). The fat content of dry food should be between twelve and sixteen percent to be considered a low-fat diet. The daily feeding guide on the package should be used as a starting point, but you'll need to adjust, as individual requirements vary greatly among pets. Beware of pet foods that merely add fiber to bulk up the food. Look for foods that have L-carnitine, which helps turn fat into energy.

It's not uncommon for veterinarians to design a weight-loss program that is sixty percent of total caloric requirement for optimal body weight for obese dogs, and sixty-six percent for obese cats. There are numerous low-calorie brands on the market today, along with prescription diets for weight loss available from your vet. Reducing diets are good because pets receive all of the vitamins, protein, minerals, and nutrients they need in fewer calories. Typically your pet will be able to eat a larger quantity of food and still lose weight. This is because a reducing diet is lower in fat and less concentrated in calories, and has a higher fiber content. There are even brands made for indoor spayed or neutered cats that are low in fat. Remember, there is considerable individual variation in caloric requirements among cats and dogs, so food intake needs to be individually adjusted to ensure appropriate weight loss.

Bear in mind that whenever you switch diets, you should do so gradually. You and your vet will decide which one is right for your particular pet and its weight-loss needs. Once you decide on an appropriate diet and a daily amount, stick to it. No cheating! If, at your first weigh-in, there has been little or no weight loss, then the daily allowance needs to be lowered (if you didn't cheat).

It really is easier than you might imagine as long as you have conviction and remember that you're extending your pet's life span and increasing its quality of life. Changes may be slow and subtle, especially in the beginning, but if you persist, you will succeed.

Diet tips

- Make sure everyone in your family knows about your pet's new diet plan and behaves accordingly.
- Keep pets away from the table at mealtime.
- Keep pets away from snacking youngsters.
- Assign one person to feed all cats and dogs in the household.
- Avoid feeding all pets from the same dish, especially cats.
- Feed pets prior to eating your own meal.
- Feed pets only at their mealtime.
- Make fresh water available at all times.
- Make sure pets don't have access to the neighbors' dog or cat food.
- Feed your pet its total allotment in two or more small meals.
- Feed all meals and treats in the pet bowl only.
- Reduce or eliminate all snacks and treats.
- Measure the exact amount of food offered at each meal.
- Substitute food rewards with attention, toys, and games.
- Feed pets separately to avoid food competition.
- Chart your pet's progress on a weekly basis.

- Keep pets out of rooms where meals are prepared.
- Never put your cat or dog on a crash diet.
- Never change diets abruptly.

Patience and common sense will lead to successful weight loss. Spending quality time with your pets is calorie-free and may even help them burn calories.

Fit, Not Fat

In any successful weight-loss program, exercise is crucial because it's the only practical way to make sure you're burning more calories than you're consuming. Physical activity is just as beneficial for pets as it is for people. For some dogs, their only exercise is a brief walk or two each day, largely to relieve themselves, not solely to encourage exercise. Most indoor cats have no reason to hunt for prey, defend their territory, or do little more than walk to their dish for a meal. Unless encouraged by their owners to exercise, most cats and dogs spend their day napping. The more weight there is to carry around, the more inactive your cat or dog becomes and the harder it gets to exercise and reduce weight. It's a vicious cycle.

You are the key to a successful fitness program for your cat or dog. You set the routine, find the motivation, use your creativity, and are responsible for getting your pet out there exercising. Try to create a routine and stick to it. Most pets won't exercise by themselves. Dogs and cats may play with each other or entertain themselves briefly with toys, but as the pet parent, it's your job to direct exercise play and keep your pets active. If you want to try something new, doggie yoga, pet treadmills, and personal pet trainers are readily available.

All exercise plans should start off slowly, initially exercising a pet only as much as they can comfortably perform—especially if your pet is fat and out of shape—working up to thirty minutes twice a day for dogs and fifteen minutes once or twice a day for cats. Once weight loss occurs, your pet should be able to exercise longer and the amount and intensity of exercise can be gradually increased. As they lose weight, most pets will experience an increase in mobility and energy level, and will look and feel better.

Canine Calisthenics

Walking

Unless your dog is already used to walking, you should begin with short walks and gradually progress to thirty-minute walks twice a day. Overexercising an obese animal can cause more harm than good. Always monitor your pet closely for signs of fatigue and stop the exercise if this occurs. Start with two easy, short walks per day—five to fifteen minutes each walk may be plenty for an obese dog—and gradually increase the intensity (if appropriate) and duration.

Swimming

Swimming is a great exercise for dogs. Swimming for just five minutes is equivalent to twenty minutes of walking. While all dogs benefit from the cardiovascular exercise of swimming, older dogs, especially those with arthritis, may benefit the most. The buoyancy of water provides a non-stress-bearing environment in which the dog can work its muscles. Swimming is also a great therapy treatment. It's often used to treat dogs after surgeries or injuries in conjunction with massage therapy.

The following is a summary of tips to safely swim your dog:

- Start slowly and never leave your pet unattended in the water.
- If your dog is old or overweight, it's a good idea to use a life jacket made for dogs. It eases the amount of work and lets them swim longer.
- Introduce puppies to water by bringing along an older water-loving dog as a role model. Puppies will generally follow the lead of elders.
- Use your own judgment about whether the water is too cold. Certain breeds can handle very cold water, but some dogs love swimming so much that they're willing to jump in regardless of the temperature, and exercising cold muscles is never good.
- Always rinse off your dog after swimming as the chlorine or salt water can dry the coat and cause skin irritation.
- Dogs with floppy ears, which are prone to ear infections, should have their ears cleaned out after swimming to prevent infection. Use an ear-cleansing solution made for dogs.
- Your dog should not swim for at least two hours after eating.

Running

Dogs make great running companions, and it's a good way to keep them slim and happy. Running is also good for their overall health, including their mental health. If you keep them active, they're less likely to be hyperactive and destructive at home.

The following is a summary of tips to safely run with your dog:

- Make sure you clear it with your vet before you start running with your dog.
- Run a short distance when you first begin, and start slowly. Try one mile to start, and see how your dog is doing the next morning. If your dog is sore or tired, you'll know you've gone too far, so cut down the distance.
- Always check the pads of your dog's feet. Dogs don't have running shoes, so they will need some time to harden up their pads. If possible, run on dirt paths or grass and be careful of burning your dog's feet on hot pavement.
- Try to exercise during the cooler parts of the day, like early morning or early evening.
- Know the signs of overheating. If your dog starts to lag behind or pant excessively, or their tongue starts hanging out, it's a warning sign that they may be overdoing it.
- Always keep your dog on a leash to prevent it from being hit by a car.
- Don't run with a dog that's too young. It's best to wait until it's at least eight months old.
- Older dogs might do better with walking instead of running.
- Use common sense. A short-legged dachshund isn't going to run as far or as fast as a greyhound or golden retriever. A Jack Russell will need much more exercise than a shih tzu.
- Never exercise a dog right after a big meal as this can lead to such life-threatening problems as bloat.

The following is a summary of tips to safely hike with your dog:

- Make sure your dog has current ID tags as well as current vaccinations.

- Make sure your dog is in shape—meaning free from hip, back, and joint problems. If you're not sure, take your pet for a checkup from the vet first.

- Make sure you have a sturdy leash and collar.

- Always carry plenty of water. I recommend carrying eight ounces of water for every hour of hiking, and a portable water dish.

- Consider buying a backpack for your dog. Even a medium-size dog can carry a bowl and a first-aid kit in its pack. A healthy, well-conditioned dog can easily carry twenty-five to thirty-three percent of its body weight in a pack. Of course, you should start out slowly and acclimate your pet to the pack prior to the hike day.

- Always stay on the trails and only hike where dogs are allowed.

- Carry a first-aid kit that contains the basics, such as bandage materials, wound disinfectant, tweezers, and your vet's phone number.

- Try to discourage your pet from drinking pond or river water. It could have giardia in it, which causes diarrhea in animals (including humans).

- Always pick up after your pet.

- Don't allow your dog to chase wildlife.

- If you plan on going for a long hike, you might consider buying some booties to protect your dog's pads.

- Avoid walking your dog on asphalt and other hot surfaces as their pads can burn easily.

- Be on the lookout for snakes. Snakebites are medical emergencies. If your pet gets bitten, you must take it to the vet as soon as possible. It can make the difference between life and death.

- Watch for signs of heatstroke. Dogs lack sweat glands and can only pant to disperse heat. This makes them susceptible to heatstroke, from which they can die. Rapid panting, a bright red tongue, and/or lagging behind are all signs of heat exhaustion.

- Put a bandanna in water and tie it around your dog's neck to help keep it cool during the hike.
- Make sure your dog has some protection against fleas and ticks.
- After the hike, remember to check your dog's coat for ticks, burrs, and foxtail grass. It's also a good idea to look between the toes and check the pads for cuts and abrasions.
- Enjoy the scenery and have as much fun on the hike as your dog does!

Other Activities

Alternative means of exercise include agility training, doggy playgroups, obedience classes, and, of course, playing fetch! (See Chapter 1 on your new four-legged friend)

Feline Fitness

Cats engage in two types of play. The first is social play, where they romp, wrestle, and chase each other, and the second is object play, where they stalk, pounce, chase, and play with an object. These are the most effective ways that you can get your cat up and moving. Be creative and try to think like a cat when creating toys for them. Keep in mind that boredom is the culprit. Instead of giving in to your frustrated feline who toe bites or vocally complains, try giving your cat attention, doing obedience work, teaching it a trick, chasing it around the house, playing with a feathered toy, or doing some other form of exercise to divert its attention from food and help it burn extra calories. With a little creativity, commitment, and determination, you can achieve a daily or twice-daily fifteen-minute flurry of activity for your cat.

The following are creative ways to exercise your cat:

- Get a kitten or a second cat that it can chase around.
- Buy interactive toys such as mechanical mice or moving toys.
- Purchase a cat video.
- Use a laser pointer.
- Bring home new toys that your cat can chase.
- Buy catnip or catnip toys.
- Play chase up and down the stairs or around the house.
- Wad up paper or foil to use as a ball.
- Buy rubber or Ping-Pong balls for your cat to chase.
- Use remote-controlled toys.
- Use a feather on a wand to entice it to play.
- Make a maze out of boxes.
- Train your cat for agility (see www.catagility.com).
- Place large containers or paper bags for cats to climb into.
- Purchase a large cat tree with several levels.
- Make an outdoor enclosure for your cat to play in.
- Increase your household activities to entice your pets to join in.
- Engage your cat in some form of exercise every day.

Scratching as Exercise

Cats have very sharp, curved nails and a natural instinct to scratch. However, you can successfully teach them to scratch their posts instead of your furniture. You can start training a kitten to use a scratching post as early as two months of age. For detailed information, see Chapter 1 on your new four-legged friend.

The Rundown

Your cat or dog may seem blissful as it gorges itself on a heaping bowl of its favorite food, but the long-term consequences of such behavior are dire. It's okay for pets to get hungry; it actually keeps them from becoming finicky eaters. The tendency to eat without experiencing true hunger is very unhealthy.

All overweight or obese cats and dogs must have a vet exam before starting treatment for steady, long-term weight reduction in which you gradually change your pet's eating and exercise habits. The earlier you catch a weight-related issue, the less life-threatening it becomes, and it's never too late for your dog or cat to benefit from a controlled weight-loss plan. Remember, too, that exercise is important because in addition to promoting weight loss, it stimulates the mind and body and makes your cat or dog feel good in general.

Your cat's or dog's health is your responsibility, and the choice is simple: You can feed your pet to create disease and premature death, or feed them properly for their age, lifestyle, and breed, keeping them active, happy, and healthy to ensure a long life and lower vet bills.

Chapter 7

How to Talk to Your Vet

Taking care of your pet involves teamwork. This team consists of all the family members—other pets included—and your veterinarian. Success depends upon the information you bring into the office and the information you take away. Pet owners often leave the vet's office without even knowing what illness their pet has, what shots or treatments were given, and what the long-term prognosis is! Communication with your vet is key.

Again, it's imperative that you bring your pet in at the first sign of disease. Don't wait until your cat or dog is deathly ill. It's both frustrating and heartbreaking to see an animal succumb to an illness that could have been successfully treated if medical care had begun sooner.

Sometimes you might be nervous and even feel intimidated bringing your pet to the vet, but it's important to remember there's no such thing as a stupid question. If your vet makes you feel that way, then it may be time to get another vet. Part of the vet's job is to educate you.

Your vet is there to diagnose, perform the correct procedures, and—hopefully with your help—detect any illnesses that may be present. Providing your vet with information is crucial to keeping your pet as healthy as possible. As the pet owner, you are the first line of defense against disease. When pets come to the clinic, their adrenaline is pumping, just like your nerves when you visit the doctor, and they don't always show the symptoms they have at home.

Think of your vet as another family doctor, one who works to keep your beloved cat or dog safe and sound. As with any doctor, you need to develop a good rapport because you're beginning a long-term, trusting relationship. It's a collaborative effort.

Cost Comparison

Like many pet owners, you've probably wondered about the cost of providing quality veterinary care for your pet. It might feel as if you're paying a lot more for your pet's health care than for your own, but chances are you have adequate health insurance and may not know the total bottom-line figure for your own medical bills. When human health-care costs are added up, including insurance, deductibles, and pharmaceutical costs, they're actually much higher than what you're paying for your pet. You would never expect your own physicians to provide a diagnosis, health care, and medication free of charge, so you can't ask your veterinarian to do this for your pet.

Veterinary care is a great deal, relatively speaking. Costs have risen very little during the last twenty to thirty years compared to human health care.

Naturally, there are differences between human medicine and veterinary medicine, but a major one is that your vet is not only your pet's primary physician, but also its radiologist, dentist, surgeon, dermatologist, cardiologist, neurologist, ophthalmologist, psychiatrist, ear/nose/throat doctor, and pharmacist. Of course, as your pet's guardian, you will ultimately determine the extent of health care given, which is an individual choice for every pet owner depending on what he or she feels is acceptable financially and emotionally. Veterinarians can only make owners aware of the services and products available and then help guide them in their choices and decisions. As the pet owner, you are given options, but you have the final say.

Getting the Most Out of Your Visit

Veterinarians are busy—but not too busy to answer all of your questions, so don't be embarrassed to ask. Be truthful about your situation as there may be alternatives or solutions to problems you are encountering, both emotionally and financially. As a pet owner, **you need to listen.** Numerous studies have shown that clients only retain twenty percent of what they hear, but eighty percent of what they see, so try not to get distracted and be sure to follow through with your pet's recommended treatment plans. Develop a good partnership with your vet. You might be confused and worried, but keep in mind that you and your vet have the same goal: to keep your pet healthy. The following information will help you get the most out of your vet visit.

Before the Visit

- Bring any paperwork you might have that pertains to your pet. This includes other veterinary records, vaccination history, and records from the shelter, pet store, or breeder.

- If you have a lot of records, it's a good idea to have this information faxed or mailed prior to your visit if possible, so your vet has time to read it.

- Bring in the detailed journal you've been keeping. This especially helps when you're nervous or upset because your pet is sick and you might not be thinking clearly.

- Bring samples if possible of any vomiting or diarrhea that is occurring.

- Don't let your pet potty before the visit, as samples may be needed.

- Try to bring in a fresh stool sample. That way, we don't have to use the "magic wand" to obtain one.

- Bring a list of all medications your pet is currently taking and the dosage. If possible, bring the medication itself.

- Write down your pet's diet. Be honest! If you're giving table scraps, say so.

- Schedule appointments and be on time, or at least call if you're running late. Vets typically book appointments every fifteen to thirty minutes, and if you show up an hour late, it really throws off the whole schedule.

- Always call ahead if you don't have an appointment, especially with an emergency, to make sure there is a veterinarian available. This also gives your vet a heads-up.

- Make a list of any abnormal changes in your pet's behavior, when it first started, and how often it's happening.

- Write down any changes in the household and be sure to mention these to your vet.

- Know your pet's birthday and if any of its siblings have been diagnosed with health problems.

- Unless instructed to do so, try not to feed your pet prior to your appointment.

Etiquette

- 🐾 Be nice to the staff. A little kindness goes a long way.
- 🐾 Try not to talk or ask questions when your vet has the stethoscope on.
- 🐾 Don't talk on your cell phone when the doctor is in the exam room with you.
- 🐾 Address your vet as "Doctor," not by their first name unless they ask you to.

Routine versus Sick Visit

There can be a difference between a routine visit, in which your pet seems healthy, and one where your pet is sick. During a routine visit, you should have more time to talk about your pet's diet, weight, and behavior problems. Also, discuss with your vet how often she thinks your pet needs to come in for an exam, based on your pet's age, previous health problems, breed, environment, or lifestyle. A healthy two-year-old Lab mix who's getting its teeth brushed daily, lots of exercise, and a high-quality diet may only need to come in once a year versus a ten-year-old poodle with a history of gum disease and a heart murmur, who may need to be seen every three to six months.

To get the best value for your money, make full use of your vet's knowledge by asking questions about all aspects of your pet's health and behavior. Most cases of owners feeling like their needs aren't being met are just plain misunderstandings, which can be resolved by talking about problems and looking for solutions.

If you're bringing your pet in because it is sick, it's important to give as accurate and thorough a history as possible to help your vet make the proper diagnosis. This includes knowing how long the diarrhea or vomiting has been occurring, if your pet's appetite is up or down, if the potty habits have changed, and so on. It can be a difficult task trying to make a diagnosis and your detailed information is crucial. Take the time to share all of your fears, needs, and wants. Ask questions. If you don't understand the treatment plan, medication, dosing, or test results, don't walk out the door nodding your head when you really don't know what's going on. Clear and concise communication is essential, especially if you're stressed or upset. The vet wants you to be an informed owner. The doctor's job is to make your pet well, and that involves you.

Scheduling Surgery

Whenever your pet has surgery, there's always an inherent risk, even for a healthy-looking animal, but the risk of anesthesia will be greatly reduced by preanesthetic diagnostics such as blood work, urinalysis, and X rays, if indicated. Your vet needs to know ahead of time if your pet has an undiagnosed illness that could complicate the procedure. A preanesthetic health screen and urinalysis will identify any underlying problems that may not be evident in the initial physical examination.

I always recommend having blood work and a urinalysis performed anytime your pet has to be anesthetized for anything. Blood work tells you how your pet is operating on the inside and is crucial in determining vital organ function. The risk of complications during surgery with anesthesia is greatly increased if your pet has an underlying illness that goes undetected. If a problem is detected prior to surgery, it may influence the type of anesthetics and/or types of monitoring devices used, as well as the medications given prior to the surgery. For example, if your pet has dental work scheduled, and the preanesthetic blood work shows a high white blood cell count, which indicates an infection in the bloodstream, most veterinarians will want to put your pet on antibiotics before, during, and after the dental work. This is critical to treating a dangerous infection from the teeth that can damage your pet's internal organs.

Reasons for a Preanesthetic Lab Workup

- 🐾 Kidney failure and liver disease can occur in young animals as well as older ones.
- 🐾 Low blood sugar increases risk.
- 🐾 Dehydration can have serious consequences.
- 🐾 Undetected anemia can have fatal consequences.
- 🐾 Serves as a baseline for future tests.
- 🐾 Gives vets and clients peace of mind.

Diagnostics

Blood Tests

Blood tests, which help determine if an animal is healthy on the inside, are essential as screening tools for senior pets, pets undergoing any and all surgical procedures, and pets with fever, chronic vomiting or diarrhea, weakness, pale gums, loss of appetite, or other medical disorders. There are hundreds of tests you can run on an animal's blood sample, but a CBC, or complete blood count, is the most common blood test performed on pets and people.

The second type of blood test commonly performed to assess the health status of cats, dogs, and people is serum blood chemistries. Blood chemistries are necessary to evaluate organ function, electrolyte status, and enzyme and hormone levels in the body. This information determines how various organs such as the kidneys, pancreas, and liver are functioning.

Urinalysis

Testing your cat or dog's urine is a very valuable diagnostic tool. A routine urinalysis will speak volumes about the condition of your cat or dog. And if something shows up in the blood sample, it can often be correlated with abnormalities that may be present in the urine. A urinalysis can aid in the diagnosis of bladder infections, diabetes, kidney disease, protein loss, liver disease, endocrine disease, and cancer. I can't tell you how many times a routine urinalysis has turned up something not so routine and has detected an illness way before the pet started to exhibit clinical signs to its owner.

I recommend a urinalysis on cats and dogs once a year until the pets reach age seven, and then, depending on the pet, I may recommend it twice a year after that. The cost, around $20 to $30, is minimal compared to the wealth of information that a urinalysis will provide. Remember, animals tend to mask their signs of illness until the problem becomes severe. Preventative medicine is the best strategy.

Fecal Exams

Microscopic examination of your pet's stool is important to diagnose a host of different illnesses and disorders including digestion abnormalities, internal bleeding, pancreatic disease, and parasites. Fecal floatation identifies the types of eggs of intestinal parasites such as hookworms, roundworms, and tapeworms. Parasites that cause diarrhea can also be identified by a fecal exam.

ECG

An ECG or electrocardiogram is an easily performed noninvasive procedure used to evaluate the electrical activity of the heart. It assesses the heart rate, rhythm, conduction, and, to some degree, the size.

Abnormalities may indicate a serious problem, and further diagnostics such as X rays and/or an ultrasound are usually indicated.

X rays

X rays routinely indicate arthritis, tumors, fractures, organ enlargement, and other abnormalities. They can help detect problems with the heart, lungs, kidneys, liver, bones, soft tissue, and intestinal tract. As pets get older, it can be helpful to obtain radiographs (i.e., X rays) of the chest and abdomen taken when your dog or cat is healthy. These can serve as a baseline to compare to after a disease process has started.

Ultrasound

An ultrasound is a noninvasive way to get a three-dimensional look inside the body. It is instrumental in diagnosing disease of the heart as it can assess the valves and movement of blood through the heart and provides precise measurements of the thickness of the various chamber walls—something X rays can't do.

Say That in English, Doc

Veterinarians go to college for a minimum of eight years, acquire a doctorate, pass a rigorous national board exam, and must meet state licensing requirements. When veterinarians are in school, everyone speaks the same technical jargon—for instance, X rays are radiographs, and cancer is neoplasia—and they're expected to use their new language. Breaking the habit can be hard. Some vets might simply be unaware that they're talking to you in technical lingo. But no matter what, your vet's job is to explain to you in clear and simple terms some pretty complicated problems. Just hearing a diagnosis of granulomatous meningoencephalomyelitis would make some pet owners faint!

Veterinarians must communicate in a professional yet meaningful way to pet owners of diverse educations and backgrounds. Medical language can be confusing, condescending, and hard to remember under emotional circumstances. That's why it's essential to ask questions, say you don't understand, or have your vet write down important information.

During the Visit

- Arrive fifteen minutes early when you come in for your very first visit. There is usually paperwork that needs to be filled out and you want to be ready when it's your pet's appointment time.
- Always bring your pet to the office on a leash or in a carrier.
- Keep dogs from visiting cat carriers with fretting felines who may not be used to dogs.
- Put only one cat in each carrier. Many cats get nervous and begin attacking their once-friendly house member in the carrier.
- Notify a receptionist or technician if your pet has an accident.
- Always let the receptionist, tech, and vet know if your dog or cat gets upset at the vet's office and may bite. Muzzle-training anxious pets is so much easier on the pet, the staff, and you.
- Remember to ask questions. Make a list ahead of time and bring it with you to ensure that everything you want to know is covered.
- Make sure to mention any changes in your pet's household or environment, like construction, moving, or any new two- or four-legged family members.
- Ask your vet to explain anything you don't understand.
- Make sure your pet has its weight and temperature taken and recorded.
- The doctor should listen to your pet's heart and lungs.
- Your pet should have its eyes, ears, nose, and teeth examined (that is, if your pet will allow it).
- Have your vet check ANY lumps or bumps that your pet might have.

- Have your vet go over any abnormal physical exam findings with you.
- Have someone go over an estimate with you prior to any diagnostic tests being performed.
- Have your vet show you and go over the results from any blood work, urinalysis, or X rays performed.
- Ask your vet to write down the diagnosis, if there is one.
- Ask for a vaccination schedule. Routine shots vary for cats and dogs, depending on their age and lifestyle.
- If time permits, go over your pet's nutritional recommendations.
- Make sure you understand all medications that are being prescribed and find out why they are being given.
- Ask to have someone demonstrate administering medication.
- Ask for a copy of your pet's lab work to keep in your file.
- Always take a business card and file it with your other vet papers.
- Schedule your pet's procedure or follow-up appointment before you leave.

After the Visit

One hundred percent compliance is important, otherwise you can have a setback in recovery and end up spending a lot more money than if you had initially followed the plan; it can even cost your pet's life. Be honest: If there's a factor that will prevent you from following your at-home instructions, say what it is. You might be short on funds; you might not understand the diagnosis; your mother may be ill and you have to spend time at the hospital—whatever it is, tell your vet so you both can come up with the best possible solution for you and your pet.

Complying with your vet's recommendations includes following treatment protocols, keeping all follow-up appointments, and giving all meds. Many clients don't follow treatment plans laid out by their vet because of the cost, or because they don't understand the plans or don't have enough time.

Also, keep in mind that it is okay to change vets. Sometimes people just don't see eye to eye. No one benefits from a poor patient–client relationship.

Specialists

During the past fifteen years there has been incredible growth in the volume of new procedures and information available to veterinarians. Consequently, it's virtually impossible for any one veterinarian to be completely versed in all areas of medical discipline. Just like in human medicine, this has led vets to become specialized, receiving advanced training in certain areas of medicine.

Specialists are veterinarians who, on top of four years of college and four years of veterinary medical school, have completed three to four years of advanced training, usually including a formal residency program that's almost identical to human physician training. In addition, they must publish new findings and successfully complete a series of challenging examinations. They can then become board certified in a clinical specialty recognized by the American Veterinary Medical Association (AVMA). Only board-certified specialists are given the title of "diplomate" in the college of their specialty. AVMA recognizes twenty-one specialty boards or colleges. Although not as many specialists exist in veterinary medicine as in human medicine, there are a growing number of veterinary experts in fields such as anesthesiology, behavior, cardiology (heart), dentistry, dermatology (skin), emergency and critical care, exotic animal medicine, internal medicine, nutrition, oncology (cancer), ophthalmology (eye), pathology, radiology (X rays), and surgery. All of these experts mean sophisticated care for your pets.

Hopefully your pet will have a long, healthy life and never need a specialist, but if one is needed, they are available. Most veterinarians recommend specialists when cases are complex, uncommon, or grave.

A referral to a specialist may also be appropriate if the usual avenues of treatments aren't working or if a diagnosis hasn't been made.

Alternative Medicine

Veterinary medicine is constantly growing and changing, just like human medicine. Dogs and cats can now enjoy a professional massage, have the crick in their back fixed, or receive acupuncture to improve their quality of life. Complementary or holistic medicine provides nonconventional treatments for a wide variety of ailments and is now offered for pets. Holistic medicine combines traditional medicine with one or more complementary therapies that address not just individual symptoms or conditions, but your pet's entire well-being.

The philosophy is to look at all aspects of the animal's life including nutrition, environment, lifestyle, and psychological state. Holistic therapy can prove beneficial in many cases. When choosing a professional to perform treatments on your pet, ask your vet for a referral and be sure the specialist has been educated in that particular medical discipline. Also inquire about alternative or holistic treatments such as acupuncture, chiropractic, massage therapy, homeopathy, and physical therapy.

Pain Management

Pets feel pain very similarly to the way we feel pain. Twenty years ago, pain management was unthinkable because there really wasn't medication available to veterinarians. All of that has changed. Veterinarians now have the best pain medicine available from nonsteroidal anti-inflammatories to narcotics. These days, it's expected for vets to prescribe pain medication after even routine procedures like a cat neuter to more sophisticated procedures like a total hip replacement. If for some reason your vet doesn't prescribe home pain meds, just ask. Don't wait until you're home with your whimpering pet and the vet clinic is closed.

The Bottom Line

Knowledge will empower you to take charge of your pet's health. That way, everyone benefits. Your pet stays healthy, your vet is happy, and you're thrilled.

Developing a good relationship with your veterinarian is vital. This is a two-way street that requires mutual respect. You are your cat's or dog's voice, so speak up! After all, you're paying for a service. Don't forget to articulate your cares, concerns, and worries to your vet.

Chapter 8

Avoiding the Emergency Room Blues

Although I have worked in veterinary emergency rooms for years, I'm still alarmed by the frequency with which pets are treated for senseless, easily avoidable accidents—pets that are inadvertently poisoned by their owners, pets given alcohol, pets given bones to eat, pets hit by cars, pets attacked by other pets. These are just some of the misfortunes that ultimately cost thousands of cats and dogs needless pain and suffering every year. The cost to owners: unnecessary regret, heartache, and substantial sums of money.

Each year thousands of pets end up at emergency clinics, where behind the scenes there is plenty of drama. No pet lover would argue that a trip to the ER is an unpleasant experience, one they want to avoid at all costs. The unfamiliar, sterile environment is tense with urgency, worry, and suffering. To make matters worse, you usually see a veterinarian you have no relationship with, and you're often asked to quickly make life-and-death decisions for your pet.

Animal emergency clinics function much like emergency hospitals for people. There are no appointments and patients are seen in the order of arrival, unless a critical case arrives that takes precedence (a triage system is used to determine the order in which patients will be treated). To expedite things, many emergency clinics take sick pets away from their owners and into the treatment area, where they can be checked in and stabilized while owners fill out paperwork. Time is of the essence, since many emergency clinics only have one doctor on duty at a time and they can be bombarded with emergencies. I've had to tell frantic pet owners on the phone that they must go to another clinic because I already had critical surgeries piling up—which brings me to a very important point: **You must call the emergency clinic ahead of time to make sure your pet can be seen.** Emergency clinics can get slammed with more than one critical case at a time and you don't want your pet to have to wait for treatment, because waiting can greatly affect the outcome. The sooner you call the clinic to inform them of what has happened to your pet, the better. Give the clinic an estimated time of your arrival, and the staff can start preparing for you. Always leave a contact number with the clinic and please call back if you decide not to come in—or, worse, if your pet doesn't survive.

Oftentimes the cases seen at emergency clinics are seasonal, which is why it's important to be aware of seasonal dangers and to be prepared for them. For example, in fall and winter, antifreeze poisonings and pancreatitis cases are rampant; in spring and summer, hit-by-car accidents and overheating are common (see Chapter 12 on seasonal disturbances).

What can you do to avoid that upsetting trip to the emergency room? It's not always easy. Pet ownership is a huge responsibility. Dogs and cats require a great deal of attention, care, and guidance. Imagine having to rely on someone for your every need. As a pet owner, you're responsible for keeping your cat or dog out of harm's way and making its safety, health, and happiness a priority. There are certainly times when accidents aren't avoidable and do happen—and in those times, it's wonderful to have emergency clinics available. Inevitably there will be times when unexpected situations arise, so you'll want to be prepared for them. However, with planning, preparation, and common sense you'll be able to minimize the number of trips to the ER.

Some measures you can take to keep your pets safe include:

- Spaying or neutering your pets
- Keeping cats indoors
- Keeping dogs on a leash at all times
- Knowing the dangerous household poisons
- Knowing which plants are dangerous
- Knowing the potential toxins in your home, yard, and garage

Signs of Poisoning

The most common signs of poisoning are salivation, incoordination, muscle tremors, seizures, vomiting, and diarrhea. If your pet exhibits any of these symptoms, it may have eaten a poisonous plant or ingested a harmful chemical. Take your dog or cat to the vet right away—don't wait. Try to take any plant material, vomitus, or chemical substances involved to the clinic with you.

Medications

Every day in this country, some unsuspecting pet owner gives his pet a pill in the hope of making his dog or cat feel better, often with disastrous results. Prescription and over-the-counter medications can be lethal to pets. And don't think that a cat or dog won't gobble down a whole bottle of pills—it has happened. Drug poisoning is the most common small-animal poison exposure. Dogs and cats don't process drugs the same way humans do, and many human medications can be fatal to pets.

Common Household Products That Are Poisonous to Pets

Adhesives	Dyes	Permanent solution
Aftershave	Eye drops	Phenol
Aleve	Fungicides	Photo developer
Antifreeze	Furniture polish	Rubbing alcohol
Aspirin	Gasoline	Shoe polish
Batteries	Glue	Soaps
Boric acid	Hair coloring	Solvent
Brake fluid	Ibuprofen	Sugarless gum
Carburetor cleaner	Kerosene	(containing xylitol)
Cleaning products	Laxatives	Suntan lotion
Crayons	Lye	Tar
Deodorants	Mineral spirits	Turpentine
Deodorizers	Nail polish	Tylenol
Detergents	Nail polish remover	Windshield wiper fluid
Disinfectants	Paint	Wood preservatives
Drain cleaners	Paint remover	

If you witness your pet ingesting household cleaning products, you can immediately flush its mouth with large amounts of water to help reduce the amount of chemical burn and thus tissue damage. Call your vet right away for additional treatment. Sometimes chemical burns don't show up right away, but clinical signs include drooling, pawing at the mouth, vomiting, lack of appetite, mouth odor, or excessive swallowing. Treatment requires immediate veterinary care. Gather the suspected poisonous substances and/or vomitus and bring them to your veterinarian along with your pet.

Garbage and Food Poisoning

Cats and dogs that eat spoiled or raw food are susceptible to food poisoning. Raw meat, for example, poses a danger of salmonella bacteria. Food poisoning in dogs and cats is similar to humans in that the toxicity is acquired by the ingestion of spoiled food and in toxins produced by the bacteria in the rotten food, which can cause serious gastrointestinal signs including vomiting, diarrhea, fever, abdominal pain, and weakness. Severely affected animals can go into shock and die as a result of the absorbed bacterial toxins in the bloodstream. Pets should never be given spoiled or raw food or allowed access to garbage cans, spoiled food, or raw food.

Lead

Cats and dogs can develop lead poisoning from ingesting lead-based paint by eating paint chips, grooming their contaminated coat, or licking their paws or feet that are covered in dust or chips from lead-based paint. Lead curtain weights at the bottom of draperies, lead fishing weights, and lead solder inside electronic equipment such as VCRs, remotes, and stereo components can all be ingested by your cat or dog. Clinical signs of lead poisoning include stomach pain, anemia, vomiting, diarrhea, lack of appetite, blood in feces, inability to sleep, depression, hysterical barking, seizures, blindness, and death. The blood test for lead toxicity in cats and dogs is the same test given for lead toxicity in humans.

Plants: Inside and Outside

Plants add beauty to your home or garden, but many of them can become deadly enemies to your cat or dog. Pets will chew on grass and plants, in part due to their curious nature, but sometimes eating plants

can be quite harmful. Ingesting a small amount of a mildly toxic plant may not always be deadly, but large or repeated doses may be extremely dangerous. Because of their small size and sensitive metabolism, pets—especially cats—tend to be highly sensitive to poisonous plants.

Given the huge number of plants in existence, it's impossible to know every single plant that may be toxic to your pet. As a general rule, plants that are listed as toxic to humans should also be considered toxic to animals. According to data compiled by the ASPCA Animal Poison Control Center from January 2001 to December 2004, **the top five deadliest plants with the potential to produce life-threatening problems are lilies, azaleas, oleander, sago palm, and castor bean.** There are a few cases of plants considered nontoxic or mildly toxic to humans that can cause serious problems in cats and dogs, such as **onion, garlic, avocados, heavenly bamboo, schefflera, dracaena, philodendron, pothos, and scindapsus.**

Therefore, any time your cat or dog ingests any type of plant material, you should be concerned, especially if your pet shows any abnormal behavior or clinical signs. After removing any remaining plant parts from your pet's mouth, you should call your vet right away.

Remember to keep all plants out of reach of your pets. Before buying a new plant, have the store label the plant with its common name and Latin name, and avoid purchasing plants that are toxic to pets. Also know the names of all your plants, both inside and outside the house. Go to the Cornell University Poisonous Plants home page at **www.ansci.cornell.edu/plant/** for a list of poisonous plants.

Pet-proofing

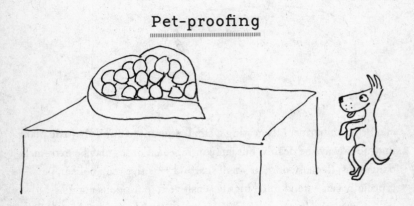

Pet-proofing your home is very similar to childproofing it. Look around your home while trying to think like your pet. Imagine what kind of trouble your cat or dog could get into. Keep in mind that pets like to check out every nook and cranny, and remember Murphy's Law: "Whatever can go wrong, will go wrong." Use your imagination and common sense to identify potential disasters waiting to happen. This is especially true for puppies and kittens or pets that are new to your home, but it applies to adult cats and dogs as well.

The following is a list of potential dangers:

- Cords of all kinds are dangerous to dogs and cats because of potential strangulation or electrocution. This includes telephone, drapery, Venetian blinds, appliance, extension, and other electrical cords.

- Plastic bags, especially those that contain food, are dangerous around cats and dogs. Pets can accidentally suffocate themselves.

- Any object smaller than your animal's mouth is fodder for ingestion: paper clips, thumbtacks, string, yarn, dental floss, rubber bands, needles and thread, buttons, staples, erasers, jewelry, marbles, fishhooks, toys with removable parts, and so on.

- Unscreened windows and balconies are dangerous as pets may fall from them and seriously injure themselves.

- Heavy objects on the edges of counters, shelves, cabinets, or tables that can fall or be pulled down by a cord can seriously injure your cat or dog.

- Open toilets, mop buckets, bathtubs, swimming pools, wading pools, and Jacuzzis all pose problems from drowning or chemical poisoning.

Emergencies

In an emergency, the best thing you can do for your pet is to be prepared, stay calm, and make quick decisions. Know where the closest emergency clinic is and if your regular vet is open, and have the addresses and phone numbers in a safe and accessible place. Also, try not to panic. Your primary objectives are to save your pet's life, prevent any further injuries, reduce pain and distress, and get your pet safely to the vet. Knowledge is power, so take the steps right now to learn how to handle an emergency with your pet. It can make the difference between life and death.

Bleeding

Severe bleeding can be life-threatening. A ten-pound cat has about 350 milliliters (ml) of blood, and a fifty-pound dog has a blood volume of 2,000 ml. Animals are at risk of dying when they lose more than thirty-five percent of their total blood volume, so the goal is to stop the bleeding. In a ten-pound cat, that's roughly 123 ml of blood lost, and in a fifty-pound dog, it's about 700 ml. With severe bleeding, you need to watch for signs of shock, which include pale gums, rapid breathing, weak pulse, cold legs or paws, and general weakness. Once an animal goes into shock, time is of the essence. Spurting blood is more critical and generally indicates a severed artery because the blood pressure is higher in arteries (carrying blood from the heart) versus in veins (carrying blood back to the heart). In either case, severe bleeding should be addressed with pressure. Place gauze and/or bandage material over the wound and apply direct pressure using your hands or fingers. This should be done for two to five minutes and then recheck. If blood soaks through the material, don't remove it—just add more material on top; that way, if clots are forming, you don't disrupt them. If there are no fractures, try to keep the bleeding area higher than the heart. If, after five minutes, the bleeding is still severe, you should take your pet to the vet immediately.

Tourniquets are dangerous and should only be used as a last resort

CAUTION

Dogs or cats that are frightened and/or in severe pain may bite their owners, so always be careful and make your safety the first priority.

as they can lead to loss of the entire limb if used improperly. If you do use a tourniquet, be sure to place it above the bleeding wound just tight enough to significantly reduce the flow of blood, and loosen it every five minutes as you transport your pet to the vet. Do not keep it on longer than twenty minutes because you can damage the blood supply to the entire limb.

Cold packs over oozing wounds can also help reduce swelling and bleeding.

With severe or constant bleeding, you should take your pet to the hospital immediately.

Broken Bones/Soft Tissue Injury

Injury to the skeletal system, which includes bones, joints, and ligaments, are very common. Bones become dislocated when you have an injury to the joint capsule and/or ligaments that hold the bones together. An injury to joint ligaments or muscle tendons themselves is called a *sprain*. A fracture occurs when bone is broken.

Some animals are very stoic, which can make it difficult to know if a limb is broken, but most pets will not put any weight on a leg that is broken, especially above the knee. With a sprain, they will limp but bear weight. Another telltale sign is to look for a leg that has a lump in it, or a paw that is facing in a slightly different direction, or a leg that appears to be dangling. Your vet should see all fractures, whether they are open and bleeding or not. If you suspect your cat or dog has a broken bone, try to immobilize your pet while holding it still and place it on a stretcher (you can use a board, a car floor mat, or even a folded blanket). By immobilizing the broken limb you are preventing any further damage to the fractured area. Do not attempt to bandage or splint a broken limb as you can actually do more harm than good, and always take your pet to the hospital immediately.

Car Accidents

It can happen in a flash: Your friend comes over, and as you open the door to greet her, your cat or dog rushes out the door. Maybe you're walking your dog and it unexpectedly tugs on the leash to investigate something interesting, causing you to accidentally drop the leash. Perhaps your pet catches the scent of a squirrel, jumps out of the car, and runs across the road in hot pursuit.

Hit-by-car accidents are all too common. One of the best preventative measures to combat this often-fatal event is to spay or neuter your pet (see Chapter 4, Love Your Pet). All dogs or cats that have been hit by a car need to see a vet right away. Internal bleeding is common from organs like the spleen, and outward clinical signs may not show up for several hours. Also, puncture wounds may close rapidly, but can lead to serious and life-threatening infections down the road.

If your pet is injured in the street, wave either a bright-colored or white cloth to attract attention and enlist someone's help to move your dog or cat to a safer spot. Even the most docile animal will bite its beloved owner when in pain, so you need to be careful when handling your pet and always think of your safety. If need be, make a muzzle out of a strip of cloth and tie it over your dog's nose, or for a cat, put a towel or coat over its face. Try to keep your pet covered for warmth, talk to them in a soothing voice, and transport them to the vet as soon as possible.

Choking

Dogs and cats will accidentally swallow toys, rawhides, pieces of food, and other numerous objects. Instead of passing down the esophagus into the stomach, an object can become lodged in front of the windpipe, obstructing air to the lungs. A dog or cat that is choking may breathe very loudly, drool, paw at its mouth, cough, gag, or become anxious and gasp for air. Oftentimes an animal will faint from

lack of oxygen. If this happens, you can gently open your pet's mouth to see if you can spot the object and remove it.

If your pet isn't breathing and you can't find what is obstructing the air passage, try a modified Heimlich maneuver to dislodge the object. With your pet's head away from you, hold your pet against you and tightly clasp your hands around its upper abdomen, just under the rib cage. For smaller dogs or cats, just use both of your hands. Or you can place your pet on its side on the floor. Then place one of your hands on top of the other. Your bottom hand should be just below the rib cage, on the midline of their abdomen. Push with your fist or lift upward to dislodge the object. This can be done three to five times with quick pushes. By squeezing forcefully, you can often dislodge the object and it will pop right out.

If your pet is small, you can also lift and suspend them with the head pointed down. For larger animals, lift the rear legs so the head is tilted down. This will sometimes dislodge an item stuck in the throat.

Another method with small animals is to place them stomach side down on your lap, keeping their head lower than their body and administer a sharp blow with the palm of your hand between the shoulder blades.

If you try these methods and are unsuccessful, you must take your pet to the vet right away.

CPR

CPR (cardiopulmonary resuscitation) is an emergency technique used to help animals or people whose heart and/or breathing has stopped. Pets that are in cardiopulmonary arrest will be unconscious and have a weak or irregular pulse, no heartbeat, and no obvious signs of breathing. Although somewhat modified, the same techniques used for people (rescue breathing and chest compressions) can be used for animals in distress. Do not attempt CPR on a conscious animal as you may get severely injured. **Try to enlist the help of others—it's best to perform CPR while you're on the way to a hospital so resuscitation can be continued with oxygen and various drugs at the veterinary hospital.**

Always follow the "ABC" order: Airway, Breathing, Circulation.

- **Airway:** You must first clear the airway to allow airflow to the lungs. With your pet on its side, gently extend the head and neck. If your pet is unconscious, pull the tongue out and, with your fingers, clear the inside of the mouth of any saliva, vomit, or foreign objects. If your pet is conscious, make sure you don't put your fingers in its mouth so you don't get bitten. Again, only perform CPR on an animal that is in full cardiopulmonary arrest.
- **Breathing:** Check to see if your pet is breathing by watching its sides for movement or holding a mirror or tissue under their nose and looking for vapor or tissue movement. If your pet is not breathing for at least fifteen seconds, proceed with artificial respiration. If you have a medium or large dog, hold its mouth closed with one hand around the muzzle. (This is unnecessary for cats and small dogs like pugs and Persians, which have little

or no nose.) Then place your mouth over your pet's nose and exhale. Breath forcefully enough to cause your pet's chest to rise a normal amount only. Don't be too forceful as you can injure the lungs in small pets. Give the animal five to ten breaths, then stop to see if the animal resumes breathing on its own. If not, continue to breathe at thirty breaths per minute for animals that weigh fewer than thirty pounds, or twenty breaths per minute for animals that weigh more than thirty pounds.

- **Circulation:** You can feel the heartbeat by placing a hand or your fingers on the chest behind the left elbow or feel for a pulse up high on the inside of either thigh. If you can't feel a heartbeat or pulse, you need to perform chest compressions. For cats or small puppies, place one hand on the chest and steady the animal with the other hand. Place the thumb on one side, fingers on the other, and *gently* press in. Note: You can cause serious chest injuries with overzealous compressions. For dogs that weigh fewer than thirty pounds, place the animal on its right side and place one hand on each side of the chest. Compress the chest a half inch to 1 inch. Perform five compressions, then give one breath, and then check for a pulse. Repeat, but be careful not to compress the chest too forcefully with small pets. For dogs that weigh more than thirty pounds, place the animal on its right side and place both hands over the area of the heart, on the chest behind the left elbow. Compress the chest 1 to 3 inches, depending on the dog's size. If you are alone, perform five compressions, then give one breath, and then check for a pulse. Repeat. With two people present, one can perform compressions while the other person gives breaths. The rate is three to five compressions for each breath. If the animal's heartbeat and spontaneous breathing fail to resume after fifteen minutes of CPR, the pet has little chance of survival.

Heatstroke

You need to gradually cool down your pet's body. Do not immerse a pet in ice-cold water because this may cause it to go into shock. Place your pet on its side and bathe its body with cool water at first, finally applying ice packs to the head and neck, and take them to the animal hospital as soon as possible. See Chapter 12 on seasonal disturbances for more information.

Seizures

Seizures are caused by abnormal stimulation that leads to involuntary contractions of muscles. They may result from epilepsy, brain tumors, poisoning, or head trauma. Dogs and cats won't swallow their tongue, so don't put your hand in the mouth of a pet that is having a seizure. Move furniture out of the way and try to keep the area as dark as possible. Seizures typically last two to three minutes, but gentle talking and stroking may help to shorten the length of the seizure. Seizures lasting longer than ten minutes should be treated as an emergency, and a veterinarian should see your pet immediately. Otherwise, wait until the seizure has subsided, then contact your veterinarian.

Shock

Pets can go into shock from infection, blood loss, injury, poisoning, heatstroke, or frostbite. When an animal is in shock, it will have rapid and shallow breathing, weakness, confusion, and pale gums. Try to keep your pet warm and quiet. Wrap your pet in a blanket or towel and take it to the hospital as soon as possible.

Come in Sooner Rather Than Later

If your cat or dog is exhibiting the following signs, you should call the vet and take your pet in right away:

- Difficulty breathing
- Difficulty urinating or defecating
- Seizures
- Fainting or collapse
- Prolonged or profuse bleeding
- Trauma of any kind, especially vehicular (even with no outward signs of injury)
- Abdominal pain, bloating, or swelling
- Heatstroke
- Hypothermia
- Repeated vomiting
- Bloody vomiting or diarrhea
- Prolonged fever
- White, blue, bright red, brown, or dark mucous membranes
- Eye disorders
- Paralysis
- Pain (severe or continuous)
- Restlessness and retching, especially in a large breed of dog
- Poison ingestion (if possible, bring the container with the name of the chemical)
- Penetrating wounds
- Dog- or cat-bite wounds

First-Aid Kit

It's a great idea to have a pet emergency kit at your home and a smaller one in your car. You can buy kits already assembled or you can put them together yourself. Use a small plastic container with a tight-fitting lid or use a tackle box for each kit. It should contain the following items:

- Phone number and directions to your veterinary hospital
- Phone number and directions to closest emergency veterinary hospital
- Phone number of poison control center
- Rectal thermometer
- K-Y jelly without spermicide
- Tweezers to remove ticks, burrs, and splinters
- Blunt-tip scissors
- Disposable latex gloves
- Syringes of various sizes
- Penlight
- Nylon slip leash
- Rubbing alcohol
- Three percent hydrogen peroxide for cleaning wounds
- Diphenhydramine or Benadryl for allergic reactions
- Antibiotic ointment for wounds
- Wound disinfectant such as Betadine or Nolvasan
- Cortisone spray or cream
- Sterile saline for flushing eyes or other areas
- Ear-cleaning solution
- Roll of 2-inch-wide gauze bandage
- Roll of 1-inch-wide bandage tape
- Roll of 2-inch-wide Vetrap (self-adhering bandaging tape)
- Gauze pads in different sizes
- Nonstick pads

- Roll of cotton
- Cotton balls
- Cotton swabs
- Soap or mild shampoo for cleaning
- Muzzles that you can buy at pet stores
- Styptic powder/sticks, Kwik-Stop, or cornstarch to control nail bleeding
- Nail clippers and metal nail file
- Magnifying glass
- Two heavy towels/blankets to use as a stretcher and to keep pet warm
- Several clean towels
- Paper towels
- Pedialyte for dehydration
- Nutri-Cal nutritional supplement
- Karo syrup for low blood sugar
- Flea comb

The Wrap-Up

Pet-proofing your home, garage, and yard can make the difference between life and death for your pet, so take a thoughtful walk around all of these areas once a month and inspect your pet's surroundings to ensure your cat or dog is safe in its own environment. As you have learned, some of the most common sources of poisoning are right in your own home and yard: medications, insecticides, rodenticides, pesticides, cleaning products, plants, ethylene glycol (antifreeze), garbage, and food poisoning. In any case of potential poisoning, it's critical to find the container of the toxic substance and know the ingredients when seeking veterinary advice. All poisons are not created equal, nor are they treated the same way. Knowing what toxic substance your pet ingested could make the difference in its survival.

Always call ahead before taking your dog or cat to the vet clinic to make sure a doctor can see your pet and to let the staff know you're on the way. Furthermore, it's much better to err on the side of caution and have all emergencies seen by a vet. Just because your pet looks fine on the outside doesn't mean everything is okay on the inside. Internal bleeding or injuries may not show external signs for several hours, and by then your pet could be in grave danger.

No question about it: With a little forethought and planning, you'll help avoid the emergency room blues. You'll be returning your pet's unconditional love—and you might even save its life.

Chapter 9

The Perfect Fit: Outfitting Your Pet

Your cat or dog should learn to wear a collar or leash with proper ID immediately and at all times. Puppies and kittens will scratch at first, but they will soon adjust to the sensation, usually within days. Of course, if the scratching persists, check the skin underneath to make sure it looks normal or try a different collar or harness. And plan on getting more than one collar if you have a puppy or kitten, because they grow so fast and may easily outgrow the first collar you buy for them.

Choosing the appropriate collar or harness for your pet is not difficult to accomplish due to the myriad of choices on the market today. However, what might look great on your pet can actually harm it. I've seen many dogs that have slipped out of their posh, gold-studded collars and been hit by cars or attacked by other dogs. So before you go to the pet store and get seduced by that expensive, bright-colored, diamond-studded, or Louis Vuitton collar, think safety first and then plunk down your hard-earned dollars for the right item that you've thoughtfully determined is not dangerous for your pet. Remember, just because it's expensive doesn't mean that it's good for your pet.

When it comes to collars, one size and one kind definitely do not fit all. Quality, functionality, comfort, and safety should drive your decision, and fashion should be secondary. Never use a makeshift collar or take your dog on a walk collarless. One Christmas Day, I was appalled to see a smartly dressed man take his dog from the car and walk it around the parking lot to go potty—with two plastic shopping bags tied together around the dog's neck, comprising a short leash and collar. The dog escaped from this contraption more than once.

Collars, harnesses, and leashes are necessary not only for controlling your pet outside of its home environment, but also for safety, identification, and traveling. One of my particular pet peeves (pardon the pun) is when owners don't make their pets wear proper identification at all times. Proper ID includes legible tags with your pet's name, phone number, and address, and the name and address of an alternate contact person in case you can't be located. An ID is critical because millions of cats and dogs end up in animal shelters across the country. A recent survey by the American Animal Hospital Association showed that approximately thirty percent of all pet owners have lost their pet at one time or another. Tragically, only about two percent of cats and roughly sixteen percent of dogs are ever reunited with their owners. Positive pet identification is the best life-insurance policy you will ever purchase because it is key to reuniting you with your lost pet.

The Fit

Every year, pets die from accidental hanging from wearing a collar that is too loose. For a proper fit, measure around your dog's or cat's neck with a cloth tape measure. Be sure to measure a few inches down from their head. Pull the tape measure so it's snug, but not too tight. Add 1 inch for small dogs and cats, and 2 to 3 inches for medium- to large-size dogs. If you're buying for a puppy or kitten, leave some room for growth. When shopping for the collar, take the tape measure or your pet with you. Some collar manufacturers measure the collar from tip to tip while others measure from the buckle to the center hole, and still others measure from the buckle to the last hole. For small dogs (less than twenty pounds) and cats, leave only one finger's width between the collar and your pet's neck. For a medium-size dog, leave two fingers' width between the collar and the neck. For very large dogs, leave two to three fingers' width between the collar and the neck, depending on the dog and type of collar. If you pull the collar toward your pet's head, it should not slip over the ears. Traditional collars should ride high on your pet's neck and not slide down near the shoulder blades.

The Purchase

Before you go out to purchase a collar or harness, keep in mind the following features: safety, size, durability, and ability to be cleaned. You should choose a collar that's the right size for your puppy, kitten, cat, or dog and make sure it fits properly.

In addition to choosing the right size, you also want to select the proper weight for your pet. The collar shouldn't be too heavy or too light for your dog or cat. The weight and width of your pet's collar should be proportional to your dog's or cat's size. Smaller, lightweight collars are good for small dogs, puppies, and cats. Wider, more durable styles are suitable for bigger, stronger pets. A large, strong dog can easily break a lightweight collar or leash, so you'll need to select a heavier, thicker material than for a smaller dog. For example, a very heavy, thick collar wouldn't be appropriate for a Maltese, and conversely, a rottweiler shouldn't be wearing a thin, rhinestone-covered collar. It should be sturdy, so if your pet lunges it won't break, but the collar should also be comfortable. Puppies and kittens do best with a soft nylon or a thin leather collar. They shouldn't have collars that are heavy or bulky for them to wear. Make sure the collar fits snugly, and cut off any extra strap that the dog or cat might chew on. Dogs with necks the same size as their heads, such as greyhounds, whippets, Irish wolfhounds, and other sight hounds, should wear harnesses or collars specifically made for their head/neck proportions, such as a martingale (see "Training Collars" section below). Small breeds of dogs with sensitive tracheas should also be walked in a harness.

Breakaway Collars

I recommend that all cats wear a breakaway collar to greatly reduce the risk of strangulation. The collar is connected with a snap-away plastic closure that's designed to break if it's subjected to a lot of tension. Cats have a curious nature, and they can get their collars caught on tree branches, fences, and deck boards outside, or bedsprings, vents, furniture, cabinet knobs, or other cabinet hardware inside if they jump. The breakaway feature allows the collar to unsnap if snagged or caught, since cats like to get themselves into and through tight spots. To get the proper fit, use a measuring tape and measure around your cat's neck, making sure you separate the hair and measure down to the skin; then add 1 inch to your measurement. You have the proper fit if you're able to get one finger between the collar and your cat's neck. Unlike with dog collars, you want the collar to be able to slip over the cat's head or break away if the collar gets caught on something. Breakaway collars should never be used for dogs as they can allow a dog to break free while on a leash.

Training Collars

It's vital to learn how to choose and use collars correctly to avoid subjecting your dog to confusion, discomfort, and injury. One common mistake that pet owners make is leaving their dog alone in a yard wearing a training collar. Many dogs have injured and even strangled themselves in their own yard. So never put your dog outside, tie it up, or leave it unattended with a training collar on. A training collar should *never* be worn other than in a training session.

Head Halter

Head halters—also called head collars—are great for dogs that pull because they are humane, safe, and easy to use. They calm boisterous dogs and can make walking your dog a pleasant rather than a frustrating experience. A head collar is like a bridle without the bit. Like a horse halter, the head collar holds the jaw and cheek, with one strap encircling the dog's nose and another strap running behind the back of the head. The leash is hooked to a ring on the nose strap under the chin. When the dog pulls, the nose loop causes the head to be pulled down gently so the dog stops pulling. This teaches the dog to walk beside you without pulling because it takes the pressure away from the dog's body and instead makes the dog lead from its head. When you guide a dog's head, the body will follow.

Once a dog has been taught not to pull, you can often go back to using a regular collar, especially if you started collar-training when the dog was very young. So head halters can be used long-term or just during the training period. They should be used to solve or prevent problems. There is a period of adjustment for this type of collar, and it can sometimes take a couple of weeks for a dog to get used to it.

Used properly, head harnesses enable you to keep and redirect your dog's attention to you, helping to give you an edge over distractions such as squirrels, rabbits, bicyclists, skaters, other approaching dogs, and humans. A head collar can reduce the pull of a 100-pound dog to that of a five-pound dog. These collars can look quite cumbersome to those who aren't used to seeing them, yet they're extremely lightweight and very gentle on the dog. Many trainers recommend this type of collar because it's effective yet gentle. The two most common brands are the Halti head collar and the Gentle Leader. It's best to take your pet with you to the pet store to ensure a proper fit. The Halti seems to fit dogs with wider muzzles, like rottweilers, a little better. Both types are well-made and durable, and cost less than $25.

Advantages of head halters include excellent control, which allows for smooth direction of dogs with no jerking motion, and because the action is smoother, corrections are more acceptable to many dogs. Harnesses also allow small and less powerful people to easily control a large, strong dog. Disadvantages: Some people don't like the muzzle appearance; head halters must be fitted correctly to be safe and effective; a second, backup collar and attached leash are recommended for safety, particularly with strong dogs that can slip out of head halters; some dogs take a while to get used to these collars and even appear stressed during the acclimation period; if misused, head halters can be dangerous; and they may not stay on dogs with short noses.

Choke Collar

The slip or choke collar, commonly used for training, consists of leather, nylon, or chain link with rings on each end. Choke collars are controversial because they work by briefly tightening—therefore punishing—when the dog needs to be corrected. Many trainers recommend purely reward-based training and are shying away from these types of collars. In any event, they are not to be used as everyday collars. They should only be used while training or walking your dog because the moving ring can get snagged on the tooth of another dog in play, causing it to pull away from danger, and as the collar tightens, both dogs may panic, which can create a dangerous situation.

Choke collars should never be used on toy breeds or dogs weighing less than twenty pounds because their tracheas are too sensitive for this type of collar. Never leave your pet unsupervised in this collar, tie a dog up with this collar, or attach tags to this type of collar. Your pet can choke to death if the collar becomes caught. Unfortunately, on numerous occasions, I have had to surgically remove a metal choke collar that was completely embedded in a dog's neck after the dog had been tied up outside with this collar on. Sometimes the dog's fur is so thick that this ghastly event goes unnoticed. An inexperienced owner should never use this collar as a substitute for proper training, discipline, or socialization.

Prong or Pinch Collar

Another kind of training collar is a pinch or prong collar. These choke collars have blunt prongs that protrude inward from the links and lie flat on your dog's neck until you pinch the dog's neck for correction or the dog pulls. When you pull the leash, the prongs press into the dog's neck, applying pressure to many points around the neck. Many people misuse or overuse this restraint, thereby reducing its effectiveness and/or causing injury to the dog, immediately or over time. These collars are controversial, too, but some experienced trainers find them useful in dealing with large, powerful dogs.

Never use this type of collar as an everyday collar. Sometimes the link can disengage, allowing the dog to get off-leash. Like many training tools, this kind of collar can be effective, ineffective, or harmful, depending on the handler and on the individual dog. This type of collar should never be used on toy breeds or dogs weighing less than twenty pounds. An inexperienced owner should never use this collar as a substitute for proper training, discipline, or socialization.

Electric Shock Collar

The electric shock collar should never be used by an inexperienced handler or on puppies as they can do much more harm than good. Experienced handlers use these collars in specialized training environments such as field training of gun dogs. An inexperienced owner should never use this collar as a substitute for proper training, discipline, or socialization. Many trainers don't recommend shock collars for training as dogs can associate the pain of the shock with whatever triggers their pulling, lunging, or other undesirable behavior instead of associating it with the behavior itself, which can cause anxiety and possibly aggression, worsening the problem.

Citronella Collar

This type of training collar is a spray collar that uses a spritz of citronella-scented liquid to annoy the dog and control barking, pulling, and unwanted or undesirable behaviors. It has a small, refillable container of citronella affixed to it that rests at the bottom of the dog's neck, just below the mouth. When triggered, such as when the dog barks excessively, the citronella is sprayed up at the dog's nose, which is annoying to the dog, but does not harm it or the environment in any way. This technique works by interrupting the unwanted behavior and changing the dog's focus rather than by inflicting pain or shock.

Martingale Collar

Martingale collars were first developed for greyhounds because their heads are smaller than their necks, allowing them to slip out of their collars. This collar is good for dogs whose heads are as wide as or smaller than their necks. It has a unique double loop system and allows your dog's collar to be loose and relaxed, but will tighten when your dog tries to back out of the collar or when you pull on the leash. This collar is different from a choke collar because you set the size to which the collar will constrict beforehand, so there's no choking involved. The loop on the martingale enables the whole collar to decrease in size when the dog pulls. This evenly distributes the pressure, easing strain on your dog's neck. The martingale collar is effective for dogs that pull, sight hounds, whippets, Irish wolfhounds, and greyhounds. Dogs should never be tied up or left alone with a martingale collar on, as they can get their lower jaw stuck in the collar, which can be fatal.

Harnesses

Unlike collars, which control a dog by attaching to the neck and/or head, a harness is placed around a cat's or dog's chest and rib cage. When you pull back on the leash, the harness tightens around the chest, controlling your pet without putting pressure on the neck or back. A properly fitted harness lets the dog or cat pull with the chest rather than the throat.

Cats can be walked for exercise with a harness as this can be used to teach them to walk on a leash. (Harnesses that are the figure-eight- or H style are made especially for cats.) The leash attaches to a ring at the tip of the dog's or cat's back, usually between the shoulder blades. For small dogs, a harness may completely replace a collar when you're walking the dog on a leash.

Harnesses are great for cats, which will slip out of a collar if being walked, and for small dogs that are prone to developing a condition called collapsing trachea. Small breeds of dogs, including the toy breeds like Pomeranians, Chihuahuas, miniature poodles, Yorkshire terriers, Lhasa apsos, shih tzus, and miniature pinchers, all have softer tracheas that will collapse in response to pressure and are often susceptible to trachea problems that can be aggravated by collar tension on the throat. These dogs may cough when excited or being walked with a traditional collar. Using a harness avoids unnecessary pressure to the tracheal rings. There are also some breeds of dogs, such as bulldogs and pugs, that have necks as wide as their heads, so you should choose a harness for them instead of a collar, from which they can readily escape. Harnesses may be a good choice for older dogs that have arthritis in their necks or pets with upper respiratory disease. When you have a dog or cat with a medical problem, be sure to take your pet and its harness to the vet for an appropriate fit.

Leashes and Leads

You'll want to select a leash—also called a lead—that's neither too heavy nor too light for your particular dog. Leads are usually four or six feet long. It's best to start puppies on shorter leads to maintain control. Long leads are good for training dogs to come to you or allowing them to roam in the park or at the beach while maintaining control. Leads are available with an extra lead section and clip for walking two dogs on the same lead.

Nylon leads are machine-washable and very durable, and come in a variety of thicknesses, lengths, styles, and colors that will even match your dog's collar. Cotton webbing leads are also washable, strong, and easy on your hands. They, too, come in a variety of lengths and colors. Leather leads are strong, hard-wearing, and long-lasting, and as the leather softens from the oils in your skin, it may become easier to grip and may be gentler on your hands.

Retractable leads are great because you can control how little or how much lead to give your dog. These are best for dogs that have already been trained to walk and heel. The nylon lead is rolled up and housed in a plastic casing that you hold in your hand. It works something like a fishing pole; you hold the lead in your hand and use it to reel in your dog if necessary. A spring-type function allows the lead to automatically lengthen or retract as you walk your dog. Retractable leads are an excellent way to walk pets as they allow up to 26 feet of freedom to roam and investigate, yet still allow the owner to stay in control. They have a one-button braking system that stops your dog from going beyond a set distance as well as a spring mechanism that allows you to adjust just how far you want to expand the lead. They also have a locking mechanism that allows you to keep your dog at consistent distances. With retractable leads, however, you do need to pay attention on busy city streets and be careful that your pet doesn't run into the street.

Identification

Pet ID Tags

Never ignore identification tags as they are a vital piece of your pet's outfit. Even if your pet is strictly an indoor pet, it must always wear a collar with current ID. If the jingling of the tags drives you nuts, buy plastic covers to minimize the sound. Never use an S hook to attach a tag to a collar because tags easily come off using this type of device. Use a slip ring like you use for your keys. Tag durability is essential. Stainless steel is probably the most durable, but if you use plastic, just make sure you check it weekly for readability. Remember, identification tags are your pet's ticket home.

Microchips

Because identification tags on a pet's collar or halter can come off, microchipping is an additional way to ensure that your pet will be returned to you if lost, but microchips should not be used as a substitute for standard ID tags. A microchip is a tiny computer chip, the size of a rice grain, with an identification number programmed into it.

These chips were originally developed to track and identify livestock. The chip is injected with a hypodermic needle deep under the skin of your pet's neck, usually between the shoulder blades. The injection itself is the same as any regular vaccination and will cause no physical side effects. A special scanner is used to send a radio signal through the skin of your pet to read the chip. The animal feels nothing as the scanner is passed over its body and the chip is read. The microchip number is then relayed to the scanner, where it is displayed. No two microchip numbers will ever be the same, so you can be assured that your pet's microchip number is totally unique. The chip itself has no power supply to replace or moving parts to wear out, and therefore can be expected to last decades, well beyond the lifespan of your pet. Your pet's number is then registered to the chip company's database, which will trace your pet back to you if found. But if you move your residence, you must contact the chip company, pay a small fee, and give them your new address and contact numbers.

The two most commonly implanted chips in the United States are from American Veterinary Identification Devices (AVID) and Home Again. All animal shelters and most veterinary clinics have scanners that will read chips from these companies. After a scan, the shelter or vet clinic calls in the code to the chip company's database of pets with identifying microchips, and the lost animal's owner will be contacted immediately, provided the owner has a current phone number or address on record.

Puppies and kittens can be microchipped as early as eight weeks old. Microchips are suitable for almost any pet, including horses, reptiles, rabbits, birds, exotics, and even fish. (I've had clients ask about chipping people, but to date, it hasn't happened—although you never know!)

A microchip is completely permanent, and can't be cut off or altered. If your pet is ever stolen and sold to a research facility, it will be returned because most research facilities won't take an animal that has a microchip implant. I've seen a small percentage of microchips move or migrate, which can make it more difficult for the scanner to pick up. However, this is rare, and if they do migrate, they don't cause any problems with your pet, but may be missed by the scanner.

Microchips are very affordable. The cost of getting your pet microchipped can range from $25 to $65, depending on where you have the procedure done.

Again, microchips should not replace a collar and identification tag. Collars and tags are the best insurance you can provide to ensure your pet's safe return should it become lost.

Chapter 10

Traveling with Your Pet

On the Road

According to an American Animal Hospital Association 2004 survey, sixty-seven percent of pet owners travel with their pets. More and more pet owners are taking their pets on the road with them, in part due to the increase in pet-friendly hotels and great new products that make traveling with your best friend easier than ever before. More hotels across the country, such as Sheraton, Westin, and W Hotel properties, are adopting pet-friendly policies. Services include everything for your pet from oversized pet pillows and plush doggie robes to check-in gift packages with a pet toy, ID tag, and turndown treat. Some hotels even have licensed dog masseuses on staff.

As with most things in life, preparation and planning are crucial because traveling with pets creates its own unique stressors. For a safe and comfortable journey, take the following precautions before you fly or drive away.

Twelve Travel Tips

Here are twelve tips to ensure a safe trip with your pet.

1. **Pets should have a complete physical exam prior to traveling.** Your pet should be deemed healthy prior to traveling, which in and of itself can create stress and bring on illness. Keep pets current on vaccinations and take along a copy of your pet's vaccination records, especially rabies, and medical records as well as medication, if necessary. This will prove to be important if your pet requires vet care while traveling. This is the time to get flea, tick, or heartworm preventative as well. If flying, obtain a health certificate from your veterinarian dated within ten days of departure.

2. **Get your pet groomed.** This should include a nail trim, anal gland expression, and flea treatment, if needed. Bring along brushes and other grooming supplies.

3. **Book lodging ahead of time.** While there are hundreds of hotels opening their doors to pets, these accommodations fill up quickly. Be sure to check on any restrictions, especially if you have a very large or active dog.

4. **Pack your pet's normal food.** Always bring more food than you think you need as well as plenty of water in case reliable water sources are not available. Never let your pet drink water from unknown sources. Stick to your pet's regular feeding routine and feed it at the end of the day or when you reach your final destination, if appropriate.

5. **Pets must wear ID at all times.** This is especially critical when they travel. Think of it as their driver's license. If your dog or cat gets lost or separated from you during the trip, you'll want whoever finds your pet to be able to contact you immediately. Make sure the information on the tag is current. It should include your pet's name; your name, address, and phone number; and the name

and address of an alternate person to contact in case you can't be located. Also, bring an extra set of tags just in case. Again, I recommend that all pets have a permanent form of identification, like a microchip.

6. **Pets should wear a travel tag.** This tag should be labeled with your cell phone number, the address and phone number of your destination(s), and any other relevant contact information.

7. **Have a pet carrier for each pet.** Keep your pet safe in a well-ventilated crate or carrier. Make sure it's large enough for your pet to stand, sit, lie down, and turn around. Be sure to get your pet acclimated to the carrier prior to traveling. Have a safety restraint on your pet if it's not in a carrier. This means keeping a leash and harness on your cat and a leash on your dog at all times.

8. **Pack familiar toys and bedding.** Your pet will enjoy its stay much better if it has a toy from home and its own bed. Pack your pet's favorite blanket and dishes, too. Remember your pet's special needs.

9. **Pack a simple first-aid kit for your pets.** The kit should include assorted bandage material, antiseptic cream, and the phone numbers of your vet, a national poison control hotline, and a twenty-four-hour emergency vet hospital in the area of your final destination (see Chapter 8 on avoiding the ER).

NEVER go anywhere with your pet without having it securely contained, either on a leash or in a carrier made for pets. Do not—and I repeat, do not—carry your pet around in, or attempt to use, a birdcage, laundry basket, shoe box, or any other container you might think temporarily appropriate. This spells immediate disaster, which will mean more vet bills, not to mention the anxiety it causes your pet.

10. **Perform a daily health check on all animals.** Pets in unfamiliar surroundings may be more susceptible to illness. Visit a local veterinarian if you notice any abnormal physical or behavioral changes (see Chapter 3, Prevention Pays).

11. **Always carry current photos of all pets that are traveling with you.** This is vital in case your pet escapes and gets lost.

12. **Bring cleaning supplies.** Pack a waste scooper, plastic bags, disinfectant to clean out crates or litter pans, and extra litter.

Crate Training

Using a proper crate or carrier is essential when traveling; never transport your pet in a clothes hamper, box, or other makeshift and unsafe contraption. Try transforming the dreaded carrier into an appealing hangout by getting your pet accustomed to it at home. This can make the difference between life and death in an emergency situation. For cats, leave the crate somewhere in your home with a towel and some catnip inside it to get your cat interested in the crate. Also practice shutting the door and moving your pet around the house. The idea is to desensitize your pet to being in and moved around in the crate. You can break most crates in half and leave the bottom half out as a bed. You want your pets to feel safe and secure in their carriers instead of panicking. Just leaving the carriers out will allow pets to explore and play around them and will really help them to adjust to the time they need to ride in one. Start training as early as possible. Crate training for puppies is an excellent way to potty-train them as well (see Chapter 1, Your New Four-Legged Friend). Leave the crate out and take off the door so it won't swing shut and frighten them. Also try feeding your pets in their carriers.

Car Travel

If you're traveling by car, safety should be a priority for your cat or dog. Pets should be in a crate, in a seat belt harness, or if they're in the back of a station wagon or SUV, behind a gate. Pets need seat belts, too. A sudden stop may send a dog or cat flying if they're sitting on your lap or sunning in the rear window. Unrestrained pets may also escape if someone opens the door. Dogs shouldn't ride in the passenger seat if it's equipped with an airbag. If your dog must ride in a truck bed, it should be in a crate that's fastened to the truck. Accidents can occur when a pet suddenly jumps on the driver, a cat crawls under your feet, or a pet distracts you in any way.

The bottom line is to never let your pets ride loose in the car. If your pet isn't used to car travel, take it for a few short rides before your trip so it will have less anxiety in a car and not always associate it with a trip to the vet.

You will need to stop every three to four hours to let your dog relieve itself and to get some fresh air. Never let your dog stick its head out of a window. Dirt and debris can enter the eyes, ears, and nose, causing injury or infection. I don't recommend leaving a pet alone in a car, but if you must, don't leave it for a long period of time, and make sure all the doors are locked and the windows are open enough to provide ventilation without enabling your pet to jump out or get its head caught.

Be very mindful of weather conditions. Make sure your pet has proper ventilation at all times, and *never* leave a pet unattended in a car when the temperature or humidity is high or near or below freezing, as pets can overheat or freeze to death. Many car companies now provide an optional "Pet Lovers Package" with their new vehicles that include pet tethers, harnesses, cushions, and gates and/or rubberized floor liners. Waterproof seat covers are also available at auto-parts stores.

Air Travel

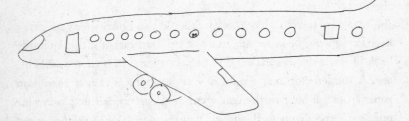

Airplanes may be the fastest way for your pet to travel, but they can also be the most dangerous. Every year, there are pets checked as cargo that end up injured, lost, or killed during transport. The USDA mandates that only dogs or cats older than eight weeks of age can travel by air and that they must be weaned at least five days prior to the flight. The USDA also prohibits the travel of pets during which they will be subjected to temperatures lower than 45°F or higher than 85°F for more than forty-five minutes while being transferred between the terminal and the plane. The prohibition for cold weather can only be waived if a veterinarian provides you with an acclimation certificate stating that the dog or cat can be exposed to lower temperatures. Rules, regulations, and guidelines are different for each airline and depend on the type of animal that will be flying. Ask the airlines what documents they require, such as vaccination records or a health certificate.

The number of pets allowed on airlines is limited, so you should make your reservations well in advance of your departure date because it is perfectly legal for an airline to turn down your request. Many of the major airlines allow cats and dogs weighing fewer than fifteen pounds to travel in pet-designed carry-on luggage that will fit under the seat in front of you. Some airlines permit pets in passenger cabins only if they are small enough to be kept within the designated space. Animals are not allowed in the overhead compartments and they must remain in their carriers until the plane lands. The size limitation does vary by airline and by aircraft, and certain carrier types, sizes, and weight restrictions may apply.

When you take your pet in the cabin with you, keep in mind that most airports will require that the pet be removed from the carrier at the security screening checkpoint so the carrier may be sent through the X-ray machine. Be sure that you have a leash or harness with you to keep your pet from escaping.

If you're traveling abroad, be sure to contact that country's consulate or embassy for information and make sure you have all the necessary paperwork and forms before entering the country; otherwise, you may not be allowed to take your pet. In addition, some countries don't allow pets into their country and others require long quarantines.

Here are some tips to keep your pets safe if they are flying in the cargo:

- Always try to book a direct flight to avoid plane changes. This reduces the risk that your pet will escape when being loaded or unloaded, end up on the wrong plane, be left on the tarmac during extreme weather conditions, or be mishandled by baggage personnel.

- If you must take a flight with a layover, schedule one that has a long enough layover for you to walk your pet. Make sure the airline will let you claim and then recheck your pet yourself. Never change planes without checking on your pet first.

- Try to book flights during off hours and avoid the busiest travel times.

- Reconfirm your flight arrangements the day before you leave to ensure there have been no unexpected flight changes or embargo rules that result in times during the year that pet travel is not allowed.

- During the summer months, many airlines won't fly pets, but if they do, be sure to choose early morning or late evening flights to avoid extreme temperatures that your pet may be subjected to while being loaded onto and off of the plane.

- During colder months, choose midday flights. The live-cargo compartments of airplanes are pressurized and kept between 50°F and 70°F, but your dog's crate might be on the runway or another area exposed to temperature extremes for a while before being loaded, especially if there is a flight delay.

- Arrive at the airport early, take your pet for one last walk, and keep your pet with you until thirty minutes before departure and personally place them in the crate yourself.

- Be sure to pick up your pet promptly upon arrival at your destination.

- Always travel on the same flight and watch at your gate to see that your pet is being loaded into the live-cargo hold. If you don't see your crate, ask the gate attendant to call the baggage area to make sure your pet is on board. Don't board the plane until you're positive your pet is on board.

- When boarding the plane, always let the flight crew and captain know that you have a pet in cargo.

- When insuring your pet, do so for an amount of $10,000. The premium for this amount of coverage is minimal, and it will ensure that your pet receives better attention with regard to safe handling.

- Don't leave toys or anything in the crate that your pet could accidentally swallow or choke on, and put a familiar blanket or something that you've worn in the crate with your pet.
- Don't give your pet a tranquilizer unless instructed by your vet. Sedatives have side effects like lowering blood pressure, which can make your pet groggy and cold. When pets are in cargo, there's no one to check on them if problems arise, and therefore it's unsafe to sedate them.

There are certain conditions that apply to your pet's crate when traveling in cargo, so call the airline beforehand to find out as many instructions as you can that pertain to the crate. The airline has the final say as to whether it will accept a particular crate.

Here are some crate guidelines:

- The crate must be large enough to allow your pet to stand without touching the top of the cage, and to turn around and lie down, but not too large for your pet in order to reduce the risk of injury during turbulence.
- Do not place more than one adult cat or dog in each crate or more than two puppies or kittens under six months of age.
- Get your pet used to the crate or carrier for at least one month prior to traveling.
- The crate should have a properly fitting kennel door that closes tightly and securely.
- The crate should have ventilation on opposite sides with exterior rims and knobs so that airflow is not impeded.
- The crate should be strong and free of interior protrusions and have handles or grips.
- The crate should have a leakproof bottom that's covered with plenty of absorbent material such as a towel.
- Clearly label the crate with your pet's name, age, breed, and special medical concerns; your name, address, cell phone

number, and destination contact number; and the travel date, airline, and flight number.

🐾 Write "Live Animal" on the top and at least one side of the crate, in letters at least one inch tall, with an arrow indicating the crate should be in an upright position. Above the crate door, write "Do not open this door without permission from owner or licensed vet." Make sure the door is securely closed but not locked.

🐾 Affix a current photograph of your pet to the top of the crate for identification purposes. This could prove to be crucial should your pet escape.

Hotel Etiquette

Keep in mind that how you and your pet behave will determine if you're allowed to come back.

🐾 Always contact lodging ahead of time to make sure the hotel is pet-friendly. Never arrive unannounced with a pet even if you've stayed at the hotel before, as policies change and they may no longer accept pets.

🐾 Ask about pet fees or deposits and the size and number of pets allowed per room.

🐾 Ask for a ground-floor room to make potty breaks easier and ask for a room where there is little foot traffic in case your dog barks at strange noises.

🐾 See if your hotel has a list of pet-sitters in case your day plans don't include your pet.

🐾 When checking in, ask about areas where you can walk your pet as well as any areas where pets are not permitted. Ask if pets are allowed in the lobby.

🐾 Make sure your pet has pottied prior to entering the hotel and keep your dog on a short leash at all times.

- Avoid leaving pets unattended in hotel rooms, but if you must, they should be crated so they don't get into trouble. Place the DO NOT DISTURB sign on the door, and inform the front desk that you don't want housekeeping or turndown service.

- Leave the television or radio on quietly for background noise. Try to make sure your dog doesn't bark while you're gone. Be prepared to change plans if your dog barks while you're away.

- While in your room, cover any furniture and beds your pet will be allowed on with sheets brought from home.

- Place your pet's food and water bowls on a mat. Litter boxes should be placed on newspaper in the bathroom to make cleanup easier.

- Wipe off muddy or dirty paws prior to entering the hotel, and if your pet should damage any property, report it immediately and volunteer to pay any costs.

- Never take your pet into a dining area, bar lounge, or pool area unless invited.

Missing Pets

Losing your pet can be a devastating experience. All pets will have plenty of opportunities to slip through your legs and out the door during their lifetime. Fortunately, there are some things you can do to ensure a safe return if it does happen.

Here are some tips to help you find your lost pet:

- Start your search immediately. Don't wait for your pet to find its way home, and don't assume that because your pet may have returned home safely in the past that it will be so lucky this time. Acting quickly can help ensure the likelihood of getting your pet back safe and sound.

- Search your property thoroughly. Sometimes cats and dogs can hide in very small places. Begin by looking in your pet's favorite areas, then look outside, under the porch, behind the shrubs, in the shed, in the trees, and on the roof.

- Start walking around the neighborhood and talk to everybody. Check backyards, garages, alleys, parks, and school yards.

- Go around the area calling out to your pet. Shake a box of biscuits or treats and/or use your pet's favorite squeaky toy to make some noise.

- Create flyers with a clear photo and detailed description of your pet. List several phone numbers where you can be reached.

- Pass out flyers and post them at post offices, gas stations, libraries, pet supply stores, veterinary clinics, grocery stores, Laundromats, convenience stores, shopping complexes, near schools, and on school and church bulletin boards.

- Place an ad in your local newspaper. Advertise in the Sunday paper as well as during the week. Keep the ad running every day for two weeks or until your pet is found.

- Check the newspaper "found" ads every day.

- Some radio stations and local schools will announce lost pet reports, so call them and find out.

- Place some of your clothes outside your home to attract your pet. The smellier, the better. Sweaty gym clothes work great.

- Call animal control, humane societies, the police, local radio stations, and veterinary clinics, including emergency hospitals, in your area.
- Look in pet shelters at least every two days. Shelters will do their best to match up the description you give of your pet. However, it can be difficult to match an owner with their pet over the phone.
- Ask postal workers, bus drivers, children, neighbors, UPS drivers, and anyone who is regularly in your neighborhood if they have seen your pet. Be sure to show them pictures.

Don't give up! Pets can return home months after being lost.

Home Alone

What should you do if you decide not to take your precious pet with you on vacation? I know people who refuse to travel because they're so worried about leaving their dog or cat behind. I can identify with them because as my dog, Duke, got older, I was reluctant to travel for fear of something happening while I was gone. However, there are several safe options for taking care of your cat or dog when you're away.

One of the best solutions is to have a trusted friend who gets along with your pet stay at your home while you're gone. Of course, it can be hard to find someone as we all lead busy lives, but I also believe in paying your friend for his or her time. This situation has worked for me on a number of occasions. Just be sure that you've signed a release for your vet that allows emergency treatment for your pet, and you can even put a credit card on file. Also, try to have your friend keep your pet on its regular feeding and walking schedules. This will help minimize stress.

Another option is to have your pet stay at a friend's home. This could work very well if your pet already visits the friend, or if you can exchange pet-care services with the owner on a relatively equal basis. This solution works best for dogs. Cats don't like changes in their home environment, so visiting another home usually isn't advisable.

Of course, you can always take your pet to a boarding kennel or vet hospital. Kennel care can be expensive, but is sometimes necessary. However, in most kennels your dog or cat may be caged a large part of the day, which can be stressful. Pets also risk picking up an illness from being in close quarters with other animals. Veterinary hospitals offer the option of superb medical and personal care, so sometimes they are the best way to go, especially if your pet has numerous medical problems.

There is also a fourth solution: a pet sitter.

The Ideal Pet Sitter

A pet sitter can look after your pet while you're traveling. The sitter doesn't stay in your home, but visits at least once a day to provide care and companionship for your cat or dog. Your pet gets to stay in the environment it knows best and will receive high-quality, personalized care. Its diet and routine will remain pretty much the same. You also get the added security of having someone bring in the mail and newspapers, water the plants, and create a lived-in look to your home that deters crime.

The ideal pet sitter is someone you and your pet know and trust. That person has to be absolutely dependable. Not only will the sitter show up on time, but will know the exact care your pet needs and provide it excellently and lovingly.

You can also hire a trustworthy professional pet sitter. Ask your veterinarian or dog trainer, or check the yellow pages under Pet Sitting Services. You can also contact the National Association of Professional Pet Sitters (800-296-PETS) or Pet Sitters International (323-983-9222) for a referral. Both organizations offer pet sitter accreditation to those who demonstrate professional experience, complete pet care-related home study courses, attend professional conferences, and abide by a code of ethics set by the organizations.

Before You Go

Arrange with your vet to authorize and pay for any necessary routine or emergency care while you're away. Make certain that your pet is current on its vaccines as well as flea, tick, and heartworm prevention. If your pet is on medication, be sure the supply won't run out when you're gone. Make sure you have enough pet food and supplies to last, adding a few weeks' worth in case you don't return on time. And remember, all pets need to be wearing current and legible forms of identification.

Chapter 11

Disaster Awareness and Preparedness

Imagine that right now you only had fifteen minutes to evacuate yourself, your family, your pets, and all necessary supplies for at least one week. Could you do it safely?

There isn't a state in the union that is immune to nature's fury—thunderstorms, blizzards, hurricanes, tornadoes, floods, heat waves, wildfires, ice storms, earthquakes. Then there are chemical spills, train derailments, acts of terrorism. Even smaller incidents such as gas leaks and minor flooding can keep you away from your animals for extended periods of time. No one is impervious to the possibility of being affected, but the key to survival in *any* disaster situation—whether natural or manmade—is to know your enemy and be prepared for yourself, your family, and your pets.

If you have never been through a disaster, it's difficult to imagine the stress, chaos, and everything that could possibly go wrong, but believe me, if you talk to people who have, they'll give you an earful. We all need to be prepared and learn how to best deal with disasters to minimize stress and possible danger to ourselves and our pets. A good rule of thumb: If it's not safe for children, it's not safe for animals.

During disaster situations, our pets—whose lives revolve around us and who depend on us for their every need—often become victims. The people they have trusted and the homes they have shared vanish, leaving them suddenly alone, frightened, hungry, thirsty, and often injured and in pain.

Planning may seem unnecessary, but it's absolutely essential in ensuring the safety and survival of your pet. We can't always prevent disasters from happening, but we can plan for the consequences, such as the loss of electricity, undrinkable water, damage to homes and community buildings, and other disruptions in our normal, everyday life that wreak havoc on us and pets that thrive under our routine. Sometimes the aftermath is worse than the disaster itself. During times of disaster, emergency systems, all lines of communication, public systems, and resources are disrupted or overburdened, and you may become isolated as inevitable turmoil results. Pets that are left to fend for themselves often die a miserable death due to predation, disease, starvation, and dehydration. So never leave your pet behind!

Now is the time to ask your local emergency management agency about your state's disaster preparedness plan. Familiarizing yourself with your community's disaster plan is an important safeguard for you and your pets. Many communities in disaster-prone areas have predesignated locations such as state fairgrounds, racetracks, shelters, stadiums, or veterinary hospitals for emergency housing of animals if a crisis arises.

Lessons from New Orleans

More than sixty-nine million American households have a pet, so planning for disasters means we must include our cats and dogs. The lessons from a tragedy like Hurricane Katrina are abundant, but one of the most important ones is to be prepared and take your pet with you at all costs. Otherwise, we end up with the debacle that occurred in New Orleans in 2005, where thousands of dogs and cats were left behind in homes or on the streets, or chained in their yards, as pet owners were forced to evacuate without their pets. The results were catastrophic.

Again, by being prepared with a well-thought-out disaster plan for each type of disaster, you can save your pet's life in any emergency. An emergency may require anything from a brief absence from your home to permanent evacuation, and each situation requires different measures to ensure your pet's safety.

Always err on the side of caution during a disaster. Many times people are told that they will only be leaving their homes for a short time, when in actuality it turns out to be weeks or days. It's better to be safe than sorry. If the emergency turns out to be a false alarm, consider it a practice run of your disaster drill.

Being prepared starts by making sure each of your pets wears some form of current, legible identification in addition to getting a microchip implant (see Chapter 9 on outfitting). When I was charged with providing veterinary care for the animals displaced by Hurricane Katrina in Louisiana at the front lines, and later in Los Angeles, the majority of animals I tended to were not wearing any form of identification; if they did have a collar and ID tag, the information was usually unreadable or incorrect. Since fewer than ten percent of the hundreds of animals I encountered had microchips or other forms of identification, trying to match owners with their pets was nearly impossible. One picture posted on a website is not enough information to adequately identify your pet. I'm sure a very small percentage of pet owners will ever be reunited with the pets they were forced to leave behind in the wake of Hurricane Katrina or Hurricane Rita.

You need to plan for two types of scenarios: evacuating your home and hunkering down at home. These take different kinds of planning. You should develop a disaster plan for each type of emergency, including earthquakes, fires, hurricanes, tornadoes, acts of terrorism or bioterrorism, and hazardous material spills. Nobody likes to think about a disaster of any kind, but if and when it happens, you'll be thankful that you were prepared.

Evacuation Kit

Assemble a portable pet disaster kit, including a first-aid kit (see p. 170 for items to include), which will help you care for your animals in the event of an emergency. The evacuation kit should be assembled in an easy-to-carry, watertight container that is ant-proof and rodent-proof. It should be stored in an easily accessible location away from areas with temperature extremes. Because a large number of fires start in the kitchen or garage, fire officials suggest avoiding these areas for storing your kits.

Replace the food, water, and medications as often as needed to maintain their quality and freshness according to expiration dates. It's a good idea to check your kit twice a year during a favorite holiday or birthday to help remind you. Keep notes in the kit as to the location of medications that are stored elsewhere due to refrigeration needs.

Consult your veterinarian for advice on making your kit for each individual animal. It's important that you are familiar with the contents of your kit and their uses.

Make an evacuation kit for each dog and cat in the household that includes the items listed below.

Food

Store a one- to two-week supply of dry and/or canned food. Place dry food in airtight containers. Use the brand that your dog or cat normally eats. If you use canned food, buy the smallest size available as opened cans of food need to be stored in a refrigerator or ice chest. Bring a spoon, non-spill food dishes, can opener (sometimes flip lids don't open properly), and plastic lids to put on open canned food. Record the diet and normal feeding amount and times for each animal, including what *not* to feed in case of allergies. Food should be replaced at least once every three to six months to prevent spoilage.

Water

Bring a one- to two-week supply of water in plastic one-gallon jugs. A forty-pound dog needs roughly one gallon of water per day; a ten-pound cat needs one quart. Store water in a dark or shaded area that's not in direct sunlight to avoid growth of bacteria or algae, and be sure to change it every three to six months. Bring a sturdy, non-spill water dish and a small container of bleach for purification. To purify water, you can mix two drops of bleach to one quart of water. Mix and seal tightly for thirty minutes prior to drinking.

Cleaning Supplies

Bring a disinfectant cleaner to clean crates and litter boxes. Also bring paper towels, a pooper-scooper, plastic bags, newspaper, trash bags, and dish soap for cleaning food and water dishes.

Litter

If you have cats, bring a one- to two-week supply of scoopable litter stored in plastic jugs. Include a small plastic litter box and litter scoop. Bring plastic bags for disposing of scooped litter.

Photographs

Have at least ten recent color pictures of all your pets. This is in case you need to distribute them to shelters if your pets get lost. Be sure to include photos of any distinguishing features your pet may have. And make sure to update your pictures from time to time, especially if you have a puppy or kitten. Include yourself or other family members in the photos, as this is vital if you need to prove ownership. Store the pictures in a resealable plastic bag.

Vaccine Records/Medical History

Make photocopies of important veterinary documents, including vaccination records (the types and dates), medical history, medical conditions, and medications. For dogs, keep a copy of your rabies certificate. Boarding facilities will require proof of current vaccinations including rabies, distemper, and bordetella for dogs. Keep records of important test results such as FeLV/FIV and heartworm as well as all medical conditions.

Veterinary Information

Have the name, address, and phone number of your veterinarian and an alternate veterinarian written legibly on a piece of paper. Write out a release statement authorizing emergency medical treatment for all of your pets. This is important in case you're not available for approval during a disaster. Have your pet insurance policy number written down and keep a copy of your driver's license as well as several waterproof marking pens (see Chapter 14 on health insurance).

Medication

List each pet separately and include dose and frequency for each medication. Be sure to keep a two-week reserve supply in your disaster kit along with directions on how to best administer. Be sure the medication doesn't expire, and provide veterinary and pharmacy contact information for refills. For cats with hairball problems, be sure to include Laxatone or Petromalt.

Proof of Ownership/Animal Information

Make copies of registration information, adoption papers, proofs of purchase, and microchip, tattoo, or other identification information. Keep a list of all dogs and cats and their species, breed, sex, color, age, and any special characteristics. Include their favorite hiding place and information on any special habits.

Collars, Harnesses, and Leashes

Your pet should wear a properly fitting collar and an ID tag at all times. This includes cats that never go outside. I recommend using a breakaway collar for cats. An extra collar or harness and leash, one for each pet, should be kept in the disaster kit as well as extra tags that you can personalize in case you have to move to a temporary location. For cats, include a properly fitting cat harness and leash so they can be safely controlled when outside of the crate. If your pet has a microchip implant—which I strongly recommend—be sure to include the national registry numbers in your kit. Also make "lost cat/dog" signs with your phone number and address. Leave several blank lines to write in the animal's description, where it was last seen, and any other pertinent information.

Identification Tags

Have identification tags including license and rabies tags, if appropriate, for each of your pets. Tags should include your name, home address, a phone number where you can be reached, and an out-of-area phone number of someone with whom you will be in contact during or soon after the disaster/evacuation.

If possible, include your veterinarian's name, location, and phone number. Some of this information could be printed in indelible ink on a piece of tape and affixed to the back of the tag.

Brushes and Combs

Include brushes for both cats and dogs.

Toys

Bring familiar items to make pets feel comfortable, such as their blankets, beds, favorite toys, and treats. Bring extra booties or sweaters if appropriate.

Grooming Supplies

Bring dry shampoo in case your pets need to be bathed, and towels for drying. Also bring ear-cleaning solution, nail clippers, muzzles, and appropriate flea, tick, and heartworm prevention. Pack dental-cleaning supplies and hot-water bottles.

Carrier

Each pet should have its own cage or carrier labeled with your contact information. All pet carriers should be in good condition with no missing parts or sharp edges. They should have the following information indelibly printed on them: your name, phone number, address, name and description of your pet, any insurance policy number, and the address, and phone number of where you or a contact person can be reached if you're not home. Never use cardboard carriers for cats because they're not sturdy enough and cats can easily escape from them. Plastic crates should be large enough to hold a food and water dish and have enough room for your dog or cat to stand up and move around. For cats, the crate should be large enough to hold a small litter box as well. Be sure the carrier has a secure locking device. An alternative to a crate is a wire collapsible cage. These are better during warm weather because they provide better venti-

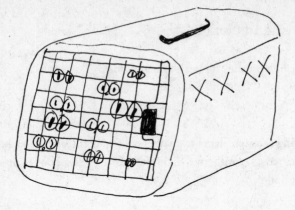

lation. For dogs, you should pack a spiral ground stake or tie-out. These should be used cautiously, though, to avoid injury. Now is the time to get your pets used to their crates, especially cats (see Chapters 1 and 9 on your new four-legged friend, for crate training and outfitting).

First-Aid Kit

See Chapter 8 on avoiding the ER for a list of items needed in your first-aid kit. In addition to the kit, bring a thick pair of gloves or wildlife gloves for restraint if you have cats.

Battery-Operated Equipment

Be sure to pack solar-powered and battery-operated radios. Include a flashlight, extra batteries, and a cell phone and charger.

List of Important Emergency Contacts

Assemble this list now before a disaster strikes. Be sure to include addresses and twenty-four-hour contact numbers if possible. This list can be used by rescue personnel responding to a disaster or by you during a disaster or an evacuation. Keep one copy near your telephone and one copy in your animal evacuation kit. Be sure to include a map of your local area and alternate evacuation routes in case of road closure.

Make a list of the following contact information:

- Phone numbers and addresses where you may be reached
- Your prearranged evacuation site
- Local contact person in case of emergency when you're not available
- Out-of-state contact person in case the disaster is far-reaching in your locale
- Your veterinarian's name, clinic address, and phone number
- Alternate veterinarian 30 to 90 miles away who provides boarding
- Local boarding facility
- Boarding facility 30 to 90 miles away
- Hotels/motels within a 90-mile radius that allow pets
- Local animal control
- Local police department
- Local fire department
- Local public health department
- Local animal shelter
- Local Red Cross chapter
- Local Humane Society
- Local Society for the Prevention of Cruelty to Animals (SPCA)
- United States Department of Agriculture Missing Pet Network (www.missingpet.net)

A Safe Place

Plan ahead for a safe place to take your pets.

- Call hotels or motels outside your immediate area and ask about their policies on accepting pets during an emergency. Keep a list of these pet-friendly places with their addresses and phone numbers.
- Make a list of boarding facilities, dog-training clubs, and veterinarians who could shelter your pets in an emergency.
- Ask friends and relatives outside the area if they could shelter your pets.
- Call local animal shelters to see if they provide emergency shelter or foster care for pets in an emergency.
- Call local emergency management officials to see if they planned for pet shelters and get directions to the locations.

First Warning

 Warnings are often issued hours and even days in advance. At the first hint of disaster, don't wait—act immediately to protect your pet, which will inevitably feel your stress and become nervous. Pets that are frightened and confused won't behave in their normal manner, so it's important for you to try to remain calm, as it will help keep your pets more relaxed.

- Bring all of your pets indoors and confine them to a small, comfortable area where you can easily reach them or place them in their crates. Do not try to hold on to any animal during a disaster such as earthquake, tornado, or hurricane.

- Put all of your evacuation kits in one central location so you don't have to search for or gather them.
- Make sure all pets have collars and ID tags on, and attach appropriate ID tags to all other collars and harnesses.
- Place any frozen or refrigerated pet food you may need in a cooler with ice.
- Attach to collar or ID tag the phone number and address of your temporary shelter, if you know it, or the contact info for a friend or relative outside the disaster area. Temporary tags can be purchased or you can write on adhesive tape on the back of the tag with an indelible or waterproof pen.
- Listen to radio stations broadcasting emergency information. Write down anything that pertains to animals, such as locations where animals may be housed.
- Contact all family members to confirm where you're going to meet.
- Check your evacuation route and confirm your shelter arrangements.
- Call ahead to confirm emergency shelter arrangements for you and your pets.

Evacuating Your Home

When an evacuation order has been issued, you'll want to evacuate your family, including your pets, as soon as possible. By leaving early, you'll decrease the chance of becoming victims of the disaster. You must have a safe place *prearranged* to take your pets. As evidenced during Hurricane Katrina, Red Cross disaster shelters will not accept pets because of health and safety regulations, so it's imperative that you have a predetermined place where you can take them. Now is the time to research your options.

After my own experience in the aftermath of Hurricane Katrina, I can't overemphasize the following: **Get out of harm's way as soon as possible and take your pets with you.** Leaving pets behind is not safe, and there is no guarantee that you will ever see them again.

Here are some evacuation tips:

- Stay calm and assess the situation.
- Bring all dogs and cats indoors.
- Make sure all pets have collars and some form of legible identification securely fastened.
- Place small pets inside individual transportable carriers immediately. If you don't, your pet may sense danger and try to hide, which makes it more difficult to catch them. Each pet should be housed separately as they can get agitated when frightened.
- Keep each dog on a leash unless they are in a crate.
- Load larger animals into cages or carriers and then into your vehicle.
- Load the animal evacuation kit and supplies into your vehicle.
- Call your prearranged animal evacuation site to confirm availability of space because if you go to a public shelter, you can't take your pet with you.
- Know which radio stations to listen to if disaster strikes, and listen for instructions on what you should do and whether special arrangements have been made for people with pets. Follow these guidelines and incorporate them into your actions.
- Have phone numbers for local police and fire stations.
- Have a full tank of gas.
- Have extra cash on hand in a safe place.
- Keep a supply of quarters to use for pay phones, as they will most likely be the first public communication to resume.
- Have a flat-tire repair kit in your car.

Hunkering Down at Home

If you plan to stay in your home during a disaster, examine it to determine the best place to keep your pet during the emergency. Make sure you have adequate provisions for all family members, including your pets. Never leave pets unattended.

- Move cages away from windows and objects that could fall on them.
- If confining pets, make sure the room is pet-proofed so they don't harm themselves.
- Gather all evacuation kits and put them in one safe, easily accessible location.
- Pets that appear calm may startle easily, so be careful that they don't escape.
- Separate dogs and cats.
- Bring pets inside immediately. Never leave a pet outside during a natural disaster of any kind.
- Stay clear of windows, fireplaces, and appliances, and keep out of the kitchen.
- Look around for things that could fall or move and avoid them.
- Secure all tall and heavy furniture that could topple over, such as bookcases, china cabinets, and wall units.
- If you bring plants inside during a storm, be sure that pets don't have access to them (see Chapter 8 on avoiding the ER for details).

Careful Planning

Here are some tips to protect your pet during a disaster:

- Have a written plan for each type of disaster.
- Make several copies of these plans so everyone knows what to do and you don't forget anything.
- Call ahead to your veterinarian and make sure you have enough of any medications your pet is currently taking.
- Again, make sure all pets are wearing current identification tags.
- Having a generator on hand is a great idea, but keep it outside and well ventilated to avoid carbon monoxide poisoning.

Potential Hazards

Fire: Put out fires in your home or neighborhood immediately, and call for help. If the fires are too big, wait for the firefighters to arrive.

Gas leak: If you smell gas or hear blowing or hissing noises, open a window and quickly leave the building with all of your pets. Turn off the gas at the outside main valve if you can, and call the gas company from a neighbor's home. If you turn off the gas for any reason, a professional must turn it back on. Therefore, shut off the main gas valve only if you suspect a leak because of broken pipes or odor. Also, don't use your kitchen stove if you suspect a gas leak.

Damaged electrical wiring: If you see sparks or broken and frayed wires, or if you smell hot insulation, turn off the electricity at the main fuse box or circuit breaker. Do not step in water to get to the fuse box or circuit breaker—call a professional, such as an electrician. Do not touch downed or damaged power lines, or any objects in contact with them.

Damaged sewage and water lines: If you suspect sewage lines are damaged, avoid using the toilets and call a plumber. If water pipes are damaged,

contact the water company and avoid using tap water for yourself or
your pets. You can obtain safe water by melting ice cubes or adding
two drops of bleach to one gallon of water, or boiling water for ten
minutes on the stove, if possible.

Damaged or downed chimneys: Approach chimneys with caution if they
are damaged, and do not use them as they could start a fire or release
poisonous gases into your house.

Fallen items: Be careful of broken glass and debris as pets may easily injure
themselves. Also be careful when opening closets and cupboards as
items may have shifted and can tumble off shelves.

Food and water supplies: Don't let pets eat or drink anything from open
containers near shattered glass or sewage.

Emergency Stickers

Be sure to pre-place permanent, waterproof "Pets Inside" stickers on your
front and back house doors or windows. These will alert emergency workers that pets are in your home. The stickers must be visible to neighbors
and rescue workers (i.e., firefighters, police officers), and if possible list the
types and number of pets in your household. These will let rescue workers
know that pets are inside your home in case you aren't there, and hopefully they will also respond faster. These stickers can be purchased through
many SPCA offices, online, and at local pet supply stores.

Disaster Strikes When You're Away

You need to have an alternate plan in case you're not home when a disaster or evacuation occurs. Your neighbors can be your best allies. Get
to know them and their pets. Hold a neighborhood meeting and discuss how you can take care of each other's pets in the event of a disaster.
Discuss what you would want to be done if you're not around when an

emergency occurs. Select a neighborhood coordinator who will be ready to assist should a disaster happen when you're not at home. Make sure this person spends much of their time at home or that they work within walking distance of your neighborhood. Select one or two backup coordinators in case the primary person is not available. Have a written plan with phone numbers, work information, emergency contact information, and veterinary information, and discuss access to house keys. Keep this list updated and distribute it to all participating neighbors. You should discuss having a plan for someone to pick up your pets and evacuation kits, and establish a predetermined meeting place outside of the likely evacuated area. The person selected should be familiar with your pets, be comfortable handling them, and also know where your crates and leashes are kept, where your evacuation kits are stored, and where your pets' favorite hiding spots are.

Have a permission slip on file with your veterinarian so he or she knows who can authorize medical treatment for your pet if you are unreachable.

Write out a detailed list of your pet's names, behaviors, special needs, likes and dislikes, and hiding spots—and keep it accessible.

To facilitate a successful rescue, provide muzzles, handling gloves, catch nets, and other animal restraints where rescue personnel can find them. Animals that are frightened can become aggressive, which can hinder the rescue process.

After the Incident

Normally quiet and loving cats and dogs may develop behavioral problems, including aggression, following a disaster. Recovery may take several days, weeks, or months.

- Check for injuries to yourself and your pets. If you have any concerns about the health of your pet, contact your vet immediately.

- Wear sturdy shoes to avoid injury from broken glass and debris.
- If you have to move to new surroundings, do not remove your pet from its crate until it is calm, and then do so in a closed room.
- Never let your pet out after a major disaster unless the environment is safe for both of you.
- Clean up spilled medicines, bleaches, gasoline, and other flammable liquids immediately before allowing pets access.
- Leave the area if you smell gas or fumes from other chemicals.
- Open closets and cupboard doors cautiously.
- Inspect all chimneys for damage prior to use.
- Inspect, or have professionals inspect, all gas, power, and sewer lines.
- Inspect your home, garage, and yard—including all windows, doors, and fences—for damage that could allow your pets to escape.
- Listen to a battery-operated radio or television for the latest emergency information.
- Stay out of buildings that look damaged.
- Use the telephone only for emergency calls so you don't tie up lines needed by rescue workers.
- Only drive if there is an emergency in order to keep roads clear for emergency vehicles.
- Return home only when it is safe for you and your pets.
- A pet's behavior may change dramatically after a disaster, so be patient and stay calm, reassuring them.
- Use care when releasing your pet from its crate. Don't release your pet and leave it unattended the first day.
- Walk pets on a leash until they become reoriented to their home.
- Avoid downed power lines and other debris in the area that pose a real danger to you and your pets.
- Don't allow pets to consume food or water that may have become contaminated.
- Let your pets get plenty of uninterrupted sleep. Encourage them to play with their favorite toys as this can help them recover faster.

- Unless it is necessary, avoid unfamiliar activities with your pet, such as bathing, excessive exercise, or diet supplements, and try to avoid changing its diet.
- Be careful using candles or oil lamps around pets and never leave these items unattended.
- Remain calm and try to stay as close to your pet's normal routine as possible. Be sure to speak to them regularly in a calm, reassuring voice.
- Be on the lookout for animals wandering the neighborhood, including wild animals and snakes.

Post-Traumatic Syndrome

If your pet seems to be suffering from post-traumatic syndrome (post-traumatic stress disorder, or PTSD), try the following:

- Contact your veterinarian if your pet has *any* medical or behavioral problems.
- Stay close to their normal routine or establish a new one and stick to it.
- Don't physically try to comfort your pets when they are worried as this can escalate anxious feelings. Instead try to distract them, using their favorite toys to play with them.
- Daily petting and brushing will help lessen their anxiety.
- Talk quietly, often, and calmly to reassure your pets.
- Engage in active play at least twice a day.
- Allow your pet to have plenty of sleep and provide familiar toys and bedding while it becomes acclimated to the surroundings.
- Make sure pets have their own safe, secure areas to stay in.
- Patience and love will get most pets through the post-traumatic period following a disaster.

No Pets Left Behind

I can't stress enough how vital it is to take your pets with you when you evacuate. However, in the event that you must leave them, make sure you leave them inside the house.

Here are some tips that should be helpful:

- Never leave your pets chained or tied up as they could easily drown or strangle themselves.
- Never leave your pets loose outside to fend for themselves. Roaming cats and dogs are often considered abandoned, and in a large disaster situation, animal control shelters have no choice but to adopt out, foster, or euthanize these pets.
- Be sure all pets left in your home are wearing a collar or harness and current, readable identification.
- Never leave pets outside during a storm or hurricane. Bring them inside and confine them to a small room—preferably with no windows, but with adequate ventilation.
- Leave familiar toys and bedding in the room.
- Keep cats and dogs separated even if they get along. Many animals can act aggressive when frightened—even to their well-known housemates.
- Leave some of your clothing, something you have recently worn, with your pets so they can smell your scent.
- If you leave a cat, leave several litter boxes filled to the top.
- If you leave your pets in the bathroom, fill the bathtub with no more than four inches of water to prevent drowning.
- Leave plenty of their regular dry food and water in sturdy non-tip containers. Never leave unfamiliar food and treats as this may lead to severe intestinal problems.
- Place a note on the front door with a phone number where you can be reached and list all pets that are inside.

If you live in a flood-prone area, give your pets a place to escape to in case of flooding. You can stack furniture or open up the attic and set a ladder under it.

Fire Prevention and Escape

No one wants to imagine his or her house on fire, but you need to take the time to prepare for this in the event it actually happens. Fires are horrible, but they're even worse for your pets because of their smaller lung capacity. They're more susceptible to smoke inhalation, and because they don't understand what's happening to them during a fire, this can be a traumatic event. Preventing fires in the first place is paramount because firefighters aren't going to endanger human lives for family pets.

Some strategies to reduce the chance of a fire happening in your house include:

- Never leave pets unattended with burning candles, oil lamps, or a lit fireplace.
- Be sure to use all electrical and heating equipment properly.
- Never leave food cooking on the stove unattended.
- Keep your pets away from outdoor grilling areas and hot coals.
- Keep fire tools such as lighters and matches in a secure place away from pets and children.
- Have the proper size fire extinguisher in your kitchen and know how to use it.
- Make sure all fireplaces have fireguards to prevent pets from dropping toys in the fire and/or getting too close to the flames.
- Space heaters should be kept at least three feet away from your pet's bedding. Never alter or remove any of the protective devices on a space heater.

Fire Escape Plan

You need to have an evacuation plan that is practiced by the whole family. When developing this plan, include your pets as family members, but remember that they are going to be frightened and may act differently during an emergency situation, so you need to keep your own safety in mind as well. One way to keep your pet safe is to have them sleep in your room, because you could be overcome by smoke in the process of searching for your pets.

You should confine your pets for safety; they will be less frightened if they are unable to see the fire. Transporting cats means putting them in their carriers, if available, or a box or pillowcase if that's all you have access to at the time. For dogs, you can snap on a leash or carry them. Know your pets' sleeping and hiding places, because during a fire your pets will be frightened and may hide.

The following tips will aid you in developing a fire escape plan for your family and pets:

- Make sure that each room where someone sleeps has a working smoke detector, and that there is one in each hallway. Check them monthly to make sure they are working.

- Have fire ladders available at second-story escape windows.

- Make sure your house numbers are clearly visible and can easily be seen from the street.

- Draw a simple house floor plan for each floor of your home. It doesn't have to be to scale, but should include all windows and doors. Mark the first and easiest way out of every room in your house—this is usually a door and is typically the way you enter the room. Using a different color, mark the second way out of every room—this is usually a window and should be the second most direct way out of the room to the outside. Avoid going through other rooms if possible.

- Walk through your plan and check every window you marked to make sure it opens properly. Check every door and make sure it can be opened easily as well. Make sure that exit doors to the outside don't have landscaping or other items that make them hard to use as an exit.

- Choose a meeting place in front of your house that's next to something permanent, like a tree, lamppost, neighbor's porch, or mailbox. Don't choose automobiles or boats as they may be moved.

- Make sure everyone understands that once you are out of the house, you stay out. No one should go back into the house for **any** reason.

- Be sure to include in your plan where your pet carriers and leashes are, and if possible have something available in every room in which to transport your pet, like a pillowcase, trash can, or carrier. Identify these items and where they are located. Have a readily accessible first-aid kit and an evacuation kit available for each pet.

- Hold a family meeting to review the plan and explain to each person what his or her role is. Designate family members to be in charge of removing pets.

- Post the plan in a place where the whole family can view it on a regular basis, such as the refrigerator or in an office on a bulletin board.

- Review and practice your plan at least twice a year. Hold fire drills. Pets should be part of the drills. Having them participate is a good opportunity for everyone to practice the plan, ask questions, and get your pets used to being quickly removed from the house. Have family members start the drill from their beds. Time your drills and try to beat your family's current record. In case you're not home when a fire breaks out, be sure to have fire stickers clearly visible that let firefighters know there are animals in the house (but be sure to remove the stickers if you move from the house).

Bioterrorism

In this day and age, bioterrorism is a concern for everyone, including your pets. This is when biological agents (living organisms or their poisons) are used by terrorists to cause illness or death in a population. There are numerous biological organisms suitable for weapons by terrorists, and they are classified into three groups: viruses, bacteria, and toxins.

Cats and dogs are subject to the same chemical and biological agents that affect people. Because pets are small and have fast metabolisms, their symptoms will appear sooner than in a person. For example, if both people and pets were exposed to anthrax at the same time, pets would come down with symptoms in several days whereas humans might not display symptoms for seven to ten days. Once chemical or biological agents have affected your pet, the symptoms vary dramatically depending on amount, time of exposure, and the specific substance that was used. If you suspect your pet has been a victim of biological agents, you need to take it to the vet immediately so it can begin treatment and any decontamination procedures that may be required.

Prepare Now

If there were only one lesson to learn from the Hurricane Katrina disaster, it would be how utterly important it is to be prepared. Your pets are counting on you to protect them, especially in the event of an emergency when they are frightened and don't understand what's happening. Hundreds of pets are lost every year to disasters, and many more  are rescued but never reunited with their owners because of lack of identification. Being prepared for a disaster can make the difference between life and death for your pets. Never leave your pets behind in a disaster situation because the chances are high that you will never see them again.

Take the time *now* to be prepared in case disaster strikes. Go over your disaster plans, which should be written out, with all of your family members and make sure everyone knows where the disaster kit is located. Practice evacuation of your family and pets until you can evacuate safely in a few minutes. Every family member should participate, including your pets. Decide ahead of time where your family will meet if you get separated and who is in charge of the pets. Planning ahead of time will greatly minimize an already hugely stressful situation. And keep in mind that animals will panic during highly unfamiliar situations, so try to stay calm and go slowly with your pets. Hopefully, you will never have to use your plan, but be prepared and remember these tips:

- Keep pets under control and safely on a leash or in a carrier.
- All pets should be wearing proper identification.
- Be sure "Pets Inside" stickers are on your doors or windows.
- Have a readily accessible evacuation kit.
- If you must evacuate, leave early and take all pets.
- All pets should be crate-trained.
- Have a disaster plan that includes all of your pets.
- Practice evacuation drills with family members and pets.
- During disasters, expect the unexpected and stay calm.
- Have clean drinking water and canned goods on hand.
- Have extra cash on hand.
- Keep all vehicles in good running condition with full tanks of gas.

Chapter 12

Seasonal Disturbances

No matter where you live, there are definite transformations of climate that can directly affect your pet, and if you're not properly prepared, these seasonal changes can send you straight to the vet hospital. Hurricane season, flea and tick season, and the holiday season are just a few reasons to be prepared.

No matter what the weather, the best way to ensure health and happiness for your pet is to keep it inside your home, where it is safe and comfortable. Prevention is always the best approach in protecting pets from hidden seasonal disturbances.

Fall

As lovely and inviting as fall is, this time of year has many dangers lurking for cats and dogs. The following are common problems that pets encounter during fall.

Antifreeze

Every year, thousands of dogs and cats die from ingesting very small amounts of this highly toxic liquid. Many pet owners unknowingly poison their own pets by leaving antifreeze out in puddles (from radiator leaks on the garage floor) or in an open container lying around, just waiting to attract and kill pets. In climates where subfreezing temperatures are common, pets may find that the only unfrozen water available is in the puddles where radiators were drained. Cats and dogs also walk through puddles and can ingest this noxious substance from licking their paws or coat. Unbelievably, pets have even been known to chew open sealed containers and ingest the contents!

Time is of the essence with this deadly liquid. Within thirty to sixty minutes of ingestion, ethylene glycol rapidly attacks the kidneys and central nervous system. Initial symptoms of poisoning include vomiting, staggering or drunk behavior, diarrhea, depression, and lack of coordination. Within six to twelve hours, pets become paralyzed, have a seizure, or fall into a coma and may die. There is antidotal treatment, but you are racing against time, because once the kidneys have been fatally damaged, your pet will die from kidney failure. If you suspect your pet has encountered antifreeze, be sure to wash your cat or dog's body and paws with soap and water before they have a chance to lick it off and rush them to the clinic immediately.

Car Engines

As warm summer nights drift into chilly fall evenings, cats, kittens, and small wildlife become very resourceful and often seek out the warmth of car engines, where they will sleep under the hoods of parked cars. Tragically, these animals become victims of heartbreaking accidents when unsuspecting owners turn on their cars before the animals have a chance to escape. I have had to pry cats from engine parts and fan belts of cars, sometimes with fatal results. So, during the fall and winter months, always bang loudly on the hood of your car or honk your horn and wait a few minutes before starting the car to allow hidden animals a chance to escape, especially if there are cats in your neighborhood, to prevent fatal consequences from moving engine parts.

Carbon Monoxide Poisoning

As temperatures drop and people start using their heaters, there is an increased risk in carbon monoxide poisoning for pets.

Dogs and cats are far more sensitive to carbon monoxide poisoning than humans due to their small lung capacity. Symptoms include drowsiness, lethargy, difficulty breathing, bright red color to the skin and gums, muscle twitching, weakness, fever, staggering, coma, and death.

If you suspect your pet has inhaled carbon monoxide fumes, take it to the vet right away. If your pet is unconscious, perform CPR immediately or, better yet, do it in the backseat of your car as someone drives you to the hospital (see Chapter 8 on avoiding the ER).

Never start your car and let it warm up in the garage unless you remove your pets, and maintain or properly vent all gas appliances. Also, install a carbon monoxide alarm in your home; it's inexpensive and widely available in stores, and could save the lives of you and your pet.

Rat/Mice Bait

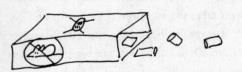

Fall is typically the time of year that we wage war on field mice, gophers, rats, and moles searching for warm lodging. For cats and dogs, this can prove to be deadly, as the products used to kill rodents in your home will also kill your pets. These products are called rodenticides, and none of them are safe for pets. Many cats and dogs—out of bore-dom, curiosity, or hunger—will readily consume these products. The poisons are usually in flimsy containers, which most pets can easily chew through to ingest the bait. Exterminators will place rodenticides in small nooks and crannies believed to be safe from our pets, often with disastrous results, as these products are made to attract rodents by their smell and taste—and will also attract your pets.

If you use these products in your home, they must be *inaccessible* to pets. Keep a record of the product(s) used and location(s) in the house, and check on them often. These poisons act by interfering with the animal's ability to utilize vitamin K. One of the key roles of vita-min K is to produce coagulation factors in the body, which cause the blood to clot when needed. Bleeding may be evident; however, most of the time the signs are subtler and include white or pale gums; weak-ness; labored breathing; bloody vomit, stool, or urine; or bruising of the skin. The antidote is vitamin K_1, given for thirty days or more, and many pets require hospitalization, blood transfusions, and fluids. In addition, there are many other types of rodenticides that can poison your cat or dog.

If you suspect your pet has ingested either a rodenticide or a ro-dent that was poisoned, take your pet to the veterinarian immediately and bring the container of the poison with you. As always, the sooner treatment begins, the more favorable the prognosis.

Grooming

While grooming your dog or cat is important all year long, there are certain times of the year when you must pay extra attention to that lustrous coat. Pets normally shed their summer coat in the fall to prepare for winter, and then shed their heavy winter coat in the spring. I don't recommend routinely shaving dogs and cats, since the hair helps insulate them against the cold and the heat. Your pet's coat provides insulation, like a jacket. When exposed to cold conditions, the hair undergoes pilo-erection, causing it to stand erect and trap the air in that layer. This air is warmed or cooled by the body and adds more insulation.

Pets, like people, are susceptible to the dangers of cold weather. Certain dog breeds with double coats, like huskies and Samoyeds, have increased protection from the elements. However, short-haired breeds of dogs, like boxers, Dalmatians, and smaller dogs, aren't "winterized" with thick fur. Therefore, these pets can benefit from wearing a warm sweater or jacket that covers their underside as well.

While the amount of shedding varies from breed to breed, daily or weekly home maintenance will keep the skin and coat healthy and pest-free. A certain amount of shedding is normal, but excessive shedding should be a cause for concern. Certain breeds tend to shed more, like retrievers, setters, spaniels, and shepherds, so their hair coats have to be combed and brushed more regularly than other breeds. Low humidity or dry air may cause your pet to experience dry skin, which frequent brushing helps alleviate by removing dead skin and stimulating oil glands. Matted hair does not insulate your pet and can be painful and lead to skin irritation.

Pets with long hair—and all cats—should be brushed at least once a week and even daily during their shedding periods. Brushing can be a bonding time for you and your pet.

Holidays: Food and Festivities

Fall signifies the beginning of the holiday season—Halloween, Thanksgiving, Christmas, Hanukkah, and New Year's Eve—each occasion presenting its own unique set of dangers. Sadly, what should be a festive occasion often devolves into a time of suffering for pets and a financial and emotional nightmare for pet owners.

Having worked in veterinary emergency rooms for many years, I can attest to the increase in business during the holidays; now, as a

shelter vet, I see larger numbers of animals at shelters during these times of the year. The holiday spikes in pet accidents are largely due to changes in routine, amplified stress, more household traffic, and an increase in food as well as in unexpected situations.

Pretty decorations and lavish meals play an important part in most holiday celebrations, but what may seem harmless and fun for you and your guests may be very harmful to your pets. So before you open that bottle of champagne and start celebrating, spend some time planning and preparing for the well-being of your cat or dog during these festive but all-too-often stressful and chaotic yearly rituals. It could save your pet's life. Go to www.DocHalligan.com for more information on specific holidays and their dangers.

Ticks

These pests appear in spring and summer, but in many areas of the country, fall is peak tick season, so you need to continue with parasite prevention. As the leaves come down, ticks will be trying to come in from the cold, so it's critical to protect your pet. See the Spring section of this chapter for details.

Standard Time

As the daylight hours become shorter, you may be walking your dog in the dark. Switch to a reflective collar for your dog and a jacket with reflective tape for you. Carry a flashlight to keep both of you safe.

Winter

Pets that are very young, thin, old, or ill have even less tolerance to the cold; small or short-haired dogs are especially vulnerable. In general, animals that are not in good health are much more susceptible to the dangers of cold weather. Certain conditions such as diabetes, heart disease, kidney disease, and hormonal imbalances lead to a compromised ability to regulate body temperature. Wind and wetness also draw heat from an animal's body and can result in dangerous consequences. But if you take certain precautions, you and your pet can have fun in the snow and enjoy this magnificent season inside your cozy home instead of spending time at the vet clinic.

As you prepare for the year's coldest days by winterizing your home, yourself, your family, and your car, don't forget to take care of your pet. The physical stress of cold temperatures can cause pets to become ill or develop infections. During extreme weather, pets should stay inside. The windchill factor can drop the outside temperature by twenty to thirty degrees, so outside temperatures of 34°F will actually feel like nearly zero degrees, which is too cold for most pets. If the temperature dips below 20°F—windchill factor or not—it's too cold for any pet to tolerate.

When you're outside playing with your pet in winter, look for signs of discomfort from the cold. If your pet starts to whine, shiver, become anxious, slow down, stop moving altogether, or look for warm places to burrow, it's a sign that it's too cold for them and they need to be brought inside to warm up. Cats and dogs can fall prey to frostbite or hypothermia with just a short exposure to subzero or extremely cold temperatures.

Frostbite

Cats and dogs have intrinsic ways of dealing with cold temperatures, but sometimes these mechanisms that keep them warm can hurt them and lead to serious damage to their extremities such as the ear tips, face, tail, and foot pads. This occurs when a pet's body becomes too cold and all the blood in the extremities gets pulled to the center of the body to keep it warm. As a result, the ears, face, paws, or tail can get cold enough that ice crystals form and can damage the tissue. Sometimes frostbite is not readily seen and the tissue damage may take several days to appear. Pets can lose their limbs, toes, and tips of their ears to this condition. Tissue that is afflicted by frostbite will be initially bright red, followed by pale white, and finally black; this dead tissue will eventually slough.

If you suspect this condition, you can warm the tissue by using warm, moist towels or by soaking the extremities—not your entire pet—in warm water for about twenty minutes to melt the ice crystals and restore circulation. Discontinue warming as soon as the affected area regains its color and *gently* dry the affected area. Frozen tissue should not be rubbed or massaged as this can cause more damage. Once your pet has warmed up, wrap it in a blanket to conserve its body heat and take it to your vet where, depending on the amount of damage, pain medication or antibiotics may be prescribed.

Hypothermia

Hypothermia is a condition that occurs when an animal is not able to keep its body temperature from falling below the normal 101°F to 102°F, which interferes with metabolic functions and adversely affects

internal organs. This is a serious condition that can cause death in your pets. Any dog or cat that spends too much time in cold temperatures, or animals with poor health and circulation that are subject to the cold, can develop this often-fatal condition. At first, animals will shiver, which is an involuntary reflex by the skeletal muscles to help generate heat and warm up the body. Subsequently, pets become weak and depressed, and eventually start showing symptoms including lethargy, stiffened muscles, decreased heart and breathing rates, shock, collapse, and unconsciousness.

If you suspect this condition in your pet, you need to take it to the vet immediately. First, wrap your pet in a blanket with hot-water bottles, or use an electric blanket that is covered in fabric (to prevent skin burns), then go to your vet right away. The vet will administer warm intravenous fluids and treatment for shock if necessary.

Paw Perils

Winter weather means hello boots, good-bye sandals—but a pet has one set of paws for its whole life. Because of this, you must pay special attention to your pet's feet, which have different elements to deal with depending on the season.

Every winter, chemicals and rock salt are used to prepare surfaces—such as roads, sidewalks, and walkways where pets commonly travel—for icy conditions. Many commercial ice-melting products contain sodium chloride, magnesium chloride, potassium chloride, calcium salts, and even urea. After walking on these surfaces, pets will groom their paws and fur and accidentally ingest these toxic substances. This can cause excessive salivation, vomiting, and diarrhea—and, in more severe cases, cardiac dysfunction, nervous system disorder, and even death. Most of these substances are caustic to your pet's paws, too.

Pets walking through snow can get packed snow or ice balls trapped between their toes. Once ice balls form, they are very painful, much like walking on rocks. When dogs develop these, they will often whine and chew at their feet. Moisture can also be trapped and cause sores and irritation, leading to infection.

After outdoor walks, be sure to wash off your pet's stomach and feet thoroughly, including between the toes, and dry them. Dog booties are available in all sizes and will protect your dog's paws from salt and chemicals on the roadways as well as from forming ice balls. If booties are not an option, you should trim the hair between your dog's toes to help alleviate the formation of ice balls. You can also apply a small amount of Vaseline to your dog's feet prior to walking to prevent snow buildup. Remove packed snow or ice from between the toes of the paw pads and wipe the paws thoroughly after every walk.

Dangerous Dish

Pets must have fresh water available at all times. They can't eat snow in sufficient amounts to prevent dehydration and can quickly suffer fatal consequences. If your pet has a water bowl outside, be sure to check it several times a day to make sure the water hasn't frozen or tipped over. Avoid using a metal dish because tongues can freeze to the metal bowl when temperatures fall below freezing, causing pain and injury. Use a non-freeze water bowl, a heavy tip-resistant plastic bowl, or a heated water dish for both food and water to prevent this problem. If you use an electrically heated bowl, make sure it's installed safely and monitored regularly.

Cozy Fires

There's nothing like a beautiful, crackling fire in the fireplace to break the winter chill and set a cozy mood, but for some pets, it can create problems as they luxuriate in its warmth. Cats and dogs that lie too close to the fire are in danger of cinders or sparks from the fireplace, not to mention burned whiskers or paws. Fumes from the fireplace may cause respiratory problems in certain pets. Be sure to keep screens around fireplaces and wood-burning stoves, and train pets to keep a safe distance. Never leave a pet alone with a fire burning in the fireplace. Space heaters can also be dangerous because pets cannot only burn themselves but also knock them over, causing a potential fire.

Wintertime means an increased risk of house fires. Candles are the leading cause of house fires, and they can easily be knocked over by jumping cats, active dogs, or wagging tails. Place all candles in heavily weighted candleholders with some form of protection, and never leave pets unattended with lit candles. Make sure that smoke detectors have fresh batteries (fire departments suggest changing the batteries every New Year's Day), and be sure to include all pets in your house fire evacuation plan and fire drills as well (see Chapter 11 on disaster preparedness).

In the Doghouse

During the winter, it's important for your dog—if it must stay outside for any period of time—to have a clean, dry, waterproof, draft-free doghouse in good repair. A doghouse should get your dog out of the elements and allow it to feel safe. It should keep your pet warm in the winter; otherwise, it could become dangerously cold. The following are some important pointers.

Size: The doghouse should be an appropriate size for your dog. Look at the amount of room your pet takes up when it curls up to lie down in your house. Draw an imaginary rectangle around your dog that's about three inches larger on all sides; that will be the ideal size for the inside of its house. The dog's body will provide the heat that will keep its house warm and toasty. If the doghouse is too large, your dog's body won't be able to provide the heat needed to keep it warm, and you'll be defeating the purpose. Conversely, a house that's too small will be uncomfortable for your dog and some of that body heat will go to waste. The house should be about 4 to 6 inches taller than your pet's shoulders. It's okay if your dog has to lower its head to enter the doghouse.

Construction: The doghouse should be made of thick, insulated plastic, wood, or insulated fiberglass. Never use a house made of metal, as this is too cold during the wintertime. The house must be able to breathe, either through the walls or via a door that is partially open or with some form of cover. If your doghouse is too airtight, this can cause problems with excess humidity. Ideally, there should be a roof over the doghouse that extends a minimum of three feet beyond the edge of the house. This will help keep rain and snow out of the inside. Igloo-shaped houses are okay, too. The doghouse door opening shouldn't be any larger than necessary to further cut down on draft. Also, the bottom of the opening should be at least four inches higher than the floor to help keep bedding inside. A cloth, carpet, canvas flap door, or metal door with vents is appropriate for the door opening; these can be purchased premade from a pet supply store. This helps reduce drafts and allows your dog's body heat to remain in the house.

Bedding: For bedding, I recommend using old blankets, towels, or pads that can be easily washed, but these items need to be monitored closely because they can trap moisture and, if soaked, can contribute to your dog getting damp and chilly. Just be sure if you use bedding to frequently change it if it gets damp, dirty, or wet. The problem with using straw, hay, or wood shavings as bedding material is that it's difficult to keep clean and can harbor ticks, mites, and fleas.

Location: The location of your doghouse is important. During the winter months, any sunshine is of benefit, so avoid placing the doghouse in shady areas. The side of the doghouse with the door should be placed opposite the direction of the prevailing winter winds.

Unsafe Outside Elements

When it is outside in the winter, always keep your pet on a leash, especially in the snow, during a snowstorm, or around bodies of water or puddles in the street. Dogs can lose their scent in winter weather and easily become lost. Some pets might panic in a snowstorm and run off. Be careful around frozen lakes, rivers, and ponds, as the ice may not be thick enough to prevent your pet from accidentally falling in and getting hurt. Don't let pets drink from any puddles, as these may be contaminated with antifreeze, oil, gasoline, windshield wiper fluid, or other chemicals.

More Fall and Winter Tips

- Windshield wiper fluid is toxic to pets if ingested and can cause acute blindness and symptoms similar to ethylene glycol (antifreeze) poisoning. As with antifreeze, time is of the essence and immediate vet care is needed to prevent fatal consequences.
- Avoid using electrical heating devices around pets, which can cause strangulation or electrocution if they get wet and/or are chewed.
- All pets—especially those with arthritis, which worsens in cold weather—need a warm place to sleep away from cold, uncarpeted floors and drafts. Areas near windows or doors that lead outdoors

may allow cold air to seep in and prevent your pet from staying warm. Keep your humidifier humming to prevent dry skin. About twenty-five to thirty percent humidity is great for most homes.

- Mothballs and moth flakes are toxic to pets, especially cats. Toxicity is caused by ingestion or by inhalation of the fumes from a large number of mothballs in a closet.
- Keep your clothes dryer door closed, as cats will jump inside looking for a warm, cozy place to sleep.
- Adjust your pet's diet. Pets that spend most of their time indoors (except for quick potty breaks outside) will need to eat less than those romping around outside, which need to burn more calories to stay warm.
- Never leave pets inside your car during the winter as they can quickly become hypothermic and freeze to death.
- Be careful of snow piling up against fences. Packed snowdrifts can allow animals to jump over fences and away from the safe confines of their yard.
- Cats and very young, sick, old, or short-haired dogs should never be left outside in winter weather without supervision.

Spring

Gardening, backyard barbecues, mountainside hikes, and days at the beach all mean lots of fun, but unfortunately spring also means lots of pests such as fleas, ticks, and mosquitoes. These unwanted visitors may seem like mere nuisances, but they can cause serious, even fatal, diseases in your pets if not dealt with properly.

Wildlife such as coyotes, foxes, bobcats, skunks, raccoons, opossums, and several rodent species, as well as other cats and dogs, can bring fleas and ticks into your yard. Pets and people can bring fleas into your home.

Interestingly, the Hartz Mountain Corporation published a study in 2002 of which major U.S. cities had the highest projected incidence of fleas, ticks, and Lyme disease. See **www.hartz.com** for a complete list.

Be aware that many of the flea, tick, and mosquito products sold at grocery and discount stores do not work and can even be harmful to your pet. Most products that are strong enough to be effective yet safe are sold only through licensed veterinarians and exterminators, who are properly trained in their use, and are regulated by the state and the Environmental Protection Agency (EPA). The EPA, not the Food and Drug Administration (FDA), oversees insecticides in general.

The best and most cost-effective way to deal with these seasonal unwanted guests is to protect your pet with year-round prevention or, at the very least, start prevention in the spring before your pet becomes infested.

Fleas

Disease-carrying fleas have menaced pets and people for centuries. As carriers of plague and disease, fleas have killed more people than all wars combined. Fortunately, common household fleas are easily controlled with preventative measures, and today there are a lot of great products out there to help prevent, kill, and control fleas.

Because the length and severity of flea-and-tick season varies across the country and changes from year to year depending on the temperature fluctuations and humidity, I recommend some form of flea control all year long. At the very least, you should start flea prevention in the spring to head off an infestation.

Learning more about fleas and their life cycle will help you understand why they become so prolific in such a short period of time and how to avoid an infestation. Although fleas thrive at 65 to 80°F with humidity levels at approximately eighty percent, they have been known to survive indoors during the winter, even in cold climates. Fleas also travel—as much as 1 mile in an hour. They will hop inside through an open door or window and are often small enough to come through a window screen. Once inside your home, there's no place a flea can't go. Fleas can be miserable for you and your pet, and not just from the bites. They can bring about a host of serious problems such as:

- **Severe anemia:** This condition is most commonly seen in very young or small pets with high numbers of fleas. Every year, kittens, puppies, and small dogs and cats suffer significant blood loss from fleabites that can actually lead to death from anemia. Signs include pale gums, weakness, and fatigue.
- **Tapeworms:** Cats and dogs develop tapeworms from ingesting a flea that is carrying the tapeworm larva.
- **Flea allergy dermatitis:** FAD is the most common allergic skin disease of dogs and cats. Animals that have flea allergy can develop a severe allergic reaction to a protein in the saliva of certain fleas that is left behind from fleabites. This condition causes severe itching, rash, and more. In dogs, it leads to hair loss and infection, usually on the rear legs or at the base of the tail; cats get scabs around the head, neck, and body. Medical treatment is needed.
- **Plague:** In rare cases, cats or dogs can get the bacteria that cause the plague from a rat flea or by ingesting a dead, infected animal. Symptoms include high fever, lethargy, and enlarged lymph nodes. Luckily, the disease is highly treatable if caught early.

It's important to realize that only five percent of the total flea population is in the form of adult fleas on your pet. The other ninety-five is in various stages: fifty percent eggs, thirty-five percent larvae, and ten percent pupae that are not readily visible to the naked eye but are in your carpet, furniture, bedding, lawn, and anywhere else your pet walks or lies down.

The key to controlling fleas is to interrupt their life cycle at an immature stage so they don't develop into adults. All pets in the household must be treated. When using preventative medication, always read all of the instructions prior to usage and never use on debilitated, very young, sick, or elderly animals without directions from your vet. Never use dog products on cats and vice versa.

Ticks

Ticks are just plain nasty! They're not insects, they're arachnids (like spiders), and are considered ectoparasites, which means they live on the outside of your pet. There are several hundred different species of ticks in the United States, with the problematic species varying from region to region. The most commonly encountered tick is the brown dog tick. Ticks are parasites and spend their entire lives looking for an unwilling host. Ticks don't jump or fly; rather, they position themselves on grass, shrubbery, or underbrush so they can hitch a ride with a passing victim, and then dig their heads in and start sucking their food of choice: blood. During feeding, ticks can swell up to more than fifty times their normal size and, like fleas, can cause a life-threatening anemia by bleeding their hosts dry. They can also transmit potentially fatal illnesses to your pet.

Ticks are most often found in and around the pet's ears, on the belly, or on the shoulders, but they can attach anywhere. A tick feeds by burying its head into the host's skin, leaving its body exposed. As it feeds, its body becomes engorged and swollen with blood. Although the body is pretty disgusting, the real danger is the tick's head, which is embedded in the skin. If you remove the tick improperly, you may end up leaving the head behind and putting your pet at risk for infection or abscess. That's why prevention is always the best approach in protecting your pets from ticks. Spring and fall are the two most active times for ticks.

In addition to prevention, whenever you take your pet on an outing in wooded or grassy areas, you need to take the time to thoroughly inspect it from head to tail as soon as possible. To prevent ticks from doing their damage, they should be removed as soon as they are observed. Because contact with ticks can be risky for humans as their body fluids can transmit disease, it's best to wear gloves and use forceps or tweezers to remove them. Grab hold of the tick where the head is right near your pet's body, as close to the skin as possible, and pull with one quick motion. Try not to jerk or twist as you pull. Place the tick in a jar with alcohol and cap it. If you suspect the tick to be a species that can carry disease, bring it with you to the vet hospital when you have your pet examined. Afterward, observe the tick to make sure the head is still attached and was removed with the body. If the head is still in your pet's skin, call your vet and bring your pet in for an inspection of the area. Either way, you should keep a close eye on the affected area for a few days to make sure the skin heals properly. It's normal for a small welt to appear in the skin where the tick was removed. Sometimes, patterns will develop around the tick bite that may alert you to a more serious disease transmitted by the tick bite; if this occurs, take your pet to the vet right away.

A tick titer is a blood test performed on your pet's blood serum that measures the production of antibodies against disease-causing organisms transmitted by ticks. The titer will help determine whether your pet has been exposed to a tick-borne disease, and if so, which ones. This is important because there are many different types of organisms that ticks can carry and not all of them spread disease. The three most prevalent diseases that are spread by ticks are Lyme disease, canine ehrlichiosis, and Rocky Mountain spotted fever. It takes about twenty-four to seventy-two hours for ticks to transfer their diseases, so that gives you time to intervene and remove the tick before it has time to hurt your pet.

Lyme Disease

Lyme disease is a bacterial disease that can cause painful disability in both humans and dogs. This disease is usually transmitted by deer ticks (some of the smallest of all ticks; no larger than the head of a pin), which tend to be found in specific regions of the United States: the Northeast, the upper Mississippi region, California, and certain areas in the South. Any potential risk to human beings from infected animals is attributable to cats, dogs, and wildlife such as foxes, raccoons, coyotes, ferrets, opossums, rodents, skunks, and bobcats bringing ticks into areas of human habitation. Dogs appear to be at greater risk than humans, although the disease has serious consequences for both.

Without treatment, Lyme disease causes problems in many parts of a dog's body including the heart, kidneys, and joints. On rare occasions it can lead to neurological disease. The most common clinical signs in dogs are high fever, swollen lymph nodes, lameness, and a loss of appetite. Dogs acquire Lyme disease when a tick carrying the *Borrelia burgdorferi* bacteria gets passed into an animal's bloodstream from a bite. The tick must remain attached to the animal's skin for at least twenty-four to seventy-two hours before the bacteria can be transmitted. In both dogs and humans, the illness is treated with antibiotics because the causative agent is sensitive to tetracycline.

The disease in humans is a multisystemic disease that can become chronic. Initial symptoms of skin rash, headache, and fever can progress to cardiac problems, arthritis, or neurologic disorders. Symptoms can develop four years after the infection.

Canine Ehrlichiosis

Ehrlichiosis is an infectious disease of dogs first observed in military dogs returning from Vietnam in the 1970s. The organism causing this disease is classified as a rickettsia, which is similar to bacteria. Certain strains are capable of infecting cats, dogs, horses, cattle, and humans in endemic regions of the Northern Hemisphere. The disease is not contagious directly from a dog to a human. The only way the disease is spread is through the bite or handling of infected ticks. The parasite *Ehrlichia canis* is found worldwide, but exists in especially heavy populations in the Gulf Coast states and in the Southwest, where the main vector, the brown dog tick *Rhipicephalus sanguineus*, is concentrated. This tick, which is larger than the deer tick, is the size of a match head or small pea when engorged.

There are three stages of the disease: acute (early disease), subclinical (no outward signs of disease), and chronic (long-standing infection). The acute phase of illness begins one to three weeks after infection, producing signs of fever, swollen lymph nodes, respiratory distress, weight loss, and bleeding disorders with pinpoint bruises on the skin and mucus membranes such as the gums. This stage lasts two to four weeks in most dogs and is the easiest time to diagnose infection. If unnoticed, however, the dog will enter into a subacute phase where clinical signs will be less obvious but not necessarily less harmful. This stage of the disease can produce significant detrimental changes in the bone marrow and immune system of infected dogs. If an animal's immune system is not able to fight off the disease, this leads to a chronic stage with irreversible damage to the kidneys and bone marrow. Lameness, anemia, blood clotting abnormalities, eye problems, swollen limbs, and nervous system disorders may occur.

Fortunately, the prognosis for patients with ehrlichiosis is good if treatment is initiated in the early stages. Doxycycline is the most frequent antibiotic used to treat this disease. Dogs with bleeding disorders usually require a blood transfusion. Dogs with weak immune systems

or that are in the last stage, which has affected the bone marrow, are
less likely to survive.

Rocky Mountain Spotted Fever

This disease affects dogs, cats, and people and is caused by another rickettsial organism, *Rickettsia rickettsii*. The illness is seasonal
with occurrences in spring through early fall. The Rocky Mountain
wood tick (*Dermacentor andersoni*) and the American dog tick (*Dermacentor variabilis*) are the main ticks carrying the disease (both are large,
typically the size of a kernel of corn when engorged), but other tick
species may carry the organism as well. Cases of human and canine
disease are most prevalent in the central and southeastern United
States.

The Center for Disease Control (CDC) reports that more than
1,200 cases of Rocky Mountain spotted fever (RMSF) occur in humans annually. This is partly due to cases where dogs have become infected with the disease and the owners are later infected, sometimes by
removing infected ticks from their pets. Fingers can become contaminated with infected tick fluids, which can transmit the disease to humans through skin abrasions or by rubbing of the eyes.

The disease can be difficult to diagnose in dogs and humans because of the vague array of clinical symptoms. RMSF organisms are
transmitted only after several hours of tick attachment and feeding. The
multiplication of the organism in small blood vessels produces profound
inflammation, with leakage of tissue fluids, swelling, and severe organ
damage. Small hemorrhages may appear as reddish-purple blotches under your pet's skin. The onset of fever five days after the tick bite is common, but clinical signs may not develop for up to four weeks. Other
clinical signs include facial or joint swelling, difficulty breathing, coughing, and neurological abnormalities. As with other infections, blood
tests are used to confirm the diagnosis. The disease is treated with antibiotics, with patients showing response in twenty-four to forty-eight

hours. People with RMSF can develop a sudden fever, severe headache, tiredness, deep muscle pain, chills, nausea, and a characteristic rash that usually begins three to twelve days after a tick bite.

The best way to prevent dogs from contracting this disease is to limit their exposure to ticks.

Mosquitoes and Heartworms

Mosquitoes are not parasites, but they, too, can cause devastating health problems. With just one bite, they can cause heartworm disease, a potentially deadly condition, in both dogs and cats. Like Lyme disease, it is completely preventable.

Heartworm (*Dirofilaria immitis*) is a blood parasite that's transmitted to dogs and cats after they've been bitten by mosquitoes that are carrying the disease. Although dogs are considered the definitive host, heartworms have been known to infect more than thirty species of animals, including cats, coyotes, foxes, wolves, ferrets, sea lions, and even humans. Heartworms are worms that squirm their way into the heart and pulmonary arteries. Adult heartworms cause disease because they live in the right side of the heart and pulmonary arteries, where they obstruct the flow of blood through the heart to the rest of the body.

The only way a pet can become infected is through the bite of an infected mosquito, where microscopic larvae are injected under the pet's skin and begin a long migratory process. It takes about six to eight months for the larvae to migrate through the tissues, eventually reaching the heart, where they will live out their life. Adult worms will reproduce inside the pet's body, with the female releasing millions of offspring into the bloodstream. Female heartworms can grow up to 14 inches long, with male worms reaching only about half that size. Dogs can harbor upward of 300 heartworms, while cats usually harbor only one to three adult worms. Overall, cats get heartworms far less often than dogs, even in heavily infected areas.

Mosquitoes become carriers after biting an animal already infected with the parasite. Mosquitoes can survive indoors, even during the winter, and can enter your house and bite your indoor-only cats and dogs. Therefore, they can pose a year-round problem for most pets.

After the initial infection, your pet may not show any clinical signs for up to two years. These parasites can cause permanent damage in your dog or cat long before any symptoms are noticed. The disease can occur at any age, but is usually diagnosed in dogs and cats three to eight years of age. The disease acts very differently in dogs than it does in cats.

Canine heartworm disease is a serious and potentially fatal disease of dogs. Every year, thousands of dogs become permanently debilitated or die from lung, heart, or circulatory problems caused by heartworms. Many dogs have heartworms for several months before symptoms are obvious and by then the disease may be difficult, if not impossible, to treat successfully. The disease is not spread from dog to dog, but rather through an intermediate host, the mosquito. Spread of the disease coincides with mosquito season in spring and fall. Adult worms cause disease by clogging the heart and the major blood vessels that leave it. They interfere with the valve action in the heart, causing the blood supply to other organs of the body to be reduced, particularly the lungs, liver, and kidneys, leading to malfunction of these organs. Clinical signs in dogs include a dull coat, lack of energy, weight loss, coughing, nervousness, difficulty breathing, fluid in the abdomen, and sometimes collapse or fainting. Severely infected dogs may die suddenly during exercise or excitement. Secondary liver and kidney disease may also occur as the liver develops cirrhosis, causing jaundice, anemia, and general weakness as toxins build in the body because the kidneys aren't working properly.

A simple blood test can diagnose the culprit. If heartworm is caught in the early stages, most dogs can be successfully treated. When the disease reaches its critical stage, damage to vital organs may be so severe that treatment is much more difficult and the possibility of complete recovery is much lower. Dogs can become reinfected, so it's essential to put all dogs in heartworm-infested areas on some form of heartworm preventative.

Infected cats may not show any clinical signs for many months, but as the adult heartworms grow in length, they can cause death (a cat's heart is very small, so harboring even one or two worms can be fatal). Clinical signs of heartworm disease in cats include heart failure, chronic coughing, wheezing, exercise intolerance, decreased appetite, weight loss, vomiting, respiratory distress, and sudden collapse or death. Strangely, some cats have only minor symptoms such as vomiting—or no clinical signs at all. In some cats, when the main arteries going to the lungs become blocked, the animal will die suddenly and the diagnosis is found on necropsy. Outdoor cats are more at risk, but since it takes so few of the heartworm parasites to cause disease in cats, even the occasional mosquito finding its way into the home can carry more than enough heartworm to be fatal. Diagnosis can be difficult and there is no effective treatment in cats, so prevention is paramount.

Prevention and Treatment

Now that you know a little more about these pests, how do you deal with them? An ounce of prevention is worth a pound of cure, and this is never truer than with fleas, ticks, heartworms, and parasites. Fortunately for your pets and your pocketbook, there are numerous good products out there to help prevent, kill, and control most of these unwelcome invaders for only pennies a day.

The problem is that many pet owners wait until they see these creatures, have an infestation, or, worse, their pet becomes sick. The cost to treat illnesses related to fleas, ticks, and heartworms can be staggering, not to mention the unthinkable suffering and possible loss of your pet. This is why prevention is so important. It makes a lot more sense to protect your pet year-round than risk your pet's life to heartworm.

In any case, you want to begin protecting your pet in the spring *before* it gets bitten, because summer will be just around the corner. Again, it's important to remember that mosquitoes can even bite indoor cats and dogs.

There are numerous products available and your vet will help you select the one that's right for your pet. In general, any medication your vet carries is safe, effective, and the best way to go. Many a cat or dog has ended up at the emergency clinic because an owner mistakenly put too much product, or the wrong product, on their poor pets, sometimes with fatal results. For example, cats are particularly sensitive to numerous insecticides including permethrin, flea products in general, and over-the-counter sprays and dips, so always make sure the age of the animal is taken into account, as well as the species.

Collar the Problem

In general, flea collars don't work. They only kill the fleas that are directly underneath them and they can be toxic to cats. However, there is a tick collar that's very effective called Preventic, made by Virbac. It contains amitraz, which actually causes embedded ticks to pull up and leave. It will poison the ticks and make them fall off within a day or so. Preventic also retards new ticks from wanting to bite your pet, is water-resistant, and is ninety-seven percent effective for up to three months. It has no effect on fleas. The collar is compatible for use with other flea-control products such as Frontline or Advantage, and can be used on puppies at least four months of age. It should never be used on cats and you have to be careful using this collar on dogs around cats, as cats can get sick from just licking the collar.

Internal Parasites

In addition to external parasites, dogs and cats (and people) are victims of several kinds of internal parasites, frequently referred to as worms. The most common are roundworms, hookworms, and tapeworms. These parasites may be transmitted to your pets by other animals contaminating the soil. The infected animals will defecate the worm or eggs that develop into microscopic larvae, which attach themselves to your pet's paws and then migrate through the body, eventually ending up in your pet's intestines. These worms can also infect humans, so treatment and eradication of the worms in the environment are critical. Early diagnosis of the presence and species of intestinal parasites is important, for not all worms respond to the same treatment. Therefore, stool samples should be taken to your veterinarian for a microscopic examination called a *fecal exam*, or *stool check*. Many veterinarians include the stool check as part of the annual health exam.

Some of the most common clinical signs of worm infections are:
- Change in appetite
- Distended abdomen
- Weakness
- Dull coat
- Diarrhea or vomiting
- Weight loss
- Scooting

I've already addressed a couple of zoonotic diseases, including Lyme disease and RMSF. Zoonotic diseases are those diseases and infections that are naturally transmitted between animals and humans. This means that zoonotic parasites can affect both pets and people. Protecting pets from zoonotic parasites greatly reduces the risk to humans. Prevention and routine screening from your veterinarian are important to protect you and your family. This should include a yearly fecal exam of all pets in the household.

Roundworms

Roundworms are the most common worms of dogs and cats. Puppies can acquire them while still in the uterus as roundworms are capable of migrating across the infected placenta and into the unborn puppies. Both puppies and kittens can get infected soon after birth through their mother's milk. In addition, roundworms can be acquired from the environment by accidental ingestion of the infective eggs in contaminated soil or by eating infected rodents.

Adult roundworms are fairly long, white, and tubular in shape and resemble half-lengths of spaghetti noodles. These worms swim inside the small intestine and feed on the animal's digested food. Roundworms can grow to be 8 to 12 centimeters long and can lead to a host of medical problems including stunted growth, weight loss, dry hair, general poor appearance, vomiting, and diarrhea. The most common manifestation from infection of multiple adults is a pot-bellied appearance due to inflammation and distention of the bowel loops. Severe infestation in puppies and kittens can lead to dehydration, intestinal blockage, and even death.

Since almost all puppies and kittens are either born with worms or infected immediately after birth—and are continuously reinfected through their mother's milk and the environment—it's important to not only begin treatment early, but to repeat treatments as well. Puppies can be dewormed as early as two to three weeks of age and should be dewormed every two weeks until they are three months of age. Nursing females should be treated concurrently with the pups. Kittens can be dewormed starting at six weeks of age, with treatment repeated every two weeks until they are twelve weeks of age. All new pets should have a fecal exam performed to check for worms in addition to a physical exam by your vet. Adult pets should be checked annually.

Roundworms of both cats and dogs pose a hazard to humans, but fortunately, most human infections with roundworms are so mild they go unnoticed and apparently produce no permanent damage. However, they have the potential to produce severe disease. Young children who play in uncovered sandboxes, litter boxes, or dirt that has been contaminated with animal feces from infected puppies or kittens are especially at risk for contracting the disease. Direct contact with infected animals *does not* produce infection, as the eggs require a three- to four-week extrinsic incubation period to become infective; thereafter, eggs in the soil remain infective for months to years. Once inside humans, the hatched larvae are unable to mature and continue to migrate through the tissues for up to six months. Eventually they lodge in various organs, particularly the lungs and liver and, less often, the brain, eyes, and other tissues. The damage is aggravated by the strong allergic inflammatory reaction the larvae provoke in human tissue. Symptoms in humans include fever, cough, and wheezing. Keeping young children away from areas contaminated with feces and encouraging them to wash their hands after playing and before eating is important in preventing the disease. All sandboxes should be covered when not in use.

Hookworms

Hookworms are parasites that get their name from the hooklike projections in their mouth that they use to attach themselves to the intestinal wall and suck blood. These worms are small and thin, but despite their small size, a large burden of worms can suck huge amounts of blood from the tiny vessels in the intestinal wall, leading to a life-threatening anemia. Dogs and cats get hookworms if they come in contact with the larvae in contaminated soil or grass. Cats can also get infected through ingestion of infected prey such as mice, and dogs can acquire infection as larvae burrow through the skin, causing inflammation.

Puppies can contract hookworms in the uterus, and both puppies and kittens can become infected from ingesting contaminated milk while nursing. A severe hookworm infestation can cause serious health problems and even death (from a severe anemia) in puppies and kittens. Other clinical signs of hookworms in dogs and cats are diarrhea, blood in the stool, weight loss, and weakness.

Hookworms are considered a human health hazard since the infective larvae can penetrate the skin and migrate locally. This is called *cutaneous larval migrans.* Clinical signs in humans are localized to the site of larval entry, particularly in the hands and feet. The lesions are usually red and very itchy. So anyone running barefoot in moist, sandy areas or in their yard or park where the grass is wet can contract visceral larval migrans from hookworm larvae.

Tapeworms

The tapeworm is a common intestinal parasite of adult cats and dogs. The adult tapeworm can reach up to 8 inches long and is made up of many small segments called *proglotids*, each about the size of a grain of white rice. Usually, single proglotid segments, which contain tapeworm eggs, break off the tail end of the tapeworm and are passed into the stool. These segments sometimes will remain visible on the pet's rear after it has had a bowel movement or be present on the stool itself. They may also crawl out of the anus when the pet is very relaxed or sleeping. In large numbers they may cause a dull coat, debilitation, and weight loss. Sometimes pets will scoot across the ground because the segments irritate the skin in this area.

There are two primary ways that dogs and cats can become infected with tapeworms. Pets can swallow a flea when they are chewing or licking themselves, and if that adult flea contains infective tapeworm larvae, then the pet will become infected with tapeworms. Less commonly, dogs and cats can become infected when they eat a rodent, which can harbor a different species of tapeworm.

Humans can become infected with tapeworms if they ingest a flea or the eggs from soil, hands, or objects contaminated by dog or cat feces. Most cases involve young children eating dirt contaminated with animal feces.

If medication is given to kill the tapeworms, but your pet continues to swallow fleas when licking itself, the tapeworms will return again and again. So it's a good idea to use flea control after deworming your pet for tapeworms.

To prevent human infection with pet-associated worms:

- Deworm puppies and kittens early and repeat every two weeks until they are twelve weeks old.
- Mother dogs and cats should be treated at the same time as the puppies and kittens.
- Keep young children away from contaminated areas and have them wash their hands after playing and before eating.
- Have new pets checked right away by your veterinarian. Ask for a fecal exam.
- Have all adult pets checked annually with yearly fecals.
- All pet feces should be disposed of promptly, especially in yards, playgrounds, and public parks.

Summer

Dogs and cats don't sweat because they don't have sweat glands in their skin and armpits like people do. During the summer months they can suffer heatstroke from overheating. This season can be downright dangerous for your cat or dog, so be prepared and protect them from the heat.

Heatstroke

Dogs and cats are very susceptible to heatstroke because they have limited mechanisms to cool themselves: panting and losing heat through their tongue, nose, and foot pads. Certain types of animals are more prone to heatstroke than others. Dogs with flat faces like pugs, bulldogs, or Boston terriers have a difficult time panting and thus can easily overheat. Also, dogs with heavy coats, older animals, obese dogs and cats, puppies and kittens under six months, pets who are ill, and pets on certain medications are at an even greater risk for overheating during the summer months.

Nearly every case of heatstroke is preventable. Exercising and being left in a car are the two most common causes of heatstroke in dogs and cats. Dogs like to keep up with you while exercising and may not readily tell you they're getting too hot until it's too late. On a 75°F day, the temperature inside a parked car—with the windows open—can quickly climb to more than 100°F and cause overheating.

Here are some of the signs associated with overheating:
- Body temperature above 104°F
- Excessive panting or openmouthed breathing
- Lethargy, daze, or collapse
- Drooling, vomiting, or diarrhea
- Depression, stupor (acting drunk), or seizures
- Increased heart rate
- Bloody diarrhea or vomiting
- Bright red tongue or gums

If left untreated, heatstroke can be fatal. The easiest way to cool your pet is to immerse it in cool water in a bathtub, kitchen sink, bucket, or swimming pool, or spray with a garden hose, and then take your pet to the vet as soon as you can. You can also use towels soaked in cool water and change them every five minutes because they will heat up fast. NEVER use ice water to immerse your pet or to moisten towels, as this can cause the reverse problem of hypothermia. Pointing a fan at your pet will help, too. If your dog or cat can drink, offer it cold water, or even ice water. If your vet is far away, keep towels soaked in cool water draped over your cat or dog until you arrive, and have the air conditioner blowing directly on your pet.

Steer Clear

Dogs and even some cats love to ride in the car, but you absolutely must resist the urge to let them accompany you during the summer months. Once temperatures soar above 75°F, your car becomes a coffin. Even with the windows open, the temperature inside a car can quickly rise to deadly conditions. NEVER leave a pet alone in the car. It only takes a few minutes for the temperature to rise above 100°F, with fatal consequences for your pet. Every summer, emergency clinics and vet hospitals treat dying pets that often cannot be saved. These tragedies are completely preventable! Unless someone will be in the car at all times with your pet with the air-conditioning on, please leave your cat or dog at home.

Walk This Way

To keep your pet from overheating, don't exercise your cat or dog during the hottest part of the day, 11 A.M. to 3 P.M., and be observant of your pet when you do take it outside. Catching heat exhaustion early is the key to success in treating this all-too-common deadly condition. Exercise your pet either early in the morning or late in the afternoon and bring plenty of water with you. Before starting your walk, give the sidewalk a test with the palm of your hand. If it's too hot to touch, it can burn your pet's foot pads and you should avoid this surface. Stick to dirt paths, grass, or concrete surfaces. Keep your pet off of asphalt, which retains heat due to its composition and dark color; the tar base can melt and stick to the pads of your pet's feet, causing burns. If you suspect that your pet has burned its paws, take your pet to the vet right away. To help cool your pet at the end of a long walk, apply a cool, wet washcloth to the foot pads.

Block That Sun

Sunlight is necessary to produce vitamin D, which helps protect the skin as well as balance the body's calcium levels and metabolism. However, too much of anything can be harmful, and too much ultraviolet (UV) radiation can cause sunburn or solar dermatitis in some animals. White cats and certain breeds of dogs, like boxers and Weimaraners, are especially vulnerable to sunburn and therefore need extra protection from the sun. Sunburn is also common in white and short-haired dogs.

Sunburn usually occurs on the abdomen, bridge of the nose, ear tips, groin, and insides of the legs. The belly is prone to sunburn because of sunlight that reflects up from the sidewalk. Dogs that spend a lot of time at beaches can get sunburned as the sun reflects up from the hot white sand. Dogs and cats don't even need to be outdoors to get sunburned because UV radiation can pass through windows. Sunburn and repeated excessive exposure to UV radiation can initially cause redness and hair loss on the ear tips, bridge of the nose, or abdomen, and may lead to skin infections, skin ulcers, and cancer.

To protect pets from sunburn and its consequences, you can apply sunblock to the small susceptible areas of the skin such as the bridge of the nose and ear tips. You can also apply sunblock along any part in the fur on your pet's head and back. For cats, sunblock is usually sufficient. You should use SPF 30 and you can mix it fifty-fifty with Vaseline. For dogs that spend a lot of time outdoors, sunblock isn't effective on the tummy, since it can rub off. There are spandex bodysuits designed to block UV radiation that will be effective in protecting your active dog from sunburn.

Insect Bites

Spiders, bees, yellow jackets, hornets, and fire ants all bask in the warmth of sunny summer days. Curious pets often get stung on the face and paws as they investigate or try to play with these stinging creatures. Most reactions manifest themselves as swelling and itching of the face, eyes, and ears or small circular areas of swelling all over the body called hives or urticaria. These symptoms are easily treated with antihistamines. However, some dogs and cats will develop life-threatening clinical signs such as breathing difficulties and swollen throats, which require immediate veterinary care; if left untreated, this can be fatal. To minimize the chance of insect bites or stings, check your yard for any nests or hives and keep pets away from these areas until you have them removed by a pest control company.

In Summary

Whether seasonal changes in your area of the world are dramatic or subtle, each season brings a whole lot of potential dangers and risks for your pets. With a little forethought and attention, you and your pets can sail smoothly through the various changing seasons and enjoy their wonder and beauty instead of suffering the consequences of being unprepared. That way, your pets will be comfortable, healthy, and happy through each spectacular season of the year.

Chapter 13

Seniors Are Special

If you're like me, you hope and pray that your pets will live forever. Unfortunately, they won't. The average life span of a dog or cat is relatively short compared to ours—about one-fourth to one-sixth that of a human. But if you're very lucky, your pet will live to a ripe old age, having enjoyed a long life. So don't despair.

I must admit I did panic when I first noticed my chocolate Lab Duke's muzzle graying and his eyebrows turning white. Still, his wonderful zest for life never diminished as time robbed him of his youthfulness. Some of my fondest memories of Duke were in his senior years: the way he walked to his food and water bowls and looked at them curiously, seeming to forget why he was there; our sacred evening walks when an especially lush lawn beckoned and he'd roll in the thick, cushy grass, murmuring softly as he turned his chocolate body blissfully; his incessant barking at me from his cozy orthopedic bed, his golden-brown eyes lovingly following me around the house as I busily finished tasks; the close bond we shared as I nurtured him during the last months of his life, pacemaker and all. Saying good-bye is never easy, but we can thumb through our treasured memories like cherished photographs because our beloved pets live on in our hearts forever, ensuring that they never truly die.

The last stage of life is the time our pets look to us for comfort and guidance to help them safely navigate the aging process. Their fur turns gray, their vision wanes, their bodies lose tone and energy, and they become more susceptible to illness, less adaptable to change, and even forgetful as time marches on. Yet although our pets grow older, the unwavering love and gratitude they offer us remains.

Sometimes it's difficult to accept the fact that life must come to an end. It's crucial to remember that your pet's quality of life is much more important than the length of its life. Loving an animal through its senior years can teach us the true meaning of love and compassion. Our pets are unselfish and caring to the end. They show us how to live, give us reasons to live, show us how quickly the years pass, and even how important it is to live each day to the fullest. So if you're fortunate enough to care for your pet into its senior years, your life will be truly blessed.

Aging Pets

According to the American Veterinary Medical Association, aging pets make up about forty-five percent of the nation's pet population. This trend, like so many others, mirrors what is happening with humans, who are living longer than ever before, thanks to monumental strides in medicine and an ever-increasing knowledge of what's good for us: exercise, a healthy diet, a positive attitude, and owning pets. Pets, too, are living much longer, higher-quality lives. Since the 1930s, the average canine and feline life span has nearly doubled from seven to thirteen years in dogs, and fourteen years in cats. This burgeoning number of senior pets and their increased longevity is due to improved veterinary technology, preventative medicine, advances in nutrition, and an increase in pet owners' knowledge of the aging process. In the United States, it's estimated that more than twenty million dogs and twenty-two million cats are considered seniors. As more dogs and cats reach an advanced age, more owners will be faced with the special demands and problems that come with it.

Understanding the aging process and the most common problems that afflict senior pets is the first step in providing the best possible care for your older animal. Pet owners need to be informed about what potential problems their aging pets might face down the line. The challenges often vary by breed and size; for instance, large breeds of dogs are predisposed to such musculoskeletal problems as arthritis, toy breeds are more prone to dental and heart disease, and cats have a higher incidence of kidney disease.

The good news is that veterinarians can rule out the vast majority of problems commonly seen with aging by using simple, noninvasive methods like blood tests, urinalysis, X rays, electrocardiograms, and ultrasound. That's one of the reasons why twice-yearly checkups, recommended by most veterinarians for senior cats and dogs, is so important to enhancing your pet's well-being. With prevention and early detection, you can get a head start on treating disease and hopefully slow down its process, or at least increase your pet's quality of life as they deal with the aging process.

Time Marches On

Aging is a natural process that begins at birth. It can be described as the sum of all physiological changes occurring in the body over time that result in functional impairment and eventually culminate in death. Although many complex physical changes accompany advancing years, age in and of itself is not a disease. Aging is a gradual process in which organs begin to deteriorate, senses begin to decline, and energy levels wane. There is a gradual decline in the body's ability to repair itself, maintain normal body functions, and adapt to stresses and changes in the environment.

Like people, pets go through life stages of growth, maturity, and aging, but passage from one stage to another is often blurred. As your pets age they will experience a number of physical and behavior changes. It seems like your pets age overnight because they age so much faster than we do—approximately six to ten times faster. Dogs and cats age at different rates depending on their species, breed, weight, genetics, environment, nutrition, veterinary care, and other individual factors.

The needs of older pets change dramatically as they age. Understanding these changes and needs, and knowing what to do to increase their quality of life, helps your pets live a fuller, longer life. For instance, older pets have become creatures of habit and enjoy predictable days, so you can minimize their stress levels by not making drastic changes in their environment or daily schedule. If changes are necessary, make them gradually, trying to maintain as much of the usual routine as possible.

As cats and dogs age, they go through changes that are remarkably similar to aging in humans, including gray hair, diminished senses, sleeping more, change in habits, difficulty in maintaining optimum weight, and wear and tear on the body. Diseases that are common among elderly people affect our aging pets as well, such as arthritis, cancer, diabetes, heart disease, kidney disease, obesity, and senility. As with people, preventive health care is the best way to keep your pets healthy and ensure that they live a long life.

Life Stages

Pets age much faster than humans. They have three life stages:

Stage 1—Puppies and kittens under one year of age.

Stage 2—Adults between the ages of one and six.

Stage 3—Seniors older than six, depending on the breed. This stage is when you will usually spend the most money on vet bills.

Life Expectancy

Most pet owners want to know about how long they can expect their cat or dog to live. I remember wondering just how long Duke would live and constantly worrying about losing him. It's much better to focus on your pet's quality of life and diagnosing disease early so you have a chance to diminish any negative effects.

Unlike most humans, dogs and cats adapt very well to the changes that come with age and are remarkable in how they handle just about anything that comes their way. Like people, though, an animal's life expectancy can vary tremendously, depending on nutrition, lifestyle, environment, genetics, and breed.

No one can accurately predict how long an individual cat or dog will live because there is always the possibility of an unpredictable illness, an accident, or a genetic predisposition to disease lurking in your pet's genes (bloodlines do tell the story, so if you have access to this information, you should ask how old the ancestors were when they died). But generally speaking, smaller breeds of dogs live longer than larger breeds, and cats live longer than dogs. Giant dog breeds like Saint Bernards and Great Danes have a life expectancy of seven to eleven years; large- and medium-size breeds, eleven to fourteen years; and small breeds like toy poodles and Chihuahuas, fifteen to eighteen years. Outdoor cats generally live three to five years, but indoor cats have a life expectancy of twelve to sixteen years—and many indoor cats are now living into their late teens and early twenties.

Life Span by Dog Breed

6–10 years: Bernese mountain dog, bulldog, Great Dane, Irish wolfhound, Newfoundland

9–11 years: Akita, boxer, bloodhound, Cavalier King Charles spaniel, Doberman pinscher, French bulldog, rottweiler, Staffordshire bull terrier

10–13 years: Afghan hound, Airedale terrier, Alaskan malamute, basset hound, Chesapeake Bay retriever, chow, cocker spaniel, dalmatian, German shepherd, golden retriever, Labrador retriever, Portuguese water dog, Scottish terrier, shar-pei, Shetland sheepdog, Welsh corgi

12–15 years: Beagle, bichon frise, collie, papillon, pug

14–16 years: Boston terrier, cairn terrier, corgi, Irish setter, Jack Russell terrier, Lhasa apso, Maltese terrier, miniature pinscher, schnauzer, shih tzu, standard poodle, West Highland white terrier, Yorkshire terrier

15–18 years: Chihuahua, dachshund, miniature and toy poodles, Pomeranian

The Senior Years

"Senior" doesn't just mean old. The term was chosen to describe the aging and older pet. Senior only means that it's time to take special considerations and precautions because of a pet's age.

The age at which a dog or cat is considered to be senior varies because individual dogs and cats age at different rates. In humans, middle age is defined as forty-five to fifty-nine years of age, senior is sixty to seventy-five years, and aged is the term applied to individuals older than seventy-five. For dogs and cats, basically the last twenty-five percent of the predicted life span for their species and breed is considered senior. Not all pets readily show the transition into their senior years, which occurs anytime between six and nine years of age.

However, there are some predictable changes that accompany this transition. In the last third of the life span, metabolic rate decreases by thirty to forty percent, body fat increases, lean body tissues decrease, and respiratory capacity and oxygen availability decrease. All of these changes limit the physical activity level of older pets. Their ability to regulate their own temperature is decreased and they are more subject to intermittent sleep. In addition, their immune system becomes less responsive, so they're more susceptible to infection, and the incidence of malignancy and cancer increase with age.

When your cat or dog reaches an age that's considered senior, you should be prepared to make some changes in the way you care for your pet. For starters, this means biannual vet exams. Just like in humans, age in animals is often relative, and a pet may not act old just because it's considered to be a senior. When an animal actually begins to experience problems because of old age, then it is considered geriatric.

Everyone has heard that old adage that a dog's age equals one year for every seven human years. This isn't quite true. The ratio is higher with youth and decreases a bit as your pet ages. At six months of age, a puppy or kitten is roughly equivalent to a teenager, and at one to two years it is fifteen to twenty-five human years old, depending on the breed. By age two, most dogs and cats have already reached adulthood, and at four, many are entering middle age. After that, they age around five human years for every year of their life, again depending on the breed and weight. Small dogs (twenty pounds or less) are considered senior between nine and thirteen years old; medium-size dogs (twenty-one to fifty pounds), nine to eleven years old; large dogs (fifty-one to ninety pounds), seven to ten years old; and giant breeds (more than 90 pounds), six to nine years old. Cats are considered senior between eight and eleven years old (for most breeds).

The following age chart shows you when your pet is considered senior (**in bold type**) and the relative human years compared to dog years.

Age Chart

Dog years	Weight			
	1–20 lbs.	21–50 lbs.	51–90 lbs.	>90 lbs.
		Age in human years		
1	18	16	15	14
2	24	22	20	19
3	28	28	30	32
4	32	33	35	37
5	36	37	40	42
6	40	42	45	49
7	44	47	50	56
8	48	51	55	64
9	52	56	61	71
10	56	60	66	78
11	60	65	72	86
12	64	69	77	93
13	68	74	82	101
14	72	78	88	108
15	76	83	99	115
16	80	87	99	—
17	84	92	104	—
18	88	96	109	—
19	92	101	115	—
20	96	105	120	—

Labors of Love

There are a number of things you can do to increase the natural life span of your pet. In addition to your once-weekly at-home exams (see Chapter 3, Prevention Pays) and brushing your pet's teeth at least three times a week, here are some other steps you should take.

Vet Exams Every Six Months for Your Senior Pet

Since pets age about six to ten times faster than we do, the potential for age-related diseases also occurs six to ten times faster. One of the most important things you can do for your senior pet is to take it in for a twice-yearly physical exam, and I recommend having a urine and blood test performed once or twice a year. A lot of illnesses that come with advanced age are hard to detect with only a physical exam, so these diagnostic tests are very important in detecting illness early, plus they establish a baseline for comparison as your pets age. Even though our pets may seem healthy based on physical appearance and activity, many clinical signs of disease don't develop until late in the disease process. Having these tests done once or twice a year helps detect any age-related disease your pet may be developing before the disease has progressed too far.

Bear in mind that a pet receiving biannual exams from the veterinarian is still only the equivalent of a senior person going in for an annual physical every three to four years. As your pet ages, the chances of its developing a life-threatening disease increases. Prevention and early detection of these diseases are imperative to extending the life span of your beloved companion. This could ultimately increase the amount of time you get to spend together, which most people would agree is just too short to begin with.

Plenty of Exercise

Routine daily exercise for cats and dogs is essential to staying healthy. The old saying "Use it or lose it" applies to pets as well as to people. Arthritis and obesity are two common problems that plague older cats and dogs, and regular exercise is vital for burning calories and reducing the pain of arthritis. Older pets that are inactive will lose muscle mass and tone, making it more difficult for them to

remain active, which causes them to gain weight, which in turn increases the workload on the heart and other vital organs. A vicious cycle develops. Exercise improves circulation, keeps joints moving, and aids in digestion. Even moderate exercise helps maintain a healthy heart and lungs and muscle tone.

Exercise is profoundly important in keeping your pet in the best shape, both physically and mentally. Physically, it helps prevent joints from locking. Following Duke's last surgery, after only three days of missing our consistent daily walks, I noticed his joints had already begun to stiffen. Two short walks are better than one long walk for the aging dog, as it puts less stress on the joints. Older pets also need more rest periods during exercise and more opportunities to go potty during the day, often every three to four hours if possible. Furthermore, keeping your pet mentally active through play helps postpone the natural decline in brainpower that comes with age.

Environment Enrichment

Make changes to the environment that will help your pet continue to function as close to normal as possible, prevent accidents, and enhance its quality of life. Look around your house to see if your flooring may be difficult to navigate, especially for dogs and cats with arthritis. Many pets with arthritis have difficulty rising or getting their feet under them as they try to get up. This is especially true for pets on tile, linoleum, and hardwood floors. Place a carpet or rug in the areas where they often lie down, and make sure the carpet or rug has an antislip backing to give the most stability and support to your pets. You can buy an antislip pad, available in a variety of sizes, to place under any rug so it doesn't move or bunch up. Hardwood and linoleum floors can make it tough for pets to get good traction, and consequently, they may slip and fall or have trouble getting up. You can solve this problem by adding throw rugs, mats, carpeting, or carpet runners.

Stairs, furniture, and cars may become obstacles for your aging cats and dogs. Buy ramps or premade steps to allow them access to their favorite sleeping spots. Many people build ramps to help pets get to different areas of the house. Be creative and use your ingenuity to design ways to decrease jumping but increase movement. Indoor and outdoor pet ramps are available to help pets get up and down stairs or on and off high objects such as beds, couches, or inside of cars. Also, stairs may pose a problem, so putting up a baby gate to limit access may help reduce the number of accidents.

A Cushioned Place for Senior Pets to Sleep

Soft bedding can help support bones and joints and keep your senior pets more comfortable. Large breeds of dogs, especially if they lie in one spot for long periods of time, can develop calluses or sores over the bony prominences of the body such as the elbows and hocks, which can then become ulcerated and infected. There is a huge assortment of orthopedic beds available for cats and dogs that range from soft lamb's wool to waterbeds, hammock beds, heated beds, and large, soft cotton styles. Ideally, the cover should be washable, and make sure it's in a place where your pet has secure footing getting into and out of the bed. The stuffing should be soft but durable to maintain its shape after repeated use. Be sure to place beds away from any areas that could be drafty, as older pets have more trouble regulating their body temperature.

Regular Grooming and Nail Trimming

Grooming is as vital to your cat or dog as it is for you to brush your hair. It's important to pets both physically and emotionally. Keeping their coat clean and free from tangles and mats helps prevent fleas,

ticks, and skin infections. The coat and skin are your pet's first line of defense against fleas, dampness, and cold, and when their skin and coat are in poor condition, it makes them vulnerable to disease and illness. Because muscle tone and circulation aren't as good as when they were younger, your senior pet can't groom itself as well. Brushing improves the circulation to the skin and keeps the coat shiny and free from tangles. Daily grooming is also a good way to examine your pet's body for any abnormalities such as lumps, bumps, or sores that may be covered up by all that beautiful fur. As your pets age, grooming becomes even more important because the skin loses its elasticity and may become thinner, making it more susceptible to injury. Their coat may also change, becoming more dry and flaky, or oily and greasy to the touch.

Cats normally spend up to thirty percent of their day engaged in some grooming activity. Older cats often groom less due to arthritis or mental changes associated with age. Many older cats may have difficulty reaching their entire body for grooming, so gently brushing them every day helps remove loose hair, preventing hairballs and making them feel better in general. This requires that you take a more active role in their daily grooming.

Look for brushes and combs that have plastic tipped teeth, as these are more comfortable to the skin. If your pet has long hair, keep the area around the rear end clipped short to prevent feces and mats in the hair that can cause skin irritations. Also, because dogs and cats have thinner, more sensitive skin, be sure to use shampoos especially formulated for pets. Human shampoo has a completely different pH level and is too harsh for your pet's skin and fur.

Older dogs and cats often have trouble with their nails because they are less active or not using the scratching post as often, so their nails don't naturally wear down. Nails may become thick and brittle with age as well. Serious problems can develop from overgrown nails, such as accidents from loss of balance and infections from nails that are allowed to grow into foot pads, so it's important to trim them on a regular basis yourself or have your groomer or vet trim them for you. Generally speaking, your pet's nails should not touch the ground when they are just standing still.

Stick to Normal Routines

Avoid making too many changes in your pet's home life and try to stick to its normal routine. Being consistent with your older pet's daily routines is vital to its physical, mental, and emotional health. Mealtime, naptime, playtime, and twice-daily walks should be done at the same times every day. Interrupting this schedule can lead to added stress. Try to keep the home environment the same as well. This means keeping food and water bowls in the same place and avoid moving furniture around too much.

Nutritional Needs for Older Pets

For the typical dog or cat, at least a third of its life is spent in its senior years. Just like people, as dogs and cats age, their metabolism slows and their caloric needs decrease. Their maintenance energy requirement decreases by about twenty percent, and because their activity level usually decreases as well, their energy needs are decreased by another ten to twenty percent. Consequently, if you continue to feed older cats and dogs the same amount you fed them when they were young, they will gain weight. Their decreasing metabolism makes it easier for dogs and cats to gain unwanted fat, which contributes to obesity, commonly seen in older pets.

Older dogs and cats need about twenty percent fewer calories but more vitamins, antioxidants, and fiber. Most senior diets are lower in calories, higher in fiber, and lower in fat, and many of them have added antioxidants. They are also formulated to be highly digestible to aid the senior pet's less efficient digestive systems, and contain highly digestible protein to help pets maintain lean body mass. Diets for senior pets should have limited or controlled amounts of sodium, phosphorus, protein, and fat, all of which can harm an older pet's health if fed in excess.

When shopping for your senior pet's food, it's important to choose a diet that suits its life stage and lifestyle—more sedentary versus still very active. With cats, the physical change often happens before you see obvious signs of aging, and switching to a senior diet can help reduce the onset of some common aging diseases like heart and kidney disease.

Additional Tips for Older Pets

- To encourage pets to drink more water, buy an automated, filtering drinking fountain. Pets like the running water and will usually drink larger amounts.
- Add extra litter boxes to accommodate your cat and/or switch to litter pans with lower sides.
- Mop up any spills around food and water bowls so pets won't slip and fall.
- Keep older pets indoors most of the time, especially in inclement weather.

- ❦ Give your pet as much human companionship as possible.
- ❦ Patience is needed to cope with aging pets because they will be slower and more forgetful and won't respond to your voice as quickly as they did when they were younger.

Sense-Ability

Dogs and cats are, above all, sensory creatures. They learn about their environment and interact with humans and other animals via their five senses: touch, taste, scent, sight, and sound. Cats and dogs rely more heavily on their senses than we do, but over a lifetime of use, the sensory organs fade. All senses diminish with age because the pathways that transmit messages from nerve endings to the brain slow down, so the senses, which receive messages from the outside, won't be as receptive as they once were. As cats and dogs age, they begin to have slower responses to external stimuli. This is usually a slow, progressive process. The best way to combat it is to keep your pet active, both physically and mentally, as activity helps keep the senses sharp. Sensory loss typically bothers the owners much more than it affects the pets because cats and dogs have an incredible ability to compensate by using their other, stronger senses—often to the point that you may not recognize an impairment until very late in your pet's life.

Vision Changes

Dogs and cats see better in the dark than we do, but they're not as able to focus sharply on detail. They do see some colors, but don't have the detailed color vision of humans. Pet's eyes change in several ways as they age, and some of these changes are similar to those in people. Nuclear sclerosis is a condition where the lens, which is normally clear, becomes hazy, inflexible, and less able to focus on close objects. This makes the eye look cloudy or blue and is a normal aging process of cats and dogs. It's very similar to the age-related condition called presbyopia in humans, which causes people over the age of forty to need reading glasses. Dogs and cats with nuclear sclerosis have more difficulty seeing at night and more trouble focusing on nearby objects, but this condition does allow light and vision to go through and thus does not severely affect their vision. This differentiates it from cataract development.

Cataracts can occur at all ages, and just like with people, they are more commonly seen with age. Certain breeds, including cocker spaniels, golden retrievers, Labrador retrievers, and poodles, are more prone to cataracts. Cataracts develop when the lens of the eye turns white or opaque, and as a result, blindness or significant loss of vision occurs due to interference of light reaching the retina. Cataracts can be slow-growing or appear to develop overnight. The most common cause of cataracts is a genetic defect. Cataracts can also develop after injury or inflammation in the eye, from diabetes, or as part of the aging process. The only treatment for cataracts is surgery, similar to that in humans, and is performed mainly on dogs.

Other age-related changes in dogs and cats' eyes include glaucoma, an increase in the pressure of the eye, which is very painful. Like cataracts, it can result in blindness. The eye is constantly producing fluid that circulates in the eye, and this fluid drains back into the bloodstream. When the fluid fails to drain properly, the pressure in the eye increases, and if left untreated can damage the retina and optic nerve, leading to blindness. Glaucoma can also occur as a result of structural changes such as lens displacement in older dogs and cats, or from causes such as inflammation or injury. This condition is most commonly seen in older pets and in particular breeds of dogs, including American and English cocker spaniels, basset hounds, beagles, chow chows, Norwegian elkhounds, and Samoyeds. Symptoms of glaucoma include squinting of the eyelids, a bulging appearance to the eye, pawing or rubbing at the eye, or behavior indicating pain in the eye. The condition is more commonly seen in older dogs or cats.

In certain breeds of dogs, tear production decreases with age, leading to a condition called dry eye, or keratoconjunctivitis sicca (KCS). This occurs commonly in dogs, but is rare in cats. This, too, is painful as lack of tears to lubricate the eyes can cause inflammation and damage to the cornea. Causes of dry eye include skin allergies, side effects of certain medications, and age. Without treatment, the cornea can become severely damaged, leading to blindness. Predisposed breeds include bulldogs, bull terriers, Cavalier King Charles spaniels, cocker spaniels, dachshunds, Lhasa apsos, miniature schnauzers, Pekingese, and West Highland terriers.

Any sudden change in vision or appearance of your cat or dog's eyes could signal an emergency and should be seen by your veterinarian immediately.

Hearing Changes

Cats and dogs have much keener hearing than we do. For example, cats can hear up to three times the range of sounds that people can, and dogs hear twice the range. Hearing loss is the most common sensory deficit in humans and may also be so in cats and dogs. As animals age, the delicate structures in the inner ear begin to lose sensitivity to vibrations. This leads to age-related hearing loss, which shows up in any animal if it lives long enough. Most dogs and cats more than ten years of age will have some loss of hearing. Hearing loss can't be predicted and it usually gets worse over time and cannot be reversed. Deafness in cats and dogs isn't life-threatening in and of itself, but it does put an animal at risk from undetected dangers such as motor vehicles and predators. Teaching your dog or cat simple hand signals when it is young can be very useful if your pet develops loss of hearing as it ages.

Hearing loss is usually gradual, so many pet owners don't recognize it until obvious signs occur, such as failure to greet you at the door or your pet startling easily. Animals that are exposed to loud noises for long periods of time, such as hunting dogs, are more prone to ear damage and thus hearing loss as nerve cells and the hearing apparatus degenerate. Ear infections can also develop more often in older dogs and cats. Additionally, as with humans, older pets can suffer from inner ear problems that may cause dizziness or loss of balance.

Most pets adjust fairly well with minor hearing impairments because they adapt by responding to body language and hand signals. With dogs, though, you need to be especially careful about keeping them on a leash when you go out for walks to protect them from automobiles and other dangers. Also, be careful about leaving aging pets outside alone near pools because they may accidentally fall in and drown.

Taste, Smell, and Touch

The senses of taste and smell usually decrease as dogs and cats age. The number of taste buds declines, and there is loss of appetite. Humans have 9,000 taste buds compared to dogs, which have 1,706, and cats, which have 473. Changes in a pet's perception of flavor are thought to reflect those experienced by aging humans. Dental disease can also affect taste as sensitive mouths and plaque buildup interfere with chewing ability and can produce unpleasant tastes and odors that make eating unpleasant. As the sense of smell declines with age, taste may become more important. Warming your pet's food can make it more appealing to your senior dog or cat's palate.

Dogs and cats have a highly developed sense of smell; a much larger area of their brain is devoted to this sense compared to humans. A dog's sense of smell is about 1,000 times stronger than ours, and a cat's is about fourteen times stronger. Disease and medication can affect the sense of smell and remain even after the disease is gone or the medication is no longer being taken. Sense of smell is extremely important for dogs, and age-related losses can result in changes in perception of food flavors and changes in food preferences. Tumors and polyps in the nose can also weaken the sense of smell. A loss of smell interferes with an older pet's perception of the world—which is another important reason to keep your pet on a leash when outside.

The one sense that doesn't diminish with age is touch. All aging pets enjoy petting, brushing and combing, kissing, and snuggling contact with you.

Down the Road

If you own a senior pet, you'll most likely encounter some of these conditions, which are common among older cats and dogs.

Arthritis

Approximately twenty-five to thirty percent of family pets suffer from arthritis. This disease causes swelling, stiffness, pain, and lameness. Arthritis is the most common source of chronic pain treated by veterinarians and the most common musculoskeletal disorder in older dogs and cats. A study conducted at the College of Veterinary Medicine at North Carolina State University found that an astounding ninety percent of cats they examined older than twelve years of age had osteoarthritis. Arthritis is seen most often in larger breeds, older dogs and cats, and pets that are overweight; however, it can affect dogs and cats of any age, size, and breed (as well as mixed breeds). Unlike dogs, cats with arthritis often show few, if any, symptoms until the condition has become severe—partly because of their habit of hiding illness—but that doesn't mean they're not suffering. You just have to look harder to discover arthritis in cats.

No pet (or human, for that matter) is immune from the disease. The physiological changes that occur in cats and dogs with arthritis are virtually identical to those in the human body. Arthritis means inflammation of the joints. A joint is a flexible connection between two bones. Its purpose is to allow movement. Some joints are relatively simple and permit only a limited range of movement, while others, such as the hip joint, are quite complex and are designed to enable the two bones to move in several directions. Dogs and cats have three types of joints: ball-and-socket joints, such as hips and shoulders; hinged joints, such as the knees and elbows; and gliding or plane joints, such as the wrists and ankles. When a joint is damaged by injury or disease, inflammation—arthritis—can occur. Arthritis can affect any joint, but those most commonly affected are the hips, spine, elbows, and knees.

Arthritis is usually divided into two types: degenerative and inflammatory. Degenerative joint disease, or osteoarthritis, is the most common type encountered in dogs and cats and results from the destruction of the cartilage that protects the bones. As cats and dogs run, jump, and play, a tremendous amount of stress is placed on all the components of the joint. Years of wear and tear break down the cartilage, leading to instability, discomfort, and eventually damage to the bone, resulting in degenerative joint disease. Osteoarthritis can also be caused by any amount of stress on malformed joints, such as in the case of hip dysplasia, where the joint sockets are abnormal. Degenerative joint disease can be either primary, where no exact cause is evident, or a secondary disease to which a cause can be diagnosed. Some of the most common causes of secondary degenerative joint disease include hip dysplasia (abnormal development of the hip joint), luxating patella (displacement of the kneecap to the side of the joint), ruptured cruciate ligaments (rupture of the cruciate ligament, which leads to instability of the knee), and trauma. A majority of the time, secondary degenerative joint disease can be prevented or stopped by surgical repair of the joint. However, one problem with degenerative arthritis is that it may not manifest until the dog or cat has had years of abnormal stress, at which point the joint is severely compromised and considerable degeneration is now present. Clinical signs include reluctance to walk, climb stairs, jump, or play; limping; difficulty rising; stiff gait; lagging behind on walks; change in personality; resistance to touch; reluctance to raise head or neck; missing the litter box; failure to groom (in cats); or exhibition of pain.

Infection or underlying immune-mediated diseases can cause

the second type of arthritis, inflammatory joint disease. Inflammatory arthritis usually affects more than one joint and is accompanied by signs of systemic illness including fever, anorexia, and generalized stiffness. This type of arthritis can either be infectious (caused by bacteria, tick-borne diseases, or fungal infections) or immune-mediated. Immune-mediated arthritis is caused by an abnormality in the immune system that can be hereditary. Rheumatoid arthritis, lupus, and unidentified immune-related arthritis all cause nondestructive joint infections.

Treatment of arthritis depends on the cause and is designed to control or eliminate the inflammation, thus reducing the pain along with stabilizing the joint, if possible. Therapy often includes a combination of exercise moderation, weight control, and anti-inflammatory medication. Pets with arthritis need to exercise to keep their joints mobile and flexible, but too much exercise can cause more destruction and pain. Weight control is important because pets that are overweight place undue stress on the joints, accelerating the disease. Anti-inflammatory medication can help ease the pain and allow for more movement and exercise in debilitated cats and dogs. But never give your pet over-the-counter medication intended for humans without first checking with your vet (see Chapter 8 on avoiding the ER). Supplements such as glucosamine and chondroitin are successful in treating arthritis in both dogs and cats, so talk to your vet about adding these supplements to your pet's diet. There are now additional therapies available that you might want to investigate, such as acupuncture and massage, which can also be effective in relieving your pet's discomfort.

Keys to Arthritis Prevention

- Keep your pets at their ideal weight.
- Give them moderate exercise at least twice a day.
- Feed the proper diet for your pet's life stage.

- Have your pets screened by your vet once or twice a year for early diagnosis and recommended therapy.
- Do not breed dogs or cats known to carry genes that predispose them to arthritis.

Seven Signs of Arthritis

1. Any lameness
2. Swelling around any joint
3. Reddening of skin around a joint
4. Pain when manipulating a joint
5. Holding up a limb and being unwilling to bear weight
6. Excessive licking or grooming of limb or joint
7. Severe pain when being touched in or around joints, including back and neck

Bloat

Canine bloat is the number one cause of death for several large and giant breeds of dogs. The breed with the highest risk is the Great Dane. Other breeds at higher-than-average risk include Akitas, bloodhounds, boxers, German shepherds, Irish setters, Irish wolfhounds, and standard poodles. Other deep-chested dogs, including mixed breeds, are also at higher risk. This painful condition, also called gastric dilatation-volvulus (GDV), is life-threatening if not treated within one to two hours. Basically, the stomach fills up with gas and the increased pressure pinches off both ends of the stomach, preventing gas from escaping. In seventy-five percent of dogs with bloat, the stomach actually twists, crimping off the blood supply and the inflow and outflow of the stomach. If not treated immediately, dogs will die from shock or a ruptured stomach.

The earliest signs of bloat are unproductive retching, restlessness, and anxiety as dogs pant and pace, unable to get relief from their excruciating pain. Their abdomens are swollen and bulging. Affected dogs drool because they can't swallow, belch, or vomit, which would help relieve the mounting pressure from the stomach gases.

Risk factors that can increase bloating include feeding a single large daily meal, age, stress, eating quickly, having a deep and narrow chest, having a relative that has had a bloat episode, and having a fearful, nervous, or aggressive temperament. For large breeds, the risk of developing bloat goes up twenty percent each year after the age of five, and for giant breeds, the risk goes up twenty percent each year after the age of three. Studies have shown that more than fifty percent of dogs with bloat will bloat again within three months, and seventy-six percent of dogs that bloat once will bloat again in their lifetime unless they have a surgery called a gastropexy, where the stomach is attached to the body wall to prevent it from twisting in the future. Some experts recommend that breeds at high risk of bloat have a preventative gastropexy performed instead of waiting for an episode of bloat. This surgery is usually performed at the time of neutering.

Cancer

Cancer is one of the leading causes of death in people and is the most common disease of older animals. Although it can occur at any age, the peak incidence in dogs and cats occurs between ten and twelve years of age. Dogs suffer from more kinds of cancer than any other domestic animal, and one in four will develop cancer in its lifetime. According to the Veterinary Cancer Society, cancer accounts for nearly half of all deaths in cats and dogs older than ten years of age. There are more than 100 different types of cancer and each one has different symptoms, rates of growth, and rates of survival. Just like in people, exposures to sunlight, smoke, asbestos, chemicals, hormones, radiation, viruses, and immune system failures can cause cancer in pets. One should never panic with a diagnosis of cancer because some forms can be cured if caught early enough, and most pets will be helped by treatment, which includes surgery, chemotherapy, radiation, cryosurgery, hyperthermia, immunotherapy, or a combination of treatments. Different breeds have tendencies to develop different kinds of cancer. Boxers and Scottish terriers, for example, are prone to skin cancer, and large breeds of dogs are more at risk for bone cancer. Breast cancer in unspayed female cats is very common, with Siamese having twice as much risk as other breeds.

Cancer is a rampant, abnormal growth of cells. It may first become apparent as a tissue mass called a tumor. A tumor is any sort of lump, bump growth, or swelling that can be categorized as either benign or malignant. Not all tumors are life-threatening. Benign tumors grow only in one isolated place whereas malignant tumors spread throughout the body. Older pets commonly develop benign skin tumors, which are easily removed, but even when more serious tumors develop, such as a brain tumor, surgical advances have given numerous cats and dogs the opportunity to get well and enjoy many more healthful years. Many cancers in pets are the same kinds that develop in people, but the most commonly encountered cancers in dogs are skin cancer, breast cancer (which accounts for over half of all cases), lymphoma, oral tumors, bone cancer, and testicular cancer. Cats can also develop the same types of cancers that affect people, but the most common ones are lymph gland cancer, skin cancer, and fibrosarcoma. Unfortunately, eighty percent of tumors found in cats are malignant. Important to remember feline leukemia virus causes ninety percent of lymph gland cancers. Other common cancers that occur in older cats include digestive tract tumors, oral tumors, and bone cancer.

For both people and animals, the sooner cancer is detected and treated, the better the chance the patient can be cured. This is another reason why a geriatric checkup every six months is good for older animals.

Symptoms of cancer include:

- Any abnormal swelling or lump that keeps growing
- Non-healing sores
- Weight loss for no apparent reason
- Loss of appetite
- Bleeding or unusual discharge from a body opening such as the nose, ear, or mouth
- A foul odor, especially from the mouth
- Difficulty eating or swallowing
- Loss of strength and disinterest in normal exercise
- Lameness or stiffness that continues
- Tiring easily
- Difficulty breathing, defecating, or urinating

Dental Disease

Hopefully, you're brushing your pet's teeth at least three times a week and taking your pet in for yearly dental exams at your vet. If not, it's never too late to start. Practicing good dental hygiene in cats and dogs is key to them living a long, healthy life. Dental care should be continuous from the time your pet is a kitten or puppy into its senior years. If not, the effects of dental neglect will be evident and potentially life-threatening. The most effective ways to prevent tartar buildup and the dangers it brings include brushing the teeth, feeding dry food, using a mouthwash, and using other oral products designed to reduce plaque buildup. See Chapter 5 on dental concerns for more information.

Diabetes

Diabetes mellitus is fairly common and occurs in cats and dogs at a rate of about one in every 400 to 500. Obese cats and dogs are especially at risk for developing diabetes. Cats weighing more than fifteen pounds are at very high risk, and the disease is most common in cats older than six years of age, with seventy-five percent of cases in cats occurring between the ages of eight and thirteen. Most dogs acquire the disease between seven and nine years of age. Although less common, it has been seen in very young dogs and cats. Neutered male cats and unspayed female dogs are also more prone to diabetes. There is no breed predilection in cats; however, the disease is seen more commonly in some breeds of dogs than others, such as beagles, cairn terriers, dachshunds, keeshonds, miniature and toy poodles, miniature pinschers, miniature schnauzers, pugs, pulis, standard poodles, and Samoyeds. Overall, female dogs are twice as likely to develop the disease as males.

Symptoms include increased thirst and urination, sugary urine, loss of house-training, increased appetite, weight loss, cataracts, and bad breath. Diabetic cats and dogs are susceptible to some of the same complications seen in diabetic people, including cataracts, infections, and pancreatitis. Treatment, just like in humans, involves diet changes and insulin injections.

Gastrointestinal Disorders

Age affects virtually every organ system including the digestive system, which becomes less efficient at breaking down food substances and then absorbing nourishment from them. Digestive problems, from stomachs that don't tolerate certain foods to intestines that fail to absorb nutrients, are more common in elderly cats and dogs. Aging pets also have reduced digestive secretions and motility, which can lead to constipation, flatulence, and abnormal digestion of nutrients. Signs of problems include diarrhea, vomiting, and gas.

Constipation is another common problem and anal glands are more susceptible to blockage or infection. Constipation can be due to a variety of problems such as insufficient fiber or water intake; aging; eating hair, bones, or other foreign objects; tumors; prostate disease; spinal cord or disc disease; or medications. Prevention of constipation includes feeding a low-fat and high-fiber diet, feeding at least twice a day to stimulate bowel movement, not giving table scraps, making sure your pet has access to plenty of fresh water, brushing your pet, and giving it regular exercise. Diet changes should be gradual or else diarrhea and/or serious stomach upset may develop. Gradually mix in the new diet with the old one during a four- or five-day period to reduce the chance of bowel problems.

Heart Disease

The American Veterinary Medical Association estimates that one out of every ten dogs suffers from some form of heart disease. Acquired heart disease and heart failure are among the most common diseases affecting older dogs. However, with better nutrition, medical care, and modern diagnostic techniques, heart disease is manageable in most cases these days, and pets with heart disease are living longer than ever before.

Factors contributing to heart disease include obesity, lack of exercise, stress, and poor diet. Early detection can save your pet's life.

Signs of heart disease include coughing, shortness of breath, tiring easily, weakness, a bluish tinge to the skin, loss of appetite, panting, rapid or slow heart rate, and swelling of the abdomen or lower limbs. Veterinary screening for heart disease includes listening to your pet's chest for heart murmurs, heart rate and rhythm abnormalities, and abnormal lung sounds; and taking X rays, electrocardiograms, and ultrasounds. Most heart disease is treatable and manageable, and with today's advanced veterinary care, the disease can be controlled or dramatically slowed.

Hyperthyroidism in Cats

Hyperthyroidism is a fairly common disease of older cats, but is rare in dogs. (Graves' disease is a similar condition in people.) On average, affected cats are about ten years old. The thyroid gland, located in the neck, plays a very important role in regulating the body's rate of metabolism. Hyperthyroidism is a disorder characterized by an over-production of thyroid hormone that leads to an excessive amount of this hormone circulating in the body, causing the body's metabolism to accelerate. The overproduction of thyroid hormone is due to a benign tumor in one or both lobes of the gland. Thyroid disease is often inter-twined with high blood pressure and kidney disease, and can result in hypertension in about one in four cats. A cat with hyperthyroidism has an increased heart rate, increased physical activity, and weight loss de-spite a voracious appetite. Hyperthyroidism can also affect the heart muscle and lead to hypertrophic cardiomyopathy. The good news is that treatment is usually very successful and involves either radioactive iodine to destroy abnormal thyroid tissues, surgery to remove the af-fected thyroid lobes, or oral medication. As with most diseases, the earlier it is diagnosed, the less the damage is done to the body and other internal organs.

Hypothyroidism in Dogs

Hypothyroidism is a disease that affects both humans and dogs (in humans, it's sometimes called Hashimoto's disease). In dogs, it's most commonly seen in middle-aged females. Certain breeds of dogs, such as cocker spaniels, dachshunds, Doberman pinschers, golden re-trievers, and Labrador retrievers, are predisposed. This condition is ex-tremely rare in cats.

The thyroid gland is one of the most important glands in the body. It's located in the neck and is composed of two lobes, one on each side of the trachea. The thyroid gland produces the hormone T4, which plays an essential role in regulating growth, metabolism, and immune system and heart functions in both people and dogs. In older dogs, a malfunctioning thyroid gland—often from the body's own immune system attacking the gland—almost always leads to hypothyroidism. In this condition, the gland puts out too little thyroid hormone, causing metabolism to slow down. When the rate of metabolism slows down, virtually every organ in the body is affected in some manner. Thyroid hormone deficiency can lead to increased susceptibility to skin and ear infections, poor skin and hair coat, hair loss, delayed hair regrowth, itching, increased skin pigmentation, decreased mental sharpness, obesity, lethargy, personality changes, poor wound healing, exercise intolerance, neuromuscular system abnormalities like gait problems, gastrointestinal problems, weakness, decreased energy, cold intolerance, high blood cholesterol, and infections.

Fortunately, once diagnosed, canine hypothyroidism is simple and inexpensive to treat. Dogs are treated the same way humans are, with an orally administered synthetic form of T4. The treatment is very effective and causes no long-term side effects.

Kidney Disease

The kidneys have two very important functions: 1) to filter the bloodstream and eliminate toxins from the body; (2) to regulate and balance body fluids. Kidneys also manufacture such various hormones as erythropoietin, which controls blood pressure and production of red blood cells. Kidney failure can cause devastating illness. It can come on suddenly due to toxins or injury, or occur slowly as the kidneys wear out. A wide range of factors including infections, injuries, cancer, parasites, and old age can cause kidney disease. It's most common in older pets and is estimated to be the number one or number two cause of death in cats and dogs.

Kidney disease is common in older cats, which may be afflicted for months to years before developing signs of disease, as both cats and dogs can lose up to seventy-five percent of kidney function before clinical signs will develop. However, blood work will detect early changes in kidney enzymes and allow management of this disease before it becomes life-threatening. Symptoms in dogs and cats include increased thirst or urination, weight loss, listlessness, nausea, dehydration, vomiting, diarrhea, constipation, mouth sores, foul-smelling breath, poor appetite, and lethargy; cats may also vocalize and urinate outside of the litter box. About twenty-five percent of cats with chronic kidney disease will develop high blood pressure. It's not uncommon for cats and dogs to have a long history of excessive water consumption when they finally come to the vet's office with other problems. Treatment of kidney disease depends on the degree of damage, but can be successful long-term.

Senility

Aging dogs and cats can suffer from a progressive neurological disorder and loss of mental sharpness called geriatric cognitive dysfunction syndrome (CDS), which is similar to Alzheimer's disease or dementia in humans and is estimated to affect ten to fifteen million pets in the United States alone. Recent studies have shown that as many as eighty percent of cats older than the age of sixteen show signs of senility. Clinical signs include poor appetite, changes in sleep patterns, decreased activity, house-training problems, anxiety or compulsive behaviors, disorientation, altered interactions with people, and loss of learned behaviors. There is no gold standard for diagnosis of CDS, and since its signs can be similar to those seen with various other illnesses, veterinarians need to perform a thorough physical exam and laboratory tests to rule out other diseases. There are non-neurological diseases that can mimic CDS, including kidney failure, liver disease, low blood sugar, arthritis, heart problems, deafness, poor vision, and hypothyroidism.

The longer a dog or cat lives, the more likely it is to acquire this disorder. The exact physiology behind senility is not completely understood, but intellectual stimulation, dietary supplements, and medication have all been shown to help maintain a healthy brain and to either help to prevent or slow down the progression of the disease. In most cases, a combination of these approaches works best. Numerous studies on human aging demonstrate that intellectual activities, new leisure activities, or hobbies can delay the onset of dementia in aging humans. Therefore, veterinarians prescribe behavioral enrichment in the form of new experiences to help keep your pet's brain active. Physically and mentally engaging your pet throughout its life helps keep its brain young and ward off the progression of age-related changes. Intellectual challenges for senior pets include simple changes in routine like walking a different route, trying different games and activities, introducing new and different toys, and social activity. Increasing dietary intake of antioxidants such as vitamins E and C and L-carnitine may help protect the brain from the adverse effects of free radicals. Some vets prescribe a human medication called Anipryl (selegiline hydrochloride, L-deprenyl hydrochloride). It has been effective in some pets, but like any medication, it can have rare side effects. If effective, it should be used for the life of the dog or cat. It takes about four weeks before any results can be expected. Anipryl is also used to treat Cushing's disease, an adrenal hormone imbalance in dogs.

Urinary Tract Disease

Aging cats almost never develop urinary incontinence; litter box problems are more often linked to senility or arthritis. However, older spayed female dogs, and to a much lesser degree, neutered male dogs, often suffer from urinary incontinence where urine will leak out when they sleep or rest as the result of a weakened urethral sphincter muscle. The reason for this is the lack of estrogen in females and testosterone in males, which can affect the tone of the bladder sphincter muscle. With a simple medication (phenylpropanolamine) that increases sphincter muscle tone, you can control or eliminate this problem.

There are numerous other causes of incontinence, including arthritis, bladder, stones, chronic kidney failure, congenital disorders, diabetes mellitus, tumors or polyps, and urinary tract infections. Therefore, dogs with this condition should have these other diseases ruled out before starting medication.

Senior Care Checklist

If your senior pet has developed one or more of the following symptoms, it needs to see a vet right away:

- Increased thirst
- Increased urination
- Increase or decrease in appetite
- Increase or decrease in weight
- Change in sleeping patterns
- Changes in behavior or activity levels
- Bad breath or swollen gums
- Excessive panting
- Coughing or exercise intolerance
- Loss of house-training
- Difficulty eating
- Tremors or shaking
- Confusion or disorientation

Saying Good-bye

One of the hardest decisions you'll ever have to make is to know when to say good-bye to your pet. Letting go is painful for so many reasons—guilty feelings over making wrong medical decisions and facing the emotional and physical voids that will be created when you lose your beloved companion and their unconditional love. Owners often ask me that heart-wrenching question, "What would you do if she were your pet?" and I always tell them the same thing: "It all comes down to your pet's quality of life." That's when I can offer my own personal and professional wisdom gathered from facing life-and-death decisions in my own life and in private practice. Although I've helped owners say

good-bye to their pets hundreds of times, it never gets any easier, but it does lend some clarity to making the right decision.

It's all about your pet. Look with your mind, heart, and soul. Is your pet suffering? Is it losing the fight? If so, you must end its ongoing pain and suffering. My own dog, Duke, fought to the very last moment of his life, tail still wagging and full of love and courage, partly because he knew I didn't want to let him go. But when I finally realized that my own struggle was actually my fear of losing him and missing his loving presence in my life, I stopped trying so hard to keep him. I released him from his pain and suffering, and I released him to leave me and to rest in peace until we meet again. Shortly thereafter, Duke peacefully and quietly passed away. When I was finally able to see through Duke's eyes, I could make the selfless decision to let him go.

One of my responsibilities as a vet is to put an end to the pain and suffering of animals by granting them a calm and gentle death through euthanasia. You need to be sure you're not prolonging your pet's life for selfish reasons, like not wanting to deal with the pain of losing someone you love. During such an emotional time it's sometimes hard to be objective, but you must look at your cat's or dog's quality of life and make decisions according to what's best for your pet. As long as you make decisions with regard to your pet's well-being, you can rest assured that the choices you make are the right ones.

Pain is physical or mental suffering caused by injury, disease, anxiety, or grief. Pets who are suffering usually stop eating and lose interest in their surroundings and family members. This can give you the signal that it is time. Never let your pet lose its dignity. Often when an animal is close to the end, and an owner is having trouble making a decision, I talk to them about the possibility of having to rush their distraught cat or dog to the emergency clinic in the middle of the night and put them down with a stranger at a highly emotional moment versus making the decision ahead of time, when the day and time can be planned, when all the words, the good-byes and I-love-yous, can be peacefully said and shared between you and your beloved pet. It's an individual decision and there is no right or wrong answer. If your pet has a terminal illness and is living on borrowed time, sometimes it's better to choose the time and the way that is least traumatic for both of you. I have tremendous respect for owners who can make that unselfish decision to help end their pet's pain before their pet is suffering and lingering in the final stages of disease and death. If you do make the decision to have your pet humanely euthanized, you can have a vet come to your home; this way your pet is in familiar surroundings and not frightened. Or you can choose to take your pet to the clinic.

It takes courage to see your pet come to the end of its journey on earth, but ask yourself these questions and the answers will lead you to making the right choice. Is my pet happy? Is my pet suffering? Is my pet's quality of life acceptable? Has my pet lost its dignity? Has my pet lost the will to live? Part of loving a pet is being willing to take the responsibility for making difficult decisions, living with the pain of those decisions because you know it was the right thing to do, and cherishing the times you had together, no matter how long or short. Don't let guilt from feeling like you were not as good of a pet parent as you should have been get in the way of making the decision that's ultimately best for your pet.

Aging Is a Part of Life

Old age is an undeniable part of living. From cancer and deterio-
rating thought processes to arthritis and diabetes, geriatric dogs and
cats develop diseases similar to those that befall humans. You're now
aware of these conditions and can take a more proactive approach toward your aging pet.

Pets age at different rates, depending on genetics, environment,
nutrition, and veterinary care. As your pet gets older, it's likely to experience age-related diseases, and you'll undoubtedly visit your veterinarian a lot more than you did in the beginning of your pet's life. I
recommend seeing your vet twice a year during your pet's senior years
and, if warranted, blood tests and urinalysis should be performed.

You can take action to extend your pet's life expectancy by diagnosing problems early, modifying your pet's diet, maintaining a healthful lifestyle and environment, and changing the way you interact with
your older pets. Our pets age much faster than we do, so it's important
to recognize signs of aging and practice preventive medicine to help
them live longer, happier lives. Since pets can't articulate their health
problems, it's important for you to recognize their symptoms and take
your pet to the veterinarian, who can help make the senior years rewarding for both you and your pet. There are definite physical conditions that affect all aging pets, but with some prudence, patience, and
common sense, you can help your cat or dog navigate their senior years
with grace and dignity.

Remember in the end that quality of life is the key to decisions
you'll be required to make on your senior pet's behalf. Your aging cat or
dog may not see as well as they did when they were young, but when
they look at you with clouding eyes, white eyebrows, and gray muzzle,
or with suffering, pleading eyes, the trust that shows through will communicate to you as clear as crystal that they love you and know you'll
do what's best for them without hesitation or regret.

Chapter 14

Health Insurance: Pros and Cons

You consider your cat or dog a member of your family, but unfortunately your pet isn't covered by your family's health plan. The sad truth is that the cost of veterinary care for your four-legged family member can amount to hundreds, if not thousands, of dollars during your pet's lifetime. Most people wouldn't dream of going without insurance for themselves and their families, but what happens when a beloved pet suddenly gets ill or has some kind of accident?

When people think of animals unnecessarily being "put to sleep," most of us envision the millions of victims of the pet overpopulation crisis that have "run out of time" at a shelter. But there is another, entirely different group of pets that are unnecessarily euthanized—those whose owners can't afford their medical treatments. Veterinary bills can add up quickly and place a large financial burden on the family budget when there's a crisis. Could your budget handle an unexpected expense of $1,500 to $5,000 or more? Pet owners must accept the probability that at one point in your pet's life, it may become sick or injured. It happens all the time. Cancer, for example, occurs more often in pets than people.

Rising Medical Expenses

Vet bills have been growing at twice the rate of inflation—or your paycheck—so your pet's health-care costs are now a bigger percentage of your take-home pay. Veterinary services have been increasing at about six percent annually since 2001, which is three to four percent higher than the average city inflation. According to the American Pet Products Manufacturing Association, Americans spent $38.4 billion on their pets—including $9.4 billion on vet care and $9.3 billion on supplies and medicine—in 2005–2006.

FACT

The average household spent $237 on vet bills for dogs in 2001—a ninety-five percent increase from 1991—and $574 is the figure for dogs and $337 for cats in 2006.

The greatest annual expense for pet owners is surgical veterinary visits, second is food, and third is routine vet services. The combined vet services (surgical and routine) add up to an average of $785 per year for dogs and $337 for cats; the average spent on food is $241 per year for dogs and $185 for cats.

Just like in human medicine, the pet industry is moving in the direction of preventative care. Furthermore, the costs are growing because vets can do more for your pets than ever before. One reason for this is the incredible advances in veterinary medicine. Medical services once thought impossible for pets are now routine. Ten years ago you couldn't get the kinds of medical technology available to pets today. Cancer treatment, pacemakers, organ transplants, CAT scans, MRIs, ultrasounds, cataract surgery, and even hip replacements are now offered in most specialty clinics. Even ducks are getting cataract surgery, and cats are getting kidney transplants and dialysis. The cost of veterinary drugs is also increasing as more human drugs are now being used to treat animals for a wide variety of illnesses. This is good news for cats and dogs, but many of these new medications and treatments are expensive. Companion animal drug sales increased nearly twenty-three percent from $2.03 billion in 2002 to $2.49 billion in 2003, according to the Animal Health Institute, which mirrors what we see with human drug costs.

This can all lead to a pet owner's worst nightmare: Your beloved pet is injured, ill, or suffering from pain and you're faced with the agonizing decision of paying unexpected, expensive vet bills you can't afford or subjecting your pet to the unthinkable "financial euthanasia" if you're unable to pay for treatment.

The responsible pet owner doesn't have trouble affording regular vet visits and routine health care—it's the unexpected, catastrophic vet bills from accidents or illness that are taking a toll. In addition, the average life expectancy for pets has greatly increased in the past twenty years, and the longer our pets live, the higher the chance that they will develop serious conditions typically associated with old age, such as diabetes, cancer, arthritis, kidney disease, and heart disease. Once-fatal conditions are now treatable at costs ranging from $1,000 to $5,000 and up. And pets' life spans will continue to increase substantially, perhaps by as much as twenty-five to thirty percent, partly due to the astounding advances in veterinary medicine.

Dogs and cats are at risk for developing all sorts of costly medical problems. It can be something as simple as a bladder infection or as severe as a life-threatening illness. Sometimes just diagnosing a problem can cost upward of $1,000. Compared to what these procedures cost in human medicine, of course, vet medicine really is a bargain.

Could you handle the costs of these medical treatments for your pet?

Kidney dialysis	$10,000 to $15,000 for four weeks
Kidney transplant	$8,000 for procedure and $4,000/year for follow-up (Note: There is a waiting list for transplants)
Open heart surgery	$6,000 to $12,000
Total hip replacement	$6,000 per hip
Ruptured disc	$5,000
Cancer treatment	$3,500 to $5,000
Hit-by-car accident	$3,100 to $5,000
Pacemaker	$3,000
Cataract surgery	$2,500
Fractured bone	$2,300 to $2,500
Knee surgery	$2,000 to $3,500
Snakebite	$1,500 to $2,000
Ingestion of a foreign body	$1,200 to $2,500
Infection	$1,000 to $2,500

Pet Insurance

Where does pet insurance come in? One way to prevent having to choose between your pet and your pocketbook during a medical emergency is to buy health insurance for your cat or dog. Far too often, pet owners must decide whether to pay for an extremely expensive medical procedure or choose financial euthanasia. An emotional decision like this can leave family members conflicted, filled with remorse, resentment, or devastation over having to put their pet down. Pet insurance can make state-of-the-art medical treatment and/or traumatic emergency care possible for many pet owners who might otherwise not be able to afford it and dramatically lessen financial euthanasia.

Total pet insurance market revenue in the United States has skyrocketed during the past ten years, increasing 342 percent from 1998 to 2002, with sales approximately $88 million in 2002 according to market trends. The current $200-million market for pet insurance is expected to grow at forty percent per year, reaching $667 million by 2007. Some analysts believe that in fifty years, pet health insurance will be universal in this country.

You have a great variety of plans to choose from. Some plans cover all types of medical expenses, including annual checkups and vaccinations, while others cover only accidents and illnesses. There's even a shelter plan for the recently adopted pet and a senior plan for older pets. Some plans offer multiple pet discounts and most plans allow you to choose your own veterinarian. Average premiums range from $120 to $500 per year, depending on your plan.

Another way to acquire pet insurance besides buying it directly from the provider is to work for a company that offers pet insurance as part of its benefits package, as some companies now offer employees an opportunity to buy insurance for their pets at a discount rate. This was unheard of in the past, but it's becoming more popular as employers recognize the importance of pets in people's lives. In fact, today, pet insurance is widely requested as a voluntary benefit, and although fewer than three percent of North American companies currently offer it, the number is growing. Employers that offer pet insurance include the State of California, the State of Delaware, the University of Ohio Alumni Association, Mercy Hospital in Florida, and The Gap in Canada. Some insurance companies have teamed up with companies like Petco and the American Kennel Club to offer coverage.

Pet insurance offers high-quality veterinary medicine to all pet owners. Since pet care can quickly get expensive, insurance can help alleviate the financial burden so owners and veterinarians can make health-care decisions for pets based on the best medical care options rather than on monetary worries.

What Is Pet Insurance?

Like all insurance, you're paying for something you may never use. But in the event you need it, you should be sure the coverage is there. Health insurance for both people and pets is a business and it stays alive by making a profit. By definition, pet insurance insures against emergency costs while charging monthly premiums whether or not claims are made. That, of course, is the essence of insurance. Either you take the risk or you pay the insurance company to take the risk on your behalf.

If you're the kind of pet owner who would stop at nothing to save or improve the life of your pet, the dollars can add up quickly. A hit-by-car accident could easily cost upward of $5,000 in vet bills, especially if your pet is in intensive care in a twenty-four-hour hospital, which costs around $500 per day. You pay for insurance in case your pet needs medical attention that you can't afford.

Pet insurance pays a portion of your vet bills in exchange for a monthly premium. Typically you pay the vet bill upfront and the insurance company reimburses you an amount that is stated in your policy.

Although there are differences, pet insurance is similar to human health insurance with deductibles, maximums, and co-pays. The portion that's paid to you is contingent on your policy and the stated conditions that are covered.

Pet insurance usually doesn't cover all treatments that your cat or dog might need. It's not inexpensive or without its share of problems. I've heard some clients complain that it has taken six to seven weeks to be reimbursed for a claim when the policy promises to pay in thirty days.

The least expensive policies run about $10 a month, with premium plans up to $50 a month or more. The cost of insurance increases as the coverage improves. That means you could easily spend up to $7,200 on premiums over your pet's lifetime.

How Pet Insurance Works

Is pet insurance worth the price? You need to weigh the cost of the insurance against the likelihood of submitting a claim. Pet insurance, like human health insurance, works best to cover unexpected and expensive situations. If your pet ends up hospitalized with a serious illness, coverage will be a godsend and can save you hundreds, if not thousands, of dollars. Pet health insurance is inexpensive compared to human health insurance.

There are two basic kinds of health plans. First, like human insurance plans, there are companies that pay a percentage of the charges after you pay a deductible first. Second, there are price-reduction plans that, for an annual fee, cover a small percentage of virtually any pet-related charges. Usually, the smaller the deductible, the higher the premium. As with human health insurance, the more expensive plans have higher limits.

Unlike human health insurance plans, though, pet insurance plans may have age restrictions, and there are limits to what a company will pay. Compared to human insurance, which offers a lifetime maximum of around $3 million, pet insurance offers a lifetime maximum of approximately $150,000. There are also per-incident limits and annual limits to what a company will pay out.

There is also pet life insurance, just like for people, where you pay a monthly or yearly premium in exchange for receiving a lump sum of money when your pet dies. There is an accidental death policy if your pet should meet with an untimely death. Some of these policies include bereavement counseling for the pet owner. Pet travel insurance is also available, which offers policies to pet owners for unexpected travel-related expenses for their pets, even if the pets are left at home.

How It All Started

Pet insurance became available in the United States in 1982 with the formation of Veterinary Pet Insurance, still the largest pet insurance company in the country. About thirty different pet insurers came and went between 1982 and 1998. Today there are only a handful of insurance companies in the United States, providing coverage to less than 0.5 percent of the pet population. Fortunately for many pets, pet insurance is catching on in the United States, and there are several different pet insurance companies, each offering numerous types of policies with varying degrees of coverage. Although only a small number of companies market nationwide plans, analysts predict an expansion of the industry in the next several years.

To Insure or Not to Insure

What do you think the odds are that your pet will have an accident or become ill? You need to carefully analyze your pet's lifestyle. Does it often get into fights with other dogs or cats, get into the garbage, have a tendency to eat nonfood items, or have a pet's family history of hip dysplasia, diabetes, or some other genetically predisposed condition? When it comes to pet insurance, you can't decide on price alone, so arm yourself with knowledge to secure the insurance policy that's best for you and your pet. I recommend that you add up how much you spend a year on veterinary care for each pet and separate the costs into routine care versus accidents and/or illness. Develop estimates for one to five years and then see how expensive the premium would be for the same period and how much of your expenses the pet insurance policy would cover. You also need to consider the age of your cat or dog and their potential to have health problems. Usually, lower monthly premiums come with higher deductibles and/or larger co-payments.

Routine Care Coverage

Routine care includes all those treatments and vet visits that you bring your pet in for every year to promote its health, including annual checkups, vaccinations, and sometimes spaying or neutering. The benefits for routine coverage include not having to worry about what's covered and what isn't. Everything is basically covered, so all you have to do is send in the itemized bills.

On the other hand, many pet owners feel pet insurance should be for expenses that are unexpected, not for routine vet visits. Since premiums have to cover the cost of claims and other expenses such as sale commissions and administrative costs, you'll pay more for a routine visit if insurance covers it than if you just pay out of pocket.

Pet Insurance Tips

- Look for a health insurer that has been in business for at least a couple of years.
- Ask your vet and other pet owners for recommendations.
- Search the Internet for complaints against or praise for the insurance company you're considering.
- Make sure the company is licensed in your state. Not all plans operate in all states. Be sure to check that your provider is licensed by the Department of Insurance and is regulated in your state.

- Contact your state's Department of Insurance about the company you're considering and any consumer complaints against it, and get the scoop on insurers operating in your state.

- Read policies very carefully for conditions and exclusions before enrolling. Many policies don't cover hereditary or congenital defects and others will cover preexisting conditions only if the dog or cat has not needed treatment in at least six months.

- Consider the specific health needs of your dog or cat.

- With new puppies or kittens, consider getting a policy that covers routine care as well as injuries and illnesses.

- Think about your pet's age. The best time to purchase a policy is when your pet is young. That way you won't have to worry if your pet develops a long-term health problem and thus has a preexisting condition.

- Consider plan affiliations. See if your employer or the pet-industry organization you belong to has an affiliation with one of the plans. Some companies make a contribution to premiums while others ensure that employees get a group rate.

- For older pets, consider policies that cover routine dental cleaning, prescription medications, and diagnostic tests such as blood tests, X rays, ultrasounds, and ECGs.

- The older your pet becomes, the more the premiums will cost, and they can be quite high for an older pet, even a healthy one.

- Read the fine print, understand the limitations, and look for exemptions.

- Talk to other pet owners with insurance.

- Consider your pet's lifestyle. Active, outdoor pets are at higher risk.

- Ask yourself if you're looking for a discount plan or a comprehensive insurance plan. These can differ. With discount-fee plans, you pay an annual fee and get discounted veterinarian and related pet services. A comprehensive pet health insurance plan would operate similarly to human health insurance.

Questions to Ask

1. Does the policy have deductibles, co-payments, and maximums, and how are they calculated? Some policies do, while others pay only a flat fee per ailment regardless of the actual cost. Does the provider pay the whole claim less the deductible or just a percentage?

2. Are there exclusions based on breed or hereditary conditions, and is my breed prone to medical conditions? What is excluded? Pet insurance exclusions can vary depending on the policy chosen. Many known hereditary conditions can exclude a pet from qualifying for coverage. Preexisting conditions such as diabetes or breed-based genetic ailments are often excluded. Preexisting conditions are typically those that have an ongoing treatment or have been treated within the past six months. Ask your insurer if they will cover your pet if the condition has been cured. Also, coverage for common exclusions can usually be included in the policy for an additional cost.

3. If your pet develops any new conditions while you have this insurance, will it be covered by the insurance for the remainder of its life?

4. How much can you safely afford for your pet's health care? Can you afford a vet bill of several thousand dollars?

5. Will your premiums increase based on your pet's age or with veterinary care inflation? What can you expect my premiums to look like as your pet ages?

6. Think about your pet's age. The older your pet, the more costly the insurance. The premium may not increase, but the deductible when making a claim for an older pet increases considerably. What ages of pets are accepted for coverage? Some policies have a limit on the age at the time coverage begins, or coverage may be dropped when the pet reaches a certain age. The age varies depending upon species, breed, and life expectancy, and if the coverage isn't cancelled, the premium may rise. Does your rate go up as your dog or

cat ages, or if it has chronic health problems? Some plans charge as much as $500 a year for older dogs.

7. Ask about exclusions. Some plans won't cover senior canines and some won't cover certain breeds.

8. Does the policy set annual, lifetime, or per-illness limits?

9. Can you choose your own veterinarian with your plan? As with human health insurance companies, some insurers mandate that you visit one of a limited number of veterinary clinics.

10. How many medical conditions are covered in the plan?

11. Does the preexisting condition list reset at the end of every policy year?

12. Which breeds are accepted?

13. Who decides what is excluded and why it is excluded?

14. What is covered and what is the amount of coverage in each policy? Some policies cover certain medical procedures only to a certain price level, while other policies cover a certain percentage of the price.

15. Does the policy cover routine exams, vaccinations, heartworm preventives, and dental cleanings? Some companies include this in the regular policy while others have this coverage available at additional cost.

16. Is there a maximum payout? Some policies may have a maximum payout per ailment, per year, or per pet.

17. For what reasons can the insurance company cancel the policy? Late payments, change in health, and/or age of the pet?

18. Are you insured against damage to property if your pet causes injury to another animal or causes an accident? Homeowner's or renter's insurance may already cover this. Be careful, though, as some insurance companies (pet, homeowner's, or renter's) will cancel the policy if your pet bites and you keep the pet.

19. What are the waiting periods? Like all insurance plans, there may be a waiting period in order for the policy to take effect and you need to know exactly when your policy starts and ends.

20. Is spaying/neutering covered?

21. Does your policy include prescription coverage?

22. Are there any illness and incident caps? There will usually be a "cap," or limit, on how much the insurance company will pay for a specific incident. For example, a broken leg may have a different cap than a neuter, so be aware of policy limits.

23. Is the company reputable and providing you with answers to *all* of your questions? Make sure you feel comfortable with the company you're interested in, since they will be handling your claims. They should be willing to answer all of your questions thoroughly.

24. What are limits on annual, per-incident, per-illness, and lifetime costs?

25. Does the insurance company offer discounts for multiple pets?

26. Will the insurance policy cover any holistic treatments?

27. What is the term of the policy?

28. Are the vaccination protocols determined by the insurance company or the veterinarian of your choice?

29. Does the definition of "accident" in the insurance policy cover what your pet may likely incur? Some pet plans won't cover injury arising from normal activity, such as joint injury from playing and poisoning from eating garbage.

30. How fast does the insurance company reimburse customers' claims and does the policy have specific claim deadlines?

Self-Insure

Another option is to self-insure. In lieu of pet insurance, you can open a savings account for your pet and deposit a few dollars into it every week to pay for unexpected vet bills. Then you'll know the money is there if you need it for your pet's health emergency. Of course, this only works if you're a disciplined person and can put the money aside in the first place. This is a step toward peace of mind, but it can be difficult not to occasionally borrow from the emergency fund. What happens when your pet's emergency savings is used up? You have to start saving all over again. In addition, since the cost of treatments can be high, you could use up all you've saved on one accident or illness and not have enough money when another one arises. That's why pet insurance is worth investigating.

A.M. Best Ratings

Founded in 1899, A. M. Best is an independent organization, not affiliated with any insurance company, that rates the financial strength of insurance companies and their ability to pay their policyholders as promised. Secure companies are awarded the top ratings: A++ and A+ is considered superior, A and A– are excellent, B++ and B+ are very good. Anything below that (B, B–, C, D) is considered "vulnerable," which means that the insurance company's promises to pay their policyholders come at some risk. Most insurance companies value their ratings. Insurance companies strive for an A rating, and while B++ and B+ are still listed as secure, you need to be very careful. To check on an insurance company's ratings, go to A. M. Best's website, **www.ambest.com.**

The following are ratings for five top companies:

Veterinary Pet Insurance of Brea, California—not rated in California, but A+ in all other states. Underwritten by Veterinary Pet Insurance Company (VPI) in California; policies outside of California are underwritten by National Casualty Company. Sells policies under VPI and is currently the largest pet insurer in the United States; Business Week Online reported in 2005 that VPI held eighty-three percent of market share in the United States. Policies are approved in all fifty states and Washington, D.C. Founded in 1980 with the support of 750 independent veterinarians. Reports a 1,000 percent increase in policies since 1998. VPI has more than 320,000 policies in force and covers more than 6,400 medical treatments for accidents and illness, with optional coverage available for preventative and routine care. VPI doesn't offer routine care in its core policy, but you can get an add-on that costs $99 per year that pays dollar amounts for specified routine care procedures.

Pethealth Inc. of Oakville, Canada—A–rated. Underwritten by Lincoln General Insurance Company. Sells pet insurance in the United States and Canada under the PetCare brand. Currently the second largest pet insurer in the United States. Founded in 1998, Pethealth is the only insurance provider offering pet insurance products in both the United States (forty-six states and Washington, D.C.) and Canada (ten provinces). Coverage for more than 6,000 illnesses but doesn't offer routine care. Petco recently began offering PetCare brand pet insurance programs. Pethealth Inc. medical plans cover more than 61,000 policies.

Pet Protect of Naples, Florida—A+ rated. Underwritten by the Insurance Corporation of Hannover. Sells pet insurance under the Pet Protect brand. Founded in 1997. A smaller company with an estimated few thousand dog and cat insurance policies in force. Pet Protect offers two plans from which to choose, but doesn't offer routine vet care coverage.

Hartville Group of Canton, Ohio—A rated. Underwritten by QBE Insurance and sold through its agency, Petsmarketing Insurance.com Agency. Sells pet insurance policies under the Petshealth Care Plan and Healthy Bark and Purr brands. A holding company specializing in niche insurance since 1998, it has coverage in more than forty-five states. It reported more than 20,000 policies in 2004.

Pet Partners of Raleigh, North Carolina—A rated. Underwritten by National Specialty Insurance Company. Sells pet insurance under the American Kennel Club (AKC) Pet Healthcare Plan and the Cat Fanciers' Association (CFA). Pet Partners is British-based and, like Pet Protect, a smaller company.

Pet HMOs

One company that sells discount plans rather than traditional insurance is Pet Assure, which sells a monthly or yearly subscription service that promises discounts on pet health care and supplies. Founded in 1995, Pet Assure requires using veterinarians on its approved list. You pay the company an annual fee of $99 per pet and receive discounts of twenty-five percent from affiliated vendors, which include veterinarians, pet sitters, and groomers. The benefit is that Pet Assure accepts pets of any age and in any health condition. There are no exclusions based on preexisting conditions or conditions inherent in a particular breed. All the other plans have exclusions. Some small, medium-size, and Fortune 500 companies now offer Pet Assure as an employee benefit.

Pet Assure works more like a health maintenance organization (HMO) with specific veterinarians and specialists in a network. As long as consumers get their treatment and medications within the network, they automatically save twenty-five percent on the full vet bill at the time of service. There are no co-pays, no deductibles, no claim forms, and no HMO referrals. Policyholders choose a vet in their network of 2,400.

There is also CareCredit, a credit card company that specializes in extending credit to clients for both human and pet health-care needs. For information, call (800) 859-9975, e-mail info@carecredit.com, or visit **www.carecredit.com**.

The Payoff

Pet owners often underestimate the costs of owning a cat or dog. But the demand for pet insurance is growing as more and more Americans choose to pay for security. Many pet owners are willing to spend a significant amount of money to keep their pets healthy and extend their lives. Some people love their pet so much that they will put their pet's needs before their own. Pet insurance can be a smart investment that can bring peace of mind and prevent considerable costs.

The pet insurance industry has steadily been improving in quality and in its offerings. New pet insurance companies keep popping up and some of the names are similar, which can make things confusing. Insurers vary in quality of coverage and claims processing and premiums, which are often based on the type of pet, its age, and the type of insurance plan you choose. Some plans cover major illnesses only, while others are more comprehensive and include routine vaccinations, heartworm prevention, and flea control. You need to decide if you prefer all-inclusive coverage that pays for everything from routine checkups and vaccinations to accidents and chronic illnesses, or if you're more comfortable with a lesser degree of coverage that just kicks in during emergencies. Some people feel that insurance is best used as protection against catastrophic expenses, not those you could easily pay out of pocket.

Pet insurance can be a lifesaver for pets with unexpected, catastrophic accidents and illness because it won't drain you financially or force you to put your pet to sleep because you couldn't afford the medical treatment. It allows you to budget for future medical expenses by spreading the cost over many years and thousands of insured pet owners. Insurance is destined to play an increasing role in the lives of pet owners and their pets, although some veterinarians are concerned that veterinary medicine is heading toward the problems of human health insurance and HMOs.

Pet insurance is no panacea. It has its problems, but for most pet owners it's worth looking into. The bottom line is that it can't hurt to get a free quote online. Keep in mind that health insurance is difficult to find for dogs and cats older than eight years of age and that age limits change from time to time.

So the question remains: Does pet insurance have real value?

Although the insured party may end up spending more or less in any given year, over a period of many years with many people contributing, the costs will equalize. Insurance may not save you money, but it will give you peace of mind. For many people, when it comes to their pets, the security that thoughtfully selected pet health insurance provides is priceless.

Epilogue: Summing Up

Owning a pet is good for you. Numerous studies have shown that people with cats and dogs live longer, healthier lives. So caring for a cat or dog just may save you money on your own healthcare costs and increase your life span. There's no doubt your pet will add many years of joy to your life, but you must be in a position to take proper care of it. Owning a dog or cat is a privilege as well as a big responsibility. It's a commitment of time and money for the lifetime of your pet.

Medical costs are a necessary expense. Due to progress in pet care, especially in food and medicine, the cost of pet ownership has increased considerably during the past ten years. Since this trend is unlikely to reverse, potential pet parents must consider their budget before taking on a new cat or dog—especially a kitten or puppy. While puppies and kittens have a way of capturing our hearts with their

FACT

The approximate cost of owning a dog from puppy to senior care—if the dog lives twelve years and weighs fifty pounds—is $18,000, and that's without any surprise vet visits or accidents.

adorable antics, precious faces, and fuzzy fur, there is no such thing as a free kitten or puppy. It costs more money to raise an animal into adulthood, so avoid impulse buying. Puppies and kittens require more routine care; therefore, the first year is more expensive.

You can avoid overspending on your pets without compromising quality care by keeping them healthy from the day you bring them home. This includes getting their vaccinations and annual exams and catching problems early so that in some cases you'll avoid problems altogether.

Knowledge and prevention will go a long way toward enhancing your pet's well-being and keeping vet bills at bay. Preventative care includes taking your pet in for yearly wellness and dental exams, and for seniors, having lab tests and urinalysis performed once or twice a year. Even though you believe your pet is healthy, yearly exams help detect problems early. I can't tell you how many times I've picked up on a potentially life-threatening illness that the pet owner didn't know about. Many early signs of illness are so subtle that it's important to have your vet's trained hands and eyes examine your pet. It's heartbreaking to watch pets get avoidable diseases when all the owners had to do was get some form of preventative medicine for their pets, like heartworm medication or a vaccination.

The cost of a veterinary visit is increasing faster than the cost of living, partially due to demand for expensive procedures, equipment,

FACT

The approximate cost of owning a cat from kitten to senior care—if the cat lives fourteen years—is $13,000, and that's without any surprise vet visits or accidents.

and the advanced medical training needed to improve the staff. You don't have to be wealthy to keep your beloved pet healthy, but before you run out and adopt or buy that beautiful four-legged furry friend, make sure your lifestyle and finances can afford the expense.

You need to be committed to your pet's care financially and emotionally. Evaluate your reasons for wanting to become a pet parent. Be sure you're getting a pet for the right reasons. Wrong reasons include feeling sorry for them, buying them because they're cute, or buying a pet for a friend.

The bottom line is that pets don't come with warranties. It's a big financial commitment over the life of a pet and one you shouldn't take lightly.

Knowledge is power. The keys to your pet's longevity are preventative medical care, common sense, and lots of TLC, and remember your pet's unconditional love is free!

For more information, visit www.DocHalligan.com.

Resources

Common Medical Terminology

Abnormal—malformation; unusual; defect

Abscess—localized collection of pus formed by the disintegration of tissue; common in cats

Acute—sudden onset

Allergies—altered reactivity following exposure to a foreign substance; common in certain breeds of dogs

Alopecia—deficiency of the hair or coat

Anemia—deficiency of red blood cells or hemoglobin; seen with chronic disease

Anorexic—lack or loss of appetite for food

Apnea—temporary halting of breathing

Atopy—hay fever or allergies in dogs

Atrophy—decrease in size of a normally developed organ or tissue; wasting

Aural hematoma—pocket of blood in one or both ears

Benign—favorable for recovery; pertains to cancer

Chronic—existing over a long period

Contagious—capable of being transmitted from animal to animal/human

Cryptorchid—animal with undescended testicles

Cyanotic—bluish discoloration of gums

Debilitation—lack or loss of strength; weakness

Defecation—elimination of waste and undigested food

Dehydration—a state when the body loses more water than it takes in

Demodex—a mite that is a parasite found in the hair follicles of the host

Dermatitis—inflammation of the skin

Dyspnea—labored or difficult breathing

Emaciation—excessive leanness; a wasted condition of the body

Euthanasia—easy or painless death

Febrile—having a fever

Foreign body—plant or mineral matter that finds its way into organs and tissues

Hemorrhagic—bloody

Hypoglycemic—abnormally low level of sugar (glucose) in the blood

Incubation period—time from when an animal comes in contact with a disease until it starts showing clinical signs of illness

Jaundice—yellowness of the skin or mucous membranes (also known as icteric)

Malignant—tending to become progressively worse, usually resulting in death; pertains to cancer

Mange—skin disease of animals caused by mites

Necrotic—pertaining to cell death

Neglect—failure to do something that a reasonable person would do

Neoplasia—any new and abnormal growth/cancer

Prognosis—forecast of the probable course and outcome of a disease and prospect of recovery

Pruritis—itching

Scabies—"sarcoptic mange," an intensely pruritic skin disease caused by a mite

Tachycardia—abnormally rapid heart rate

Trauma—wound or injury produced by external force

Zoonotic—disease of animals transmitted to man

Veterinary Associations

American Veterinary Medical Association: **www.avma.org**

American Veterinary Chiropractic Association: **www.animalchiropractic.org**

Academy of Veterinary Homeopathy: **www.theavh.org**

American Holistic Veterinary Medical Association: **www.ahvma.org**
American Academy of Veterinary Acupuncture: **www.aava.org**
International Veterinary Acupuncture Society: **www.ivas.org**

Websites for nutritional requirements in cats and the role of vitamins and minerals in their diet:
http://dels.nas.edu/banr/cd_cat_vit.html
http://www.merckvetmanual.com/mvm/htm/bc/tmgn48.htm

Websites for nutritional requirements in dogs and the role of vitamins and minerals in their diet:
http://dels.nas.edu/banr/cd_dog_vit.html
http://www.merckvetmanual.com/mvm/htm/bc/tmgn47.htm

Poison Hotlines

Animal Poison Hotline: (888) 232-8870
ASPCA Animal Poison Control Center: (888) 426-4435
National Animal Poison Control Center: (800) 548-2423
University of Illinois: (900) 680-0000

Vet Schools

Many vet schools operate a low cost or reduced cost clinic. By letting your pet be seen by vet students in training you'll be rewarded with lower vet bills without compromising the care your pet receives.

The following is a list of U.S. vet schools and their teaching hospitals:

Auburn University
College of Veterinary Medicine
Small Animal Teaching Hospital
Hoerlein Hall
Auburn, AL 36849-5523
(334) 844-4690
www.vetmed.auburn.edu

Colorado State University
College of Veterinary Medicine &
Biomedical Sciences
James L. Voss Teaching Hospital
300 West Drake Drive
Fort Collins, CO 80523-1620
(970) 221-4535
www.cvmbs.colostate.edu

Cornell University
College of Veterinary Medicine
Hospital for Animals
Box 20
Ithaca, NY 14853-6401
(607) 253-3060
www.vet.cornell.edu

Iowa State University
College of Veterinary Medicine
Veterinary Teaching Hospital
Ames, IA 50010
(515) 294-4900
www.vetmed.iastate.edu

Kansas State University
College of Veterinary Medicine
Veterinary Medical Teaching Hospital
1800 Denison Avenue
Manhattan, KS 66506
(785) 532-5690
www.vet.ksu.edu

Louisiana State University
School of Veterinary Medicine
Veterinary Teaching Hospital and Clinics
Skip Bertman Drive
Baton Rouge, LA 70803
(225) 578-9600
www.vetmed.lsu.edu

Michigan State University
College of Veterinary Medicine
Veterinary Teaching Hospital
G100 Vet Med Center
East Lansing, MI 48824-1314
(517) 355-2964
www.cvm.msu.edu

Mississippi State University
College of Veterinary Medicine
Animal Health Services
P.O. Box 6100
Mississippi State, MS 39762-6100
(662) 325-3432
www.cvm.msstate.edu

North Carolina State University
College of Veterinary Medicine
Veterinary Teaching Hospital
4700 Hillsborough Street
Raleigh, NC 27606
(919) 513-6911
www.cvm.ncsu.edu

Ohio State University
College of Veterinary Medicine
Veterinary Teaching Hospital
601 Vernon L. Tharp Street
Columbus, OH 43201
(614) 292-3551
www.vet.ohio-state.edu

Oklahoma State University
Center for Veterinary Health Sciences
Boren Veterinary Medical Teaching Hospital
Stillwater, OK 74078
(405) 744-7000
www.cvm.okstate.edu

Oregon State University
College of Veterinary Medicine
Lois Bates Acheson Veterinary Teaching Hospital
200 Magruder Hall
Corvallis, OR 97331-4801
(541) 737-4812
www.vet.oregonstate.edu

Purdue University
School of Veterinary Medicine
Veterinary Teaching Hospital
625 S. Harrison Street
West Lafayette, IN 47907
(765) 494-1107
www.vet.purdue.edu

Texas A&M University
College of Veterinary Medicine &
Biomedical Sciences
Office of the Dean
Suite 101—VMA
College Station, TX 77843-4461
(979) 845-2351
www.cvm.tamu.edu

Tufts University
Cummings School of Veterinary Medicine
Tufts New England Veterinary Medical Center
200 Westboro Road
North Grafton, MA 01536
(508) 839-5395
http://vet.tufts.edu

Tuskegee University
College of Veterinary Medicine
Tuskegee, AL 36088
(334) 727-8174
www.tuskegee.edu

University of California, Davis
School of Veterinary Medicine
Veterinary Medical Teaching Hospital
University of California
One Shields Avenue
Davis, CA 95616
(530) 752-1393
www.vetmed.ucdavis.edu

University of Florida
College of Veterinary Medicine
Small Animal Hospital
P.O. Box 100125
Gainesville, FL 32610
(352) 392-4700
www.vetmed.ufl.edu

University of Georgia
College of Veterinary Medicine
Small Animal Teaching Hospital
Athens, GA 30602-7391
(706) 542-5289
www.vet.uga.edu

University of Illinois at Urbana-Champaign
College of Veterinary Medicine
Veterinary Teaching Hospital
Urbana, IL 61802
(217) 333-5300
www.cvm.uiuc.edu

University of Minnesota
College of Veterinary Medicine
1365 Gortner Avenue
St. Paul, MN 55108
(612) 624-4747
www.cvm.umn.edu

University of Missouri-Columbia
College of Veterinary Medicine
Veterinary Medical Teaching Hospital
1600 East Rollins
Columbia, MO 65211
(573) 882-7821
www.cvm.missouri.edu

University of Pennsylvania
School of Veterinary Medicine
The Matthew J. Ryan Veterinary Hospital
3800 Spruce Street
Philadelphia, PA 19104
(215) 898-4680
www.vet.upenn.edu

University of Tennessee
College of Veterinary Medicine
Small Animal Clinic
2407 River Drive
Knoxville, TN 37996-4550
(865) 974-8387
www.vet.utk.edu

University of Wisconsin—Madison
School of Veterinary Medicine
Veterinary Medical Teaching Hospital
2015 Linden Drive
Madison, WI 53706-1102
(608) 263-7600
www.vetmed.wisc.edu

Virginia-Maryland Regional
College of Veterinary Medicine
Virginia Tech
Veterinary Teaching Hospital
Duckpond Drive
Blacksburg, VA 24061
(540) 231-4621
www.vetmed.vt.edu

Washington State University
College of Veterinary Medicine
Veterinary Teaching Hospital
Pullman, WA 99164-7060
(509) 335-0711
www.vetmed.wsu.edu

Western University of Health Sciences
College of Veterinary Medicine
309 East Second Street
Pomona, CA 91766-1854
(909) 469-5628
www.westernu.edu

Acknowledgments

First and foremost, I would like to thank Liz Halligan for all of her love, support, and endless hours on the telephone. This book would never have happened without her. She is truly an amazing woman! Also, a big hug to Cary and Jonathan Halligan for allowing me to take up so much of Liz's time, and for their unwavering encouragement as well. Next, I would like to thank my editor, Melissa Brandzel, whose expertise made this book an easy and enjoyable read, and who is also an amazing cohort to work with.

I would especially like to thank my wonderful agent, Alice Martell, who inspired me to write the best book I possibly could. Also, a big thank you to Matthew Benjamin, my amazing editor at HarperCollins, whose tireless editing skills were hugely appreciated, and who made my first book-writing experience thoroughly enjoyable.

Thanks to Deborah Keaton for her brilliance as a graphic designer as well as her amazing intuitive abilities, and to Liz Wells for her incredible illustrations and extreme talent as an artist.

I would also like to thank Elizabeth McMillian for her inspiration, encouragement, and guidance in making this book a reality. Next, I want to thank Summer Gourdin for her beautiful friendship as well as her insight into recognizing the strong demand for pet parents' thirst for knowledge.

A huge thanks to Pat Broeske, my teacher and mentor at UCLA, who inspired me to strive for excellence via her tremendous passion for writing. Also, a big thank-you to everyone at VCA Petville Animal

Hospital, who put up with my endless neuroticism and drive to make my dream become a reality.

And last, but certainly not least, I want to thank Mark Puopolo and his mother, Sonia (may she rest in peace), for believing in me and encouraging me to follow my dreams. Their inspirational words "If you can dream it, you can live it" kept me on course.

Index